Periodicals and Publishers

PRINT NETWORKS
PREVIOUS TITLES IN THE SERIES

This series publishes papers given at the annual
Print Networks Conference on the History of the British Book Trade

EDITED BY PETER ISAAC & BARRY MCKAY

Images and Texts: Their Production & Distribution in the 18th & 19th Centuries
St. Paul's Bibliographies & Oak Knoll Press, 1997

The Reach of Print: Making, Selling and Using Books
St. Paul's Bibliographies & Oak Knoll Press, 1998

The Human Face of the Book Trade: Print Culture and its Creators
St. Paul's Bibliographies & Oak Knoll Press, 1999

The Mighty Engine: The Printing Press and its Impact
St. Paul's Bibliographies & Oak Knoll Press, 2000

The Moving Market: Continuity and Change in the Book Trade
Oak Knoll Press, 2001

EDITED BY BARRY MCKAY, JOHN HINKS & MAUREEN BELL

Light on the Book Trade: Essays in Honour of Peter Isaac
Oak Knoll Press & The British Library, 2004

EDITED BY JOHN HINKS & CATHERINE ARMSTRONG

Printing Places: Locations of Book Production & Distribution since 1500
Oak Knoll Press & The British Library, 2005

Worlds of Print: Diversity in the Book Trade
Oak Knoll Press & The British Library, 2006

Book Trade Connections from the Seventeenth to the Twentieth Centuries
Oak Knoll Press & The British Library, 2008

Periodicals and Publishers
THE NEWSPAPER AND JOURNAL TRADE
1750–1914

Edited by
John Hinks, Catherine Armstrong
& Matthew Day

OAK KNOLL PRESS
&
THE BRITISH LIBRARY
2009

© The Contributors 2009

First Published in 2009 by
Oak Knoll Press
310 Delaware Street
New Castle, DE 19720
and
The British Library
96 Euston Road
London NW1 2DB

Cataloguing-in-Publication Data
A CIP Record for this book is available
from both the Library of Congress
and The British Library

ISBN 978-1-58456-266-5 (Oak Knoll)
ISBN 978-0-7123-5074-7 (British Library)

Designed and composed by Catherine Armstrong

Printed in the United States of America by
Sheridan Books, Ann Arbor

Contents

Introduction

JOHN HINKS

THIS IS THE FIRST of the ten *Print Networks* volumes to combine selected papers from three of our annual conferences: Dublin 2006, Chester 2007 and Lincoln 2008. This reflects a new editorial intent to identify broad themes for the volumes, rather than simply offering the 'proceedings' of a single conference. Future *Print Networks* conferences will also aim to be broadly thematic. As ever, the focus of both conferences and published volumes is the history of the book trade – the production, distribution and readership of texts, especially in print but also in manuscript – primarily, though not exclusively, with a British focus. *Print Networks* papers have usually tended towards an emphasis on book-trade practitioners in provincial towns and the relationships, often amicable, sometimes not, between them and members of the London trade. The multiple meanings of 'provincial', discussed in a perceptive keynote essay by Iain Beavan, resonate throughout this collection. The other main focus of this volume is the publication of newspapers and periodicals, an important part of the activities of many book-trade people, both metropolitan and provincial, especially during and since the 'long eighteenth century'. Essays deal with many parts of the British Isles and there are several on an Irish theme from our memorable conference in July 2006 at Trinity College, Dublin.

The essays in this collection reflect the broad chronological scope of the *Print Networks* conferences, ranging from *c*. 1740 to the early twentieth century. By the latter half of the eighteenth century most British provincial towns apart from the smallest had at least one local weekly newspaper, some had several competing titles. By the early twentieth century, the newspaper business had progressed beyond the wildest dreams of the pioneers: production was increasingly mechanized, while the gathering and presentation of news had developed to meet the growing appetite of readers for current news and information. At national and local level, weekly newspapers were now complemented by a wide range of daily titles, many of them peddling their own brand of politics. By the start of the First World War, readers had an unprecedented choice of papers, while producers faced ever increasing challenges from competition and technological innovation. Alongside a growing demand for up-to-the-minute news, there developed a voracious market for periodicals reflecting a wide range of interests. The work, and thought, that went into the production of both serious journals and popular magazines is discussed in a number of these essays.

The history of the book is currently thriving as an exciting and fruitful field of study – thankfully not as a discrete academic discipline – and within this broad, interdisciplinary field, the history of the book *trade* flourishes too. It is good to see the work of promising young scholars represented in this collection, alongside that of more seasoned contributors.

With this volume, Catherine Armstrong has chosen to end her editorial involvement with the *Print Networks* series. I wish to record my thanks for her imagination and efficiency, and her good humour, all of which will be greatly missed. At the same time, I am delighted to welcome Matthew Day into the editorial harness and I look forward to working with him on future volumes. Once again, the editors extend their gratitude to Maureen Bell, not only for her exemplary proofreading but also for advice and 'moral support' without which the *Print Networks* series would be immeasurably poorer.

Contributors

Catherine Armstrong is a Lecturer in American History at Manchester Metropolitan University. Her first monograph entitled *Writing North America in the Seventeenth Century* was published in 2007 by Ashgate. Her book trade interests centre on transatlantic cultural connections between England and North America during the seventeenth and eighteenth centuries.

Iain Beavan has recently retired as Keeper of Rare Books, Historic Collections, University of Aberdeen. He has written widely on aspects of the Scottish book trade, and continues to pursue his research interests in print culture.

Stephen W. Brown is the Master of Champlain College at Trent University in Ontario Canada and the 3M Fellow in the Department of English. The author of over fifty articles and book chapters and editor of the manuscripts of the Scottish eighteenth-century printer, William Smellie, he is currently engaged as co-editor of volume two of the Edinburgh History of the Book in Scotland.

Stephen Colclough is a lecturer in the School of English, University of Bangor. He is a contributor to *The Cambridge History of the Book in Britain* and the author of *Consuming Texts: Readers and Reading Communities 1695-1870* (Palgrave, 2007).

Matthew Day is Head of English at Bishop Grosseteste University College, Lincoln. He has research interests in print culture and early modern travel and their intersection. He has published on censorship, paratextuality and the reception of early modern travel narratives during the eighteenth century.

Victoria Gardner recently gained her doctorate on provincial newspaper proprietors (1760-1820) from St. John's College, Oxford. She is particularly interested in the evolution of the national newspaper trade, its occupations and networks, over the later eighteenth century.

John Hinks is an Honorary Fellow at the Centre for Urban History, University of Leicester, where he is researching networks and communities in the British book trade. At the University of Birmingham he is an Honorary Research Fellow in English and a Visiting Lecturer in History, where he teaches early modern cultural history.

Graham Hogg works as a senior curator in Rare Book Collections at the National Library of Scotland. His interest in the career of George Miller arose from ongoing research into the development of printing in Scotland, which celebrated its 500th anniversary in 2008.

Máire Kennedy is Divisional Librarian with Dublin City Libraries in charge of Special Collections (early printed books and manuscripts). A book based on her PhD thesis *French Books in Eighteenth-Century Ireland* was published by the Voltaire Foundation in 2001. She has also published widely in Irish and international journals.

Jennifer Moore is currently an editorial assistant and researcher with the Irish Historic Towns Atlas in the Royal Irish Academy. Her PhD thesis, at the University of Limerick, deals with provincial print culture, their networks, and the power of the printer in civic urban governance.

Lisa Peters is the law librarian at the University of Chester. Her main research interest is North Wales newspaper history.

Michael Powell is Librarian of Chetham's Library, Manchester. He has published a number of papers in previous *Print Networks* volumes on aspects of the book trade in Manchester.

Kath Skinner is a learning resources assistant at the University of Chester. She is interested in Victorian literature, especially child-parent relationships.

Ria Snowdon was a fellow at the Print Networks and Texts, Ma(r)kers, Markets Joint Conference in 2008. Her research focuses on Georgian women and the business of print, particularly proprietors of newspapers.

Elizabeth Tilley is a lecturer in the Department of English, National University of Ireland, Galway. She is an associate editor of the *Dictionary of Nineteenth-Century Journalism* and publishes on Irish periodicals and book history.

Terry Wyke teaches Social and Economic History at Manchester Metropolitan University.

Forever Provincial?: A North British Lament

IAIN BEAVAN

THIS PAPER RAISES a number of questions relating to recent approaches and modes of thought in some limited areas of print culture, and is as concerned about the words used to discuss and describe the British book trade as it is about its actual history. It neither prescribes nor proscribes any particular vocabulary, but rather looks at some of the consequences and implications inherent in the concepts employed to analyse the British book trade. Arguments are advanced to suggest that the widely accepted model of the eighteenth- and early nineteenth-century British book trade stands in need of minor adjustment; but, more fundamentally, unless book-trade historians look carefully at the concept of provinciality, differences of view over its applicability that first appeared over 300 years ago will continue to find expression.

The provincial and metropolitan trades

The classic statements of the bipartite (though interdependent) nature of the English book trade have been made by Pollard and (more implicitly) by Wiles, both overshadowed by Feather's hugely influential full-scale study.[1] Indeed, this view of the past

[1] The author is grateful to Pearson Education for permission to quote from the Oliver & Boyd papers; to the National Library of Scotland for permission to quote from material under its charge; and to Prof Peter Davidson for his many intriguing observations, and whose *The Universal Baroque* (Manchester, 2007) has wrestled with the concept of provinciality in a very different context. J. Feather, *The Provincial Book Trade in Eighteenth-Century England* (Cambridge, 1985); G. Pollard, 'The English Market for Printed Books', *Publishing History*, 4 (1978), pp. 7-48; R. M. Wiles, 'The Relish for Reading in Provincial England Two Centuries Ago', in *The Widening Circle; Essays on the*

nature of the English book trade has become an orthodoxy underpinning much subsequent research and debate. Given the clarity of these formative studies, it is possible to draw out some of the more general salient features of the model of the eighteenth- and early nineteenth-century British book trade.

i.   The expression 'provincial book trade' can be defined geographically, as being a stated distance from the main locus of (economic, commercial or political) power or government – in this context, London.

ii.   There are fundamental differences in character between the provincial and metropolitan trades, one being that 'the provincial book trade was essentially passive' and that 'the heart of the provincial trade has always been in distribution rather than production'.[2]

iii. Although there are many examples that can be brought forward of provincial printers arranging for the regional distribution of their books, most were for local distribution and sale only. [3]

iv. Distribution of printed material was largely (though not entirely) one-way, from London to the provinces, and the major London houses could fairly be described as 'merchants of culture' distributing 'metropolitan printed culture' throughout the country, and 'smoothing the path which enabled a metropolitan culture to reach the provinces'.[4]

Circulation of Literature in Eighteenth-Century Europe, ed. by P. J. Korshin, (Philadelphia, 1976), pp. 87-115.

[2]   J. Feather, 'The Merchants of Culture: Bookselling in Early Industrial England', *Studies in Voltaire and the Eighteenth Century*, 217 (1983), pp. 11-21 (p. 19); J. Feather, 'The History of the English Provincial Book Trade: a Research Agenda', in *Light on the Book Trade*, ed. by B. McKay, J. Hinks and M. Bell (New Castle, DE., London), 2004, pp. 1-12 (p. 2).

[3]   Feather, *Provincial Trade*, ch. 6., and esp. p. 117 on the provincial imprint as 'value judgement'.

[4]   Feather, 'Merchants', pp. 18, 20.

And on the books themselves:

v. Overwhelmingly, a provincially published book was 'an indicator of provincial taste and culture' and of 'limited [local] interest.'[5] Moreover, the provinces reflected metropolitan culture, and it was only towards the end of the eighteenth century that 'imitation gave way to competition'.[6] This view is entirely consistent with a broader historical assessment that, in England, 'provincial towns gained stature as foci of polite society, consumption, communications and the arts. In search of cultural identity, burghers did not trumpet their 'provinciality'...[but] mimicked the capital'.[7] Feather however, sees a somewhat looser relationship, with 'provincial cultural and economic life...a vigorous entity in its own right, separate from that of London and yet intimately related to it'.[8]

vi. Genres typically found amongst provincially published books were: antiquarian studies and local histories, directories and almanacs, topographical material and guidebooks, local flora and fauna, poetic effusions, sermons, denominational disputes, newspapers and magazines, chapbooks, possibly schoolbooks, and material in non-standard English, or indeed other languages (Scots, Manx, Gaelic, Welsh).

Negative connotations of the word, 'provincial'

Problems arise because of the connotations associated with the adjective 'provincial' – a feature of the word that has been acknowledged and commented upon by many commentators, including, recently, John Feather. The literary scholar Raymond

---

[5] Feather, 'Merchants', p.19.

[6] Feather, *Provincial Trade*, p. 124.

[7] R. Porter, *English Society in the Eighteenth Century*, rev. ed. (London, 1990), p. 40

[8] Feather, 'History of the English Provincial Book Trade', p. 1.

Williams noted that 'metropolitan and provincial were increasingly used to indicate a contrast between refined or sophisticated tastes and manners, and relatively crude and limited manners and ideas...Thus provincial and regional are terms of relative inferiority to an assumed centre, in dominant usage'.[9] In a more directly literary context, Robin Gilmour traced the negative connotations of 'provincial' to the eighteenth century and the 'self-consciously metropolitan bias of high Augustan culture' citing definitions in Johnson's *Dictionary* (1755) to support his case.[10]

Some scholars may have shied away from the centrism implicit in, and the judgemental nature of, the word 'provincial', but it was explicitly spelt out by Wiles who noted, in 1976, 'Although the term 'provincial' as applied to cultural matters commonly implies some degree of inferiority, one must not assume that readers living in the country were not quite so intelligent as those living in London, or that provincial readers were generally satisfied with second-rate publications'.[11]

Wiles, however, perhaps unintentionally condescendingly, rescued the provincial reader from any lack of refinement or intelligence by drawing attention to the availability and demand for books, magazines and newspapers emanating largely from London.

Questions for the orthodox model

The orthodox model, with its central dependence on the concept of provinciality, can be questioned in a number of different ways, some relating to its adequacy to assimilate all features of

---

[9]   R. Williams, *Keywords: a Vocabulary of Culture and Society*, rev. ed. (London, 1988), pp. 265-6.

[10]   R. Gilmour, 'Regional and Provincial in Victorian Literature', in *The Literature of Region and Nation*, ed. by R. P. Draper (Basingstoke, 1989), pp. 51-60 (p. 51).

[11]   Wiles, 'Relish', p. 87.

the English (and, more broadly British) book trade, and others relating to the meanings of terms used.

(a) How adequate is the model in itself?

i. What of provincial publications and their 'limited interest'? Leading scholars, notably Peter Isaac, have brought forward many examples of important and influential texts printed outside the capital cities, yet such instances are liable to being put aside as exceptional. [12] But there is little doubt that even the types of material usually identified as associated with provincial publication are manifestly incomplete. Feather has noted correctly that 'provincial shops stocked a great number of...practical books'. [13] But from whence did these books originate? It is true that books on navigation and seamanship were also published in London, yet it is equally true that many were produced in the major seaports of Britain, where demand would be greatest, and the books' usefulness most immediately appreciated. [14] Books on accountancy, whilst making no direct contribution to *belles-lettres* or to advanced abstract thought, were crucial for the efficiency and effectiveness of regional economies, and were also published throughout British commercial centres as well as in London. [15]

---

[12] P. Isaac, 'The English Provincial Book Trade: a Northern Mosaic', *Papers of the Bibliographical Society of America*, 95 (2001), pp. 410-41.

[13] Feather, 'Merchants', p. 14; J. Feather, *A History of British Publishing*, 2nd ed. (Abingdon, 2006), p. 85.

[14] Examples include Henry Clarke, *The Seaman's Desiderata* (Bristol, 1800); *Instructions for Merchants, Ship-owners, Ship-masters...2nd ed.*, (Plymouth, [1787]), John Draper, *The Navigator's Veni-mecum; or, Complete System of the Art of Navigation* (Whitehaven, 1773); William Chambers, *The Useful Navigator* (Whitehaven, 1774); Thomas Haselden, *The Seaman's Daily Assistant* (Glasgow, 1788); Darcy Lever, *The Young Sea Officer's Sheet Anchor* (Leeds, 1808).

[15] See, Thomas Lazonby, *Merchants Accounts; or, The Italian Method of Book-keeping*, 18th ed. (York, 1757); William Jackson, *Book-keeping in the True Ital-*

The extent to which practical law books and law manuals were printed outside London has probably been underestimated. Again, although many were indeed printed and distributed from the capital, many were not. John Hewitt's *A Guide for Constables and all Peace Officers* was printed in 1779 by Robert Martin in Birmingham; *The Young Clerk's vade mecum; or, Compleat English Law-Tutor* went through several editions in Belfast between 1742 and 1792; and *The Magistrate's Assistant*, by Samuel Glasse, a clergyman and active magistrate himself, was printed in a number of editions in Gloucester by Robert Raikes II from c. 1784 to 1799. This last example is interesting, as Raikes managed to negotiate a distribution agreement for the second and subsequent editions with G. G. & J. Robinson, and others, in London, which rather suggests that the text had a value on a national level also.

ii. Is the 'provincial' / 'metropolitan' model entirely adequate?

Do (within the British context) the two categories cover the totality of possibilities? Possibly not, as there are quite obvious and straightforward examples that do not appear to fit the orthodox model comfortably. Given that local histories, guide books and other texts relating to a particular locality (and published in that same locality) are usually regarded as provincial, how should book-trade historians categorize such books when they relate to London, and have only limited immediate usefulness beyond the capital? This is not a rhetorical question, as there are many such texts: indeed they form a general class of books that tend to be overlooked. *The Builder's Price-Book* (London: I. & J. Taylor, 1776; latest ed. traced in this form, 1801); the substantial, 330-page quarto, The London Society of Cabinet-Makers' *London Book of Prices, and Designs of Cabinet Work*, (2nd ed., 1793);

---

ian Form (Cork, 1792); Edmund Fitzgerald, *An Epitome of the Elements of Italian Book-keeping* (Whitehaven, 1771).

Charles Hallifax's *Constable's Sure Guide; or, every Constable his Own Lawyer* (printed for S. Bladon in Paternoster-Row, 1791), with chapters on the powers and duties of constables in the City of London, and Westminster; *An Historical Description of Westminster Abbey, its Monuments and Curiosities... Designed Chiefly as a Guide to Strangers* (London: Minerva P., for Newman & Co., 1814) are all cases in point. So are we obliged to make a distinction between metropolitan books that were subject to widespread distribution, and, conversely, metropolitan books for local distribution only? The question is one ultimately of scholarly utility, and there is a danger of unnecessarily creating new categories, but it is very clear that printers in London were producing material (concerned with London and its environs) of immediate relevance only to its immediate area, and primarily for local or localised consumption.

iii. Where do we look for evidence of a 'provincial' book? Imprints are highly important, but they are only one type of evidence – and one that is based on decisions and agreements reached before the release of the book to the trade.[16] But what if there were commercial agreements drawn up for the large-scale distribution of books not reflected in an imprint? These could be either pre- or post-publication, though they are most likely to have occurred after release for sale.

The examples that follow are of texts that might be considered, if not 'provincial', then at least 'Scottish', but were also ordered in large numbers by London printers and booksellers. Oliver & Boyd entered into a series of exchange agreements with printers and publishers in London that involved large cash values. In June 1815, Oliver & Boyd's traveller agreed to exchange material to the value of £307 15s 6d. with Newman & Co. of the

---

16 J. Feather, 'The Commerce of Letters: the Study of the Eighteenth-Century Book Trade', *Eighteenth-Century Studies*, 17 (1984), pp. 405-24 (p. 413).

Minerva Press, and to the value of £139 with Dean & Munday of Threadneedle Street. This latter transaction included no fewer than sixteen gross of the first three volumes of Oliver & Boyd's series, *The Little Warbler*, some of which were subsequently advertised by the London firm.[17] Large-scale transactions such as these are hidden from view in that they are not necessarily represented on any title-page imprint, yet they prompt a reassessment of the status of the books themselves, and the limits of their availability.[18] It could be reasonably argued that the most such examples might achieve is a modification of the 'metropolitan'/'provincial' model. This may be correct, but such examples certainly cast doubt on the reliability of imprints to indicate anything like the extent of large-scale, widespread distribution.

(b) Describing aspects of the eighteenth-century trade

i.   What counts as 'metropolitan culture'? A rough working definition might include those sets of attitudes, values, aspirations, social institutions and behaviour patterns embedded in, and expressed through, those publications that the London trade thought saleable and worthy of widespread distribution.[19] Yet some caution may be needed here as such a working definition may be seen as slipping inexorably beyond questions of the eco-

---

[17] Volumes from the *Little Warbler* series are included in the 'List of pamphlets, spelling-books, & c. printed and sold by Dean & Munday' as advertised on the original paper covers of their edition of Walter Scott's *The Abbot*, 1820.

[18] Imprint from the undated 1808/09 edition of Oliver & Boyd's *Little Warbler*. vol. V: *Jacobite Songs* reads 'Edinburgh: printed by Oliver & Boyd, Netherbow', 140pp. The titles in the series were reissued many times between at least 1808 and the early 1820s. For the traveller's log book, London, 1815, see the Oliver & Boyd papers, Acc 5000/1110, in the National Library of Scotland.

[19] Based loosely on P. Burke, *Popular Culture in Early Modern Europe* (Aldershot, 1988), p. [xi].

nomic structure of the trade in itself to a much broader (and infinitely more thorny) issue bearing on the flow and movement of intellectual thought and of the appropriation, adoption, and acceptance of ideas in and beyond the metropolis. The London trade made rigorous commercial decisions about what would turn a profit, and what might fail as a publication: what they published both reflected and influenced taste. If by 'metropolitan culture' is meant, simply, that which the London trade thought saleable, then this is to say very little, but if 'metropolitan culture' is meant to extend to the ideas and values embedded in the publications themselves, then the phrase in the context of the British book trade is in need of further analysis and elucidation.

Such analysis might acknowledge the flow of ideas that emanated outside London, became accepted and established in the capital, then spread back out to other parts of Britain (and beyond) in printed form. Instances abound: the architect James Gibb (or Gibbs) became hugely fashionable in eighteenth-century London. He wrote *A Book of Architecture*, printed in London in 1728, which has been described as 'arguably the most influential pattern book in the history of British architecture... [and] was used throughout Britain and its colonies'.[20] His architectural ideas may have become British by adoption but he was educated in Scotland and his formative years were spent in Italy. David Hume and George Turnbull, both eighteenth-century Scottish philosophers educated in Scotland and profoundly influenced by Scottish and continental thought, had their efforts first published not in Scotland but in London, by John Noon. Dr William Alexander, probably of Halifax, was educated at Edinburgh University and subsequently moved to London. His writings include *Experimental Essays* (London: printed for Dilly,

---

[20] T. Friedman, 'Gibbs [Gibb], James, (1682-1784)', in *Oxford Dictionary of National Biography*. http://www.oxforddnb.com/

1768), and *The History of Women from the Earliest Antiquity to the Present Time*, 1779 (and later editions), first published by Strachan and Cadell: a book that has been described as deserving of 'a place among Enlightenment histories of civil society' and 'influenced by Montesquieu and the *encyclopédistes*' and 'contemporary Scottish historians'.[21] James Oswald, composer, musician and music publisher, moved from Edinburgh to London in 1741, where he not only contributed to, but further stimulated the vogue for 'Scotch Song' which 'flooded the London market...to such an extent that the English almost forgot that they had any traditional or folk-songs of their own'.[22] While these (and many other) examples do not directly affect the adequacy of the economic model, they nevertheless raise some real debate over the cultural genesis of many metropolitan-published books: the interplay of ideas was considerably more complicated and subtle than might be concluded from the simple 'metropolitan culture'/'provincial culture' dichotomy implied by the model.[23]

ii. The appropriate application of adjectives like 'provincial' is acutely time-dependent and reflects contemporaneous constitutional and political realities. Privileged status is usually accorded to Dublin and Edinburgh as books produced in either city are not normally regarded as provincial. The reasons for this are largely attributable to the fact that both cities (depending on the period in question) were either seats of Parliament or of government, or both, and were the bases of His (or Her) Majesties'

---

[21] J. Rendall, 'Alexander, William (bap. 1742?)' in *Oxford Dictionary of National Biography*. http://www.oxforddnb.com/

[22] R. Fiske, *Scotland in Music: a European Enthusiasm* (Cambridge, 1983), p. ix and ch.1.

[23] J. Feather, 'The Country Trade in Books', in *Spreading the Word: the Distribution Networks of Print, 1550-1850*, ed. by R. Myers and M. Harris (Winchester, 1990), pp. 165-83 (p. 171).

Printers in Scotland and Ireland. Nevertheless it is possible for commentators to contort themselves even with the use of the word 'provincial' based entirely on temporal geopolitical facts. Before he started printing in Aberdeen, Edward Raban had worked in Edinburgh and St Andrews. Is Raban therefore to be categorized as a 'provincial' printer? In so far as he started work in Edinburgh, then presumably not, but he (equally presumably) became 'provincial' by moving on to St Andrews and Aberdeen.

Morrison & Co., printers in Perth in the 1790s, might contentiously be regarded as doubly provincial: first, in respect of the relationship between Perth and Edinburgh; but also because of the relationship between Perth and London, capital of the relatively newly created Great Britain. Such a description in regard to Morrison & Co. would be rightly looked upon with discomfort, but one consequence of the use of the word, 'provincial' indicates such a logical end point.

Pejorative provinciality or assertion of cultural difference?

While the points raised above suggest the need for some adjustment to the 'provincial/metropolitan' model, a more fundamental problem resides in any analysis of the British book trade (including and going beyond the 'orthodox model') that relies fundamentally on a term like 'provincial'. One way of countering any difficulty surrounding the use of 'provincial' that has been adopted is essentially to acknowledge and deplore its unfortunate connotations, and minimize them whilst still retaining the adjective for analytical purposes.[24]

But it still has a problem of applicability, and how in particular to describe Scotland, which after the Act of Union became part of Great Britain. Commentators on the British book trade understandably choose not to describe Scotland as 'a province'

---

[24] See Feather, 'History of the English Book Trade', p. 1.

and have claimed that whilst 'the London book trade has always dominated British publishing...from the middle of the eighteenth century onwards it was never without competition', and that the challenge came about because of the 'development of the provincial, Scottish and Irish trades'. Moreover, 'Edinburgh publishing was important in the Scottish domestic market'.[25]

But has the 'provinciality' problem really gone away? By the mid- eighteenth century, London was no more to be completely identified with English printing and publishing than Edinburgh was with the Scottish trade. And if printing in, for example, Birmingham was 'provincial', how should printing and publishing in Glasgow be categorized? But we are left with an open question: if the role of helping support a distinctive culture is allowed for Edinburgh are there other British cities to which a similar status can be attributed? Newcastle may be a candidate, as its regional economic role within the northern English book trade has long been recognized, and its cultural distinctiveness has been emphasized.[26]

Even if the term 'provincial' is now avoided in respect of Scotland, or, more specifically, Edinburgh, this was not the case in the eighteenth century and somewhat later. Charles Elliot, the highly respected Edinburgh-based bookseller, was prepared to pay authors handsomely for their work and notably succeeded in negotiating distribution arrangements for his publications with members of the London trade (who were only too pleased to have a share of the sales). Elliot recorded, perhaps sardonically,

---

[25] Feather, *History of British Publishing*, pp. 78-9, 85.

[26] J. Smith, 'Books and Culture in Late-Eighteenth- and Early-Nineteenth-Century Newcastle', in *The Moving Market: Continuity and Change in the Book Trade*, ed. by P. Isaac and B. McKay (New Castle, Del., London, 2001), pp. 1-12. The adjective 'distinctive' is again not exactly without problems. It could convincingly be argued that to be simultaneously 'distinctive' and 'provincial' is not contradictory.

that 'the London gentlemen thought it strange that a Country Bookseller (so they are pleased to call the vendors of books in the Metropolis of Scotland) should outbid them in the purchase of Dr. Cullen's Practice of Physic'.[27] Indeed, the views of 'the London gentlemen' as given by Elliot are a good example of that metropolitan bias characterised by Gilmour.[28]

Many local publications were more positively perceived as an assertion and affirmation of a particular locality's – or indeed, a particular nation's – sense of identity, that diverged from that embedded in so many publications published in and from London. One eighteenth-century challenge for Scotland was not so much how North Britain was to be measured and assessed against South Britain, but how both Scotland (North Britain) and England and Wales (South Britain) were to be integrated into Britain as a whole and how to achieve a 'furthering of the Scottish cultural presence under the aegis of Britishness'.[29]

Local publications can reinforce a sense of sameness, or similarity across regions: Nonconformist debates and the acceptance

---

[27] Quoted in W. McDougall, 'Charles Elliot's Medical Publications and the International Book Trade', in *Science and Medicine in the Scottish Enlightenment*, ed. by C. Withers and P. Wood (East Linton, 2002), pp. 215-54 (p. 221). Robert Cadell, the Edinburgh publisher of Scott, saw himself as a 'Provincial Publisher'. See Cadell's letter of 1832 to J. G. Lockhart as cited in Jane Millgate, *Scott's Last Edition: a Study in Publishing History* (Edinburgh, 1987), p. 126.

[28] Gilmour, 'Regional and Provincial', p. 51, draws a suggestive distinction between 'provincial' and 'regional' and notes: '"Regional" and "regionalism"...are at least neutral and more usually positive terms, suggesting valid and vigorous differences from metropolitan norms – attractive modes of speech, custom, landscape, culture'.

[29] R. Crawford, *Devolving English Literature*, 2nd ed. (Edinburgh, 2000), pp. 49-50, where he quotes the concerns of the poet, James Thomson that there was an attitude commonly encountered that Britain and England were identical, 'The English People are not a little vain of Themselves, and their Country. Brittania [*sic*] too includes our native Country, Scotland' (p. 49).

of Nonconformist theology provide one example of this. Or perhaps such publications can mark off a particular region as having a degree of religious individuality. A simple, almost commonplace example might be: *A Collection of Spiritual Hymns and Songs on Various Religious Subjects*, printed by James Chalmers & Co, Aberdeen in 1802, the first thirteen pieces of which were 'composed and dictated by the late most worthy and venerable Bishop Geddes'.[30] The work has all the signs of a 'standard' provincial publication, and is one of a very large class of religious texts produced outside London and Edinburgh. However, the work is also a small but important indicator of the continuing existence and tradition of adherence to Roman Catholicism in north-east Scotland. The work itself was produced by the Chalmers family, Presbyterians, semi-official civic printers, and the largest firm in Aberdeen. Yet Geddes himself had been Superior of Scalan, a discreetly organised Roman Catholic seminary in a remote part of Banffshire, and subsequently became rector of the Scots College in Valladolid.

To complicate matters, a book could be simultaneously local and essentially British. Guidebooks and travellers' companions (the latter more for the man of business than the enquiring visitor) of the late eighteenth century and following decades are cases in point. Although these texts have only local or regional applicability, at a more generalized level their very production stands as a statement of the existence and coherence of Britain, and of its diplomatic and political stance, as access for visitors to the European Continent had become very restricted because of war and revolution.[31]

---

[30] *A Collection of Spiritual Hymns and Songs on Various Religious Subjects*, printed by James Chalmers & Co. (Aberdeen, 1802), p. 42.

[31] See J. Smith, *A Month in France and Switzerland during the Autumn of 1824* (London, 1825), p. 1 for travelling difficulties of the preceding period.

'Local' poetry has been described as provincial, especially so if in a form of non-standard or dialect English, or in another language, such as Scots. Behind this description lay the 'Anglocentricity...particularly located in...London...the place to which the eighteenth-century teachers of Rhetoric looked for their standards of language'.[32] Yet not everybody subscribed to the 'high Augustan culture' at the time, and even amongst those who did so, their commitment was not necessarily unqualified.[33] Certainly many Scots consciously modified their forms of speech and writing so as to approach the desired Anglocentric level of elegance and refinement. The poet and philosopher James Beattie was one such, whose *List of Two Hundred Scoticisms* (Aberdeen, 1779) was followed eight years later by *Scoticisms...designed to Correct Improprieties of Speech and Writing* (Edinburgh, 1787), though this is best seen not so much as a gesture towards Anglocentricity, but rather a pro-British stance.[34] Others found no difficulty, no incongruity, in moving between English and Scots as a written medium. Alexander Murray's *History of the European Languages* (Edinburgh: pr. for Constable & Hurst Robinson & Co., London, 1823) included some introductory autobiographical passages. Brought up in Galloway, his reading for many years consisted of school books, and 'ballads and penny-histories'.[35]

---

[32] Crawford, *Devolving*, pp. 7, 13.

[33] D. Hewitt, 'Scoticisms and Cultural Conflict' in *Literature of Region and Nation*, ed. by Draper, pp. 125-35 (p. 129) has observed, in the context of eighteenth-century poetry in Scots, 'The poetry itself constitutes a rejection of the arguments in favour of English, but within the poetry there are clear statements about Scots as the language of Scotland'.

[34] Hewitt, 'Scoticisms', pp. 129, 134 noted that the Scottish literati, 'in spite of their championing of English, found that they were employing a foreign tongue that restricted their self-expression'.

[35] Alexander Murray, *History of the European Languages* (Edinburgh: pr. for Constable & Hurst Robinson & Co., London, 1823), p. xliii.

His first serious attempt to get into print was with a translation of 'a MS. Volume of the Lectures of Arnold Drackenburg...on the Lives and Writings of the Roman Authors', yet, as he had doubts about the success of the translation he 'likewise composed a number of Poems, chiefly in the Scottish dialect, and most of them very indifferent...but...I collected by myself and friends four or five hundred subscriptions'. What is significant here and elsewhere in Murray's autobiography is his assessment of the poems in Scots: certainly 'indifferent', 'incorrect, stupid and silly' but never actually inappropriate.[36] The status of the Scots language, which, in printed contexts, survived notably in poetic discourse, was intimately related to the status of Scotland itself. [37]

Andrew Shirreffs, bookseller, printer and poet addressed the Country Club of Aberdeenshire in his introduction to his comedy, *Jamie and Bess or the Laird in Disguise* (Aberdeen, 1787) and suggested that:

Had my performance been written in the most elegant and polished language...it could have been addressed to none, with more propriety, than to you. But such as it is, that Patriotic spirit which you inherit...and which you have on so many occasions so eminently displayed, will probably dispose you to favour a Performance written in the Scots dialect.

Shirreffs' *Poems Chiefly in the Scottish Dialect* was published in Edinburgh in 1790. Like the Edinburgh edition of Burns pub-

---

[36] Murray, *History of the European Languages*, pp. lxvi-lxvii, xxxiii.

[37] See A. Hook, 'Introduction', in *The History of Scottish Literature*, vol. 2: 1660-1800, ed. by A. Hook (Aberdeen, 1987) pp. 3-4, where he poses a series of questions: 'Was standard English to be the language of Scotland outside the Gaelic-speaking areas...? Yes and no was the characteristic eighteenth-century answer...Scottish self-consciousness in this area was extraordinarily acute. Language often appears to be the point at which a more generalized cultural uneasiness becomes specific.'

lished three years earlier, and under the aegis of the same book-seller, William Creech, Shirreffs' *Poems* was published by sub-scription. At least 110 copies went to the Edinburgh booksellers, and another 100 to the trade in London, and over 125 to the West Indies. But why so many to the Caribbean? By 1790 Scots had both benefited from, and significantly contributed to, British imperialism and trade for nearly eighty years. Business was defi-nitely British and commanded (and duly received) its own loyalty. Yet simultaneously the book's subscribers in the West Indies, primarily Jamaica, appear to have maintained – perhaps forged – their sense of identity by buying copies of a work in Scots. The same phenomenon is apparent, though less clearly, with David Morison's *Poems, Chiefly in the Scottish Dialect* (Mon-trose: pr. by David Buchanan, 1790). Again financed by subscription, eleven copies went to Gothenburg in Sweden, where there was a long-standing community of traders (including many of Scottish background) in wood and iron ore.[38] Shirreffs' *Poems* appealed to others, also, such as Jonathan Troup who studied medicine in Aberdeen and Edinburgh, and who was by 1791 practising in Dominica. His diaries indicate that his reading was varied and wide and included Hugh Blair's *Sermons*, James Fordyce's *Addresses to Young Men* (1777), Johann Zimmermann's *Solitude* (prob.1791 edition), and the then recently published *Po-ems* of Andrew Shirreffs.[39]

While it must readily be conceded that readership patterns in the Caribbean have no obvious bearing on the structure of the British book trade, the presence of, and demonstrable demand for, these 'provincial' books in Scots reflect a positive sense of a

---

[38] J. Ashton, *Lives and Livelihoods in Little London: the Story of the British in Gothenburg*, 1621-2001 (Savedalen, 2003).

[39] W. Cranna, 'A list of books read by Jonathan Troup from 1791 to 1796, extracted from his diary', Aberdeen University MS 2391.

cultural identity amongst those wishing to obtain copies. And to call these Scots poems 'provincial' (with all its depreciatory connotations) – whether or not they had any literary merit – would be to understate their overall cultural significance.

As Francis Jeffrey, lawyer (later judge), critic and editor observed in the context of a long review of *The Reliques of Robert Burns*:

This Scotch is not to be considered as a provincial dialect, – the vehicle only of rustic vulgarity and rude local humour. It is the language of a whole country, – long an independent kingdom, and still separate in laws, character and manners'. It is by no means peculiar to the vulgar; but is the common speech of the whole nation in early life, – and with many of its most exalted and accomplished individuals throughout their whole existence. [40]

Works in Scots were published in England also, and decades before William Davison of Alnwick printed his editions of Burns's *Poetical Works* in 1808 and Thomas Donaldson's *Poems, Chiefly in the Scotish Dialect,* a year later. At least one London bookseller, Thomas Jauncy, at the Angel, acted as publisher and bookseller for some of the works of the Scottish poet, Allan Ramsay (d.1758). In 1720 alone he sold Ramsay's *Prospect of Plenty,* his *Poem on the South-Sea* and *Wealth or the Woody.* Jauncy's open letter to the readers of *The Doleful Swains,* composed by the Scots-born poet and playwright, Joseph Mitchell, is surprising in its even-handed distinction between South Britain and (by implication) North Britain:

After the author of the following Pastoral Poem, Originally compos'd in the Natural Simplicity of the Scots vulgar Dialect, was prevail'd on to allow me to Publish it; he was also perswaded to favour us with a

---

[40] 'Review of *Reliques of Robert Burns*', *Edinburgh Review*, 15 (1809), pp. 249-76 (p. 259). Cited in Hewitt, 'Scoticisms', pp. 133-4.

Translation of it into proper English. His South-British Readers, for whose sake the Version was made, may therefore be assured it is as just and literal as the Nature of the Thing could allow.

There are also many examples of the use of non-standard English in eighteenth-century publications emanating from English towns and cities.[41] And by the early nineteenth century, articles were being published in 'metropolitan' magazines using English dialect.[42] Again, commentators are presented to an extent with the same problem. Such publications are undoubtedly geopolitically provincial. Yet are they 'provincial' in the sense of being of 'limited interest'; and, even if they are, to what extent were (and still are) such works to be seen as an expression of a non-metropolitan culture?[43]

Do we live with 'provincial'?

This paper does not attempt to expunge the word, 'provincial' (and cognate forms) from discussions of British book-trade history. The word has become firmly embedded in relevant

---

[41] For example, Rev. Robert Nelson, *A Choice Collection of Poems in Cumberland Dialect* (Sunderland, [1780?]); A.W., *The Westmorland Dialect, in Three Familiar Dialogues, in which an Attempt is made to Illustrate the Provincial Idiom* (Kendal, pr. by James Ashburner, 1790); Rev. Thomas Browne, *Poems on Several Occasions*, which makes use of Yorkshire dialect, was printed in Manchester, 1800 for Vernor & Hood, London, and sold also in Liverpool and Hull. On Tim Bobbin and his Lancashire dialect writings, see R. Poole, 'Collier, John [pseud. Tim Bobbin'], in *Oxford Dictionary of National Biography*, http://www.oxforddnb.com/

[42] For example, 'The Parson's Tale in the Provincial Dialect of the Barony of Kendal, Westmorland', *The Lady's Monthly Magazine*, March 1803, pp. 187-89.

[43] See P. Borsay's view in his introduction to R. Porter's 'Science, Provincial Culture and Public Opinion in Enlightenment England' in *The Eighteenth-Century Town: a Reader in English Urban History, 1688-1820*, ed. by P. Borsay (London, 1990), p. 243, that the influence of the metropolis may be overstated by some historians, and too little regard given to 'the more regionally orientated county towns and provincial capitals.'

specialized discussions and, within the overall topic, is used in historical, economic, political, and cultural contexts, all frequently overlapping and inter-linked.[44] However it does carry with it a cluster of pejorative connotations, which have descended from at least the eighteenth century. If not avoided, they will remain to obscure and stalk future discussion and debate.

---

[44] See M. Suarez, 'Historiographical Problems and Possibilities in Book History and National histories of the Book', *Studies in Bibliography*, 56 (2003-04), pp. 141-70, especially the section on 'boundaries (pp. 147-50).

The Market for Murder and Edinburgh's Eighteenth-Century Book Trade

STEPHEN W. BROWN

O N 18 NOVEMBER 1765 the publishers of the *Scots Magazine*, the *Edinburgh Weekly Journal*, the *Edinburgh Evening Courant*, and the *Caledonian Mercury* were summoned by the Lord Advocate to appear before the high court of the justiciary to answer for having printed a controversial document known as the *Opinion* of Mr M'Carty, a London lawyer, who had questioned the legitimacy of both the proceedings and the outcome of a notorious incest/murder trial conducted in Edinburgh in August of that year.[1] The court's official record for the publishers' trial on 25 November – afterwards printed *with* permission in the *Weekly Journal* and the *Scots Magazine* – reports the admission of guilt by the appellants and especially William Auld, then proprietor of the *Weekly Journal*, who was the first by several days to publish the offending *Opinion*.[2] Auld no doubt knew who had solicited M'Carty's *Opinion*

---

[1] The *Opinion* had been printed by the *Weekly Journal*, the *Edinburgh Evening Courant*, the *Caledonian Mercury* and the *Scots Magazine* on 2 October, 7 October, 9 October and 23 October 1765, respectively, with an appearance in the *London Chronicle*, 12 October 1765, attributed to the *Courant* and the *Mercury*. The *Weekly Journal* did not have a London circulation. M'Carty's *Opinion* was itself dated 14 September 1765.

[2] The *Proceedings of the High Court of Justiciary in Relation to the Publication of Mr M'Carty's 'Opinion'* appeared 27 November and 4 December (November issue) in the *Weekly Journal* and the *Scots Magazine*. The *Scots Magazine's* summary of the *Proceedings* is reprinted as 'Appendix VIII' in the *Trial of Katharine Nairn*, ed. William Roughead, *Notable British Trials* (Edinburgh, 1926), pp. 199-204. A further account with more of a book trade slant is available in W. J. Couper, *The Edinburgh Periodical Press*, 2 vols (Sterling, 1908), vol. 1, pp. 102-04 and vol. 2, pp. 94-5. See also Hugo Arnot, *History of Edinburgh* (Edinburgh, 1779), pp. 270-1.

– and had received it himself directly from that individual. Auld indicated by way of some modest defence that 'there had been a great many copies...dispersed and going about in the city of Edinburgh in different hands' of which he 'procured two copies...and did cause [to] print the same...[and] now is sensible he was wrong in so doing, and is sorry therefor'.[3]

The others (the *Courant*'s Robert Fleming, the *Mercury*'s Walter Ruddiman, and William Sands, Alexander Murray and James Cochran of the *Scots Magazine*) all insisted that they only printed the libellous text to keep up competitively with Auld; their fault was simply that 'they did severally cause to reprint and publish, by themselves or servants, the said Opinion'.[4] After severely rebuking the publishers but issuing neither a fine nor a prison sentence, the Lord Advocate himself is recorded to have 'stood up and took notice' that he was motivated in bringing the charges because, among other things, 'the publication in question was a kind of challenge to enter into a paper-war in the newspapers' and 'he had thought himself bound, by the duty of his office, to take notice of this publication; submitting the matter entirely to the court'.[5] Alexander Donaldson, the publisher of Edinburgh's fourth newspaper, the newly established *Edinburgh Advertiser*, who alone declined to follow William Auld in printing M'Carty's *Opinion*, was praised by the justiciary for his commendable discretion, although his motives, as we shall see, were not altruistic. Among 'the erring publishers', however, Auld received the 'severest censure' not only for initiating the publication of the M'Carty document but for further aggravating the court by being the only publisher to advertise in his paper for Edinburgh 'gentlemen of the law' to come forward and offer

[3]   Roughead, *Notable British Trials*, p. 201.

[4]   Roughead, *Notable British Trials*, p. 201.

[5]   *Scots Magazine*, vol. 27, p. 564.

their views on the jury's verdict.[6]

The Lord Advocate's decision – especially its precedent suggesting that the court should intervene in 'paper-war[s]' – would become one of several crisis points in the historic debate around the liberty of the press in Scotland. Hugo Arnot, who was personally acquainted with the whole affair from the incest/murder trial through to the case against the newspapers, dedicates several pages to it in his 1779 *History of Edinburgh*, finally observing that 'nothing could be more dastardly than this submission of the printers' whose 'abject timidity alone' makes way for 'usurpation and tyranny'.[7] In his seminal study of Edinburgh's periodical press, W. J. Couper concurs with Arnot and insists that the court was not so much disturbed by M'Carty's opinion as by 'the boldness with which papers circulating widely among the citizens dared to criticize the doings of the authorities'.[8]

But examined from another angle, the issue may have more to do with the liberty of the *purse* than of the *press*. The scandalous case about which M'Carty had expressed his 'opinion', the incest/murder trial of Katharine Nairn and her brother-in-law Lieutenant Patrick Ogilvie of the 89th regiment of foot, contained all the elements of classic tabloid journalism. On 13 January 1765 Thomas Ogilvie, a gouty, over-weight and eccentric bachelor laird married a pretty local girl, Katharine Nairn, considerably his junior, and she promptly fell in love with his younger soldier brother, Patrick, a dashing and handsome lieutenant residing with the newlyweds in the family home at Eastmiln. A third brother, the wastrel Alexander, had gone to Edinburgh to study medicine but turned instead to gambling, drinking, and whoring, eventually setting up house with his cousin Anne Clark. But when Alexander married a stableman's

---

6   Couper, *The Edinburgh Periodical Press*, vol. 2, pp. 94-5.

7   Arnot, *History of Edinburgh*, p. 271.

8   Couper, *The Edinburgh Periodical Press*, vol. 1, pp. 104-05.

daughter, the conniving Anne was sent to live with Thomas and Katharine in Eastmiln, sometime in March 1765, where she eventually figured prominently as the prosecution's much maligned star witness at the incest/murder trial. It was she who would claim to have seen Katharine and the Lieutenant kissing on 19 May 1765, and who would testify to Katharine's having received a parcel of arsenic from Patrick on 5 June, which Katharine confessed to Anne she planned to use to poison her husband – or, at least, that was what Anne would claim in her deposition. Anne Clark's own morally suspect conduct and her scheming alliance with the third Ogilvie brother Alexander, who stood to inherit the estate should his two siblings be removed and who raised the alarm against Katharine on 11 June five days after his brother's death, made her the public's *bête noir*. When Katharine and Patrick were found guilty of both incest and murder on 14 August, Katharine was discovered to be pregnant; her capital sentence consequently delayed, she would eventually escape Edinburgh's Tollbooth prison on 15 March 1766, disguised in some accounts as a young soldier and in others in the garb of one of the midwives who regularly visited her. Whatever the masquerade, it succeeded and she was never heard from again. Her abandoned child died just a week after the mother's flight on 23 March. Patrick received four reprieves from the King before being hanged on 13 November 1765, and Alexander, after inheriting the estate, was arrested, tried, and exiled for seven years for bigamy, having been found to have married his cousin Anne before his matrimonial union with the stableman's daughter.[9] The social standing of the pannels (the accused) and the intricate family politics at play in this extraordinary affair predictably attracted widespread public interest, but the Edinburgh newspapers mostly responded with delicacy: there was a clear reluctance to

---

[9]   Timeline derived from newspaper accounts and Roughead, pp. 65-6.

print the actual details of the case on the part of the city's two most established papers, the *Courant* and the *Mercury*, and the bulk of the most controversial coverage before, during, and after the matter came to court was provided by the *Weekly Journal*, originally part of the lucrative publishing empire of the Ruddiman family but now owned solely by William Auld.[10] Auld was among Edinburgh's more successful printers, and he was obviously ambitious to become a publisher. Acquiring the *Weekly Journal* was a first step in that direction, and he would subsequently put his name to several profitable literary properties, including the bestselling *Account of the Trial of Katharine Nairn and Lieutenant Patrick Ogilvie* (1765).[11]

---

[10] Walter Ruddiman Jr was William Auld's partner from the founding of the *Weekly Journal* in 1757, the same year that he launched the monthly *Edinburgh Magazine* in direct competition with the *Scots Magazine*. Auld would become a partner in that second venture in 1761, when his name appears with Ruddiman's on all the issues forming volume five. In 1762, when the *Magazine* was withdrawn, Ruddiman also left the *Journal*, but he would combine his experiences with the weekly newspaper and the monthly magazine when he created something of a new periodical genre in 1768 with the *Weekly Magazine, or Edinburgh Amusement*, which cleverly included news with the usual magazine fare, thus competing with the newspapers while avoiding the stamp tax – which he did successfully for nearly a decade. When Ruddiman left the *Journal*, William's brother Robert, a lawyer in Aberdeen, provided financing as a silent partner until William Smellie joined in 1765, to be followed quickly by the bookseller John Balfour. Both William Auld and William Smellie had been apprentices with the firm of Hamilton, Balfour and Neill. With the establishment of Ruddiman's *Weekly Magazine*, the *Journal* rapidly lost its advertising income and ceased publishing not long after Smellie and Balfour withdrew from the partnership in early 1771. Smellie's surviving correspondence with both Auld brothers in the Archives of the Society of Antiquaries of Scotland (National Museums of Scotland) indicates that by 1770 the *Journal*'s finances were in disarray, and the periodical is not listed among Auld's properties in the extensive depositions from a legal suit brought against Auld in October 1773 (National Archives of Scotland, CS 271/41914).

[11] Auld was the essential link in passing along *The Rudiments of Architecture*, which he acquired in 1772 after its first edition (published by subscription and printed by Auld) sold out. He then printed a quick and highly profitable sec-

Were it not for Auld, the trial of Katharine Nairn and Patrick Ogilvie would never have become a *cause célèbre* for liberty of the press. Edinburgh's three other newspapers (the *Courant*, the *Mercury*, and the *Advertiser*) published only the abstract of the indictment (as approved by the court clerk) and the written replies of the two defendants, along with the guilty verdict, carefully worded to favour the jury's decision. They would no doubt have left the matter alone at that point, had Auld's *Weekly Journal* not persisted by raising questions about the trial's improprieties and ultimately turning to the critical opinion of the London lawyer M'Carty to support the notion that an injustice had occurred. The trial itself thus became as notorious as the crime.

The court was in session for some twenty-two consecutive hours, during which time the jury and the judges openly consorted and socialized. Katharine Nairn's defence was led by none other than Henry Dundas (the future Viscount Melville), appointed city assessor just after the trial[12] and brother to the Lord

---

ond edition in 1773. The text ultimately became the joint property of James Dickson and Charles Elliot in 1778. But Auld's most successful literary property was the *Free Masons Pocket Companion* which he first issued jointly with fellow-freemason Walter Ruddiman Jr in 1761, then in partnership with William Smellie (also a freemason) in 1765, before his famous sole-proprietor third edition of 1772, entitled *The History of Masonry*, which became Scotland's standard freemason's handbook until at least 1792. Along with the *Weekly Journal* (1757-72) and the *Edinburgh Magazine* (1761), Auld also had partial or full ownership of at least three other periodical titles: the *Scots Farmer* (1772), the *Gentleman and Lady's Weekly Magazine* (1774-5), and the *North British Intelligencer* (1776-77). Auld joined John Mennons (later founding publisher of the *Glasgow Advertiser*, 1783, subsequently the *Herald*) and Walter Ruddiman Jr as the major players in Scotland's magazine trade in the 1760s and 1770s.

[12] *Edinburgh Advertiser*, Tuesday 13 August to Friday 16 August: 'Wednesday last the town-council of this city, made choice of Henry Dundas, Esq; Advocate, brother to the Lord President, to be one of the assessors of this city' (p. 4). Dundas was married on 16 August, immediately after the conclusion of the trial.

President, whose extended family were in the midst of establishing a political dynasty that would control Scotland for half a century.[13] Dundas raised compelling questions about the propriety of the proceedings, and no doubt saw the trial as a showcase to establish his credentials as a clever and resourceful interpreter of the law who would not hesitate to go over the heads of those he found blocking his way. It is quite likely that Dundas himself procured M'Carty's *Opinion*, and, after circulating it in the capital, went to Auld as someone who had already shown discomfort with the justiciary's conduct during the trial and would see the opportunity to print the *Opinion* as a way of sustaining interest in the case while trumping his newspaper competitors. At any rate, the aspersions consequently cast on the Scottish justiciary caused Edinburgh greater shame than the incestuous conduct of the fratricide Ogilvie.

But what were William Auld's motives in pursuing the story so relentlessly, other than preparing a market for a monograph account of the sensational trial? How did his coverage of the trial differ from that of his fellow newspapermen? And was his contrition before the Lord Advocate genuine? Answering these questions touches on two seldom discussed areas of Edinburgh's eighteenth-century book trade: one, the mutually acknowledged patterns followed by the city's newspapers in purveying the news; and the other, the way in which newspaper publishers turned scandal into profit.

The trial of Katharine Nairn and Patrick Ogilvie first became news with the announcement in the press of their arrest and indictment in June 1765, but no more than a perfunctory notice of the affair is taken by any of the Edinburgh papers at this point, and it is left at that, until the trial commenced on 12 August. But during the period between the indictment and the trial, William

---

[13] Michael Fry, *The Dundas Despotism* (Edinburgh, 1992). See pp. 23-4 for a brief discussion of the trial and its place in Henry Dundas's early career.

Auld, alone among the city's newspaper publishers, had personal access to the high court's preparations for the trial since his brother and then silent partner in the *Weekly Journal*, Robert, was enlisted by the Crown to interview witnesses against Nairn and Ogilvie. It was Robert Auld who first deponed Anne Clark, eventually the most controversial individual associated with the case. It is reasonable to assume that Robert shared information from these interviews with his brother in anticipation of the notoriety that would accrue around the affair. And this may well have been the first impetus in suggesting to William Auld that the sale of a book-length account of the trial would be profitable; alternatively, it may have been Auld's soon-to-be partner, the bookseller John Balfour – he would purchase Robert's share of the *Weekly Journal* in 1766 – who got the idea for a book about the trial since his long-term partner Gavin Hamilton was to be one of the jurymen.[14] No doubt both circumstances convinced Auld to proceed with the monograph account, which appeared immediately after the trial and, as we shall see, sold well enough to merit two editions in quick succession. Consequently, as the trial progressed and became a topic in the papers, Auld had a unique incentive among the city's publishers to keep the public interest alive in order to create a market for his book about the proceedings.

When the trial opened on 12 August, the papers and the *Scots Magazine* all printed – as was customary in high-profile criminal cases – an abstract of the official indictment along with the written defences of both Nairn and Ogilvie. These ran to seven

---

[14] As previously noted, both William Auld and William Smellie had been apprenticed with the publishing firm of John Balfour, Gavin Hamilton and Patrick Neill. Since Balfour shared the imprint of *An Account of the Trial of Katharine Nairn and Patrick Ogilvie* (1765) with Auld and Smellie, and since Gavin Hamilton, Balfour's partner, served on the jury while Auld's brother (and former partner) Robert worked for the Crown in the case, we are presented here with a scenario of business intimacy that typifies the close-knit and familial nature of Edinburgh's book trade in the mid-eighteenth century.

columns in the *Courant*, the *Mercury*, and the *Journal*, and ten pages in the *Scots Magazine*. All five venues also remarked upon the unusual duration of the proceedings. The prosecution's case was complete by 3pm on the Tuesday (13 August) with the defence then continuing until 2am on the Wednesday (14 August), when the jury were 'inclosed' (sequestered), returning their verdict at 4pm that same day. According to Scottish law at the time, the whole proceedings continued without adjournments, other than refreshments. Each newspaper account is prefaced with an editorial justification for publishing the official records of the trial at such length. The *Courant* observes that:

Some weeks ago Katharine Nairn relict of Thomas Ogilvie of Eastmiln, and Patrick Ogilvie Lieutenant in the 89th regiment of foot were committed prisoners to the tollbooth of Edinburgh, being accused at the instance of his Majesty's advocate, of the crimes of **INCEST** and **MURDER**. As this unhappy affair now excites the general attention, we shall here (*however disagreeable we judge the task*) [italics mine] present our readers with an abstract of the Indictment together with the printed Defences offered for the Pannels....It is hoped that the publication of this Abstract will both gratify the public curiosity, and prevent that inundation of vague and uncertain reports concerning this unhappy affair, which are flying through every corner of the country.[15]

The *Caledonian Mercury* and the *Edinburgh Advertiser* print a similar preamble to their publication of the Abstract and Defences, but without the telling phrase 'however disagreeable we find the task', which is exclusive to the editor of the *Courant*. In all three instances the words 'incest' and 'murder' are printed in bold upper-case characters. All three papers talk about the stir caused by the charges; the *Advertiser* writes that the 'great deal of noise' surrounding these 'horrid crimes' is such that the newspapers must 'gratify the public curiosity, until the issue of the cause

---

[15] *Edinburgh Evening Courant*, 10 August 1765.

is known'.[16] In his preamble to the abstract in the *Weekly Journal*, Auld echoes precisely the wording of his three competitors about 'gratify[ing] public curiosity' and joins the *Courant* and *Mercury* in a desire to 'prevent inundation[s] of vague and uncertain reports', but he does not moralize, declining to talk about 'horrid' crimes, nor does he offer disclaimers about the disagreeableness of journalism having to deal in such events.[17]

During the trial the *Advertiser*, the *Courant*, and the *Mercury* apologized for going to press before the latest official updates from the proceedings had been announced, and they observed somewhat self-righteously that it would be improper to speculate on the prolonged proceedings. Again, the *Weekly Journal* takes a different tack by delaying going to print until trial updates are available and confirmed by the court clerk. Thus the *Journal* reports on 14 August 'we hope our Readers will excuse our late Publication of our Paper for this Night owing to our earnest desire to gratify our Readers with the event of this important trial.'[18] Consequently, Auld is the first to print the verdict and, perhaps more significantly, to assert that irregularites in the court, arising from what the *Weekly Journal* called 'informalities in the course of the trial' (or consorting among the prosecutors, jurors and judges), may entitle the two defendants to an 'arrest of judgment'.[19] Auld is so keen to demonstrate the up-to-dateness of his report that he provides a precise time for this news item, 'Wednesday night, eight o'clock', and his note about the prolongation of the trial on account of the objections by the defence is datelined 'nine this evening'.[20] Auld clearly delayed printing that day's paper until some time afterwards, around ten o'clock that

---

[16] *Edinburgh Advertiser*, 11 August 1765, p. 97.

[17] *Edinburgh Weekly Journal*, 7 August 1765, pp. 1-2.

[18] *Edinburgh Weekly Journal*, 14 August 1765, p. 1.

[19] *Edinburgh Weekly Journal*, 14 August 1765, p. 1.

[20] *Edinburgh Weekly Journal*, 14 August 1765, p. 2.

night. But what is obviously breaking news for Auld becomes old news for his competition who are fully a day to three days behind him in publishing these particulars. The *Advertiser* prints the verdict on 15 August, but the *Courant* and the *Mercury* do not report the trial's final outcome until 17 August. None of these three papers shows any concern over the verdict nor do they mention anything about improprieties in the conduct of the court itself.

The arrest of judgment was denied and sentence was passed on the defendants on 15 August, despite Henry Dundas challenging the objectivity of a jury that openly conversed with the judges and dined with them during breaks in the proceedings, and his insistence that under Scottish law two capital indictments (incest and murder) could not be treated in a single trial. When the sentence of the court was published in the press, Auld again dissented from the common approach of his fellow newspaper publishers. The *Courant*, *Mercury*, and *Advertiser* quote the pronouncement in full, emphasizing the dreadfulness of Patrick Ogilvie's fate and announcing the shocking discovery of Katharine Nairn's pregnancy, although even that was uncertain since the midwives who examined her could not be sure of her condition and were given three months to observe her before swearing oaths to her pregnancy before the court. The *Courant* observes that the Lieutenant would be

carried back to prison, there to be fed on bread and water, till Wednesday the 25th day of September next, and between the hours of two and four o'clock to be carried to the Grass-market and there to be hanged upon a gibbet till dead; and thereafter his body to be given to Dr Alexander Monro, professor of Anatomy, to be publickly dissected.[21]

The accounts in the *Advertiser* and the *Mercury* are similar, although they do not identify Dr Monro, whose name and

---

[21] *Edinburgh Evening Courant*, 17 August 1765, p. 2.

academic title bring such striking *gravitas* to the *Courant's* record, saying only that Ogilvie's body will 'be given to the
surgeons to be dissected'.[22]

Both the latter papers also take the *Courant's* lead in publishing an editorial defence of the character and testimony of
Ogilvie's cousin, Anne Clark, whose reputation had been questioned with good cause by Henry Dundas, although her
apparently perjured evidence on behalf of the prosecution still
carried the day against the two accused. Thus the *Courant* writes
on 17 August:

It is to be observed that notwithstanding the attack made upon the
character of Miss Anne Clark in the printed defences, no evidence
whatever was adduced to impeach her character; and instead of har-
bouring malice against the prisoners, it appeared she had withdrawn
herself from the place of her abode and concealed herself in different
places under a false name, in order to avoid giving evidence against
them; and that she was not recovered till the warrants issued by the
Court forced her from her concealment.[23]

The *Weekly Journal* makes no attempt to rehabilitate Clark in
this way, and when the *Scots Magazine* finally begins its account
of the trial with a long article at the beginning of October,[24] its

---

[22] *Caledonian Mercury*, 17 August 1765, p. 3; *Edinburgh Advertiser*, Tuesday
August 13 to Friday August 16, p. 6.

[23] *Edinburgh Evening Courant*, 17 August 1765, p. 2.

[24] The *Scots Magazine* is delayed in its coverage of the trial because its
monthly numbers appear some six weeks after the fact, but it nevertheless
provides the most thorough coverage and one sees Smellie compiling the
monograph for the *Account* as he edits the *Magazine*. Nairn/Ogilvie first appear in the *Scots Magazine* in July with ten pages covering the arrest and
indictment, followed by the M'Carty *Opinion* in September, an initial five
pages on the trial itself in October with a further twenty-four pages on the
trial in November (including three pages on the court's proceedings against
the publishers of the *Opinion*), and a concluding six pages on the trail in December. March 1766 sees two more pages on Katharine Nairn's escape. The
Scots Magazine does not cover the trial in its August number, instead dedicat-

editor William Smellie – who, as we have already heard, was also editing the *Weekly Journal* for Auld and would become his partner in the autumn of 1765 – reprints this paragraph but with a careful attribution to the *Courant* and the *Mercury* that cannily separates the *Scots Magazine* from the sympathetic portrayal of Clark promoted by these two newspapers.[25]

While Katharine Nairn was awaiting confirmation of a pregnancy that would postpone her execution, Patrick Ogilvie received four royal reprieves, an indication not only of the doubts surrounding his trial but even more so of the defence team's connections and reputation in London. It is at this point that the infamous M'Carty *Opinion* is first solicited, then circulated in manuscript around those in Edinburgh sympathetic to Ogilvie and inclined toward the rising Dundas dynasty. When it appears in the *Weekly Journal* on 2 October, it does so carefully framed by two editorial paragraphs. The editor introduces M'Carty's analysis with a reference to the 'unfortunate Mr. Ogilvie', an epithet in bold contrast to the *Courant*'s 'horrid' murderer. He then goes on to justify the *Weekly Journal*'s publication of M'Carty's critique of the trial as an explanation of the King and his Privy Council's intervention on Ogilvie's behalf, asserting that M'Carty, 'an eminent English Counsellor ... points out to us the reasons of granting a reprieve to this unfortunate

---

ing nearly twenty pages (including an advertisement from the Faculty of Advocates) to the contentious issue of changes in the laws on entailments. The crisis over entailments with its extraordinary implications for Scotland's landed money was the primary interest of all of Edinburgh's newspapers except the *Weekly Journal* throughout the summer of 1765. It was only Auld and Smellie who brought the incest/murder trial to the foreground of the capital's imagination, perhaps providing some relief from the more serious matter of the entails.

[25] *Scots Magazine*, vol. 27, pp. 513-17. The one major analysis of the Nairn/Ogilvie trial by the lawyer William Roughead (*The Trial of Katharine Nairn*, pp. 1-64) is reluctant to speculate about Clark's veracity, but nonetheless studiously casts doubt on her testimony (pp. 34-8).

Gentleman'. The editor thus concludes his short commentary with a second expression of sympathy for the Lieutenant. At the end of the three-column opinion, the editor inserts another paragraph soliciting 'any Gentleman of the law' among his readers to 'take the trouble of transmitting to the Publishers his Observations upon it'[26] (that is, the verdict and M'Carty's critique of it).

When the *Courant*, *Mercury*, and *Scots Magazine* reprint M'Carty's *Opinion* on October 7, 9, and 23 respectively, only the *Scots Magazine* refers sympathetically to Ogilvie and none calls for further commentary from Edinburgh's legal community on the trial and the reprieve. The *Weekly Journal*'s editorializing went a long way towards antagonizing the high court magistrates, who clearly saw it as a direct challenge. This becomes all the more apparent when one reads M'Carty's *Opinion* as it was printed in the other papers, objectively presented and lacking an editor's commentary. The *Journal*'s actual editorial texts were likely written by William Smellie, or so his surviving correspondence with Auld suggests,[27] and this would explain the apparent inclination of the *Scots Magazine* to sympathize with the *Weekly Journal*, since Smellie was simultaneously editor of both periodicals in 1765. Curiously, Smellie prints the M'Carty *Opinion* one month before he gives the readers of the *Scots Magazine* an account of the trial itself. The *Opinion* becomes the lead article in the magazine's September issue (published 23 October), with the trial narrative not coming out until the October number appeared in November. It seems that Smellie made the decision to print M'Carty in the space he had already provided for an ac-

---

[26] *Edinburgh Weekly Journal*, 2 October 1765, p. 1.

[27] William Kerr does not print this material in his *Memoirs of the Life and Writings of William Smellie* (Edinburgh, 1811), but correspondence in the archives of the Society of Antiquaries of Scotland clearly indicates that from early in 1765 Smellie was editing the *Weekly Journal* for Auld. National Museums of Scotland, William Smellie Manuscript Papers, Book Trade Correspondence: Robert and William Auld.

count of the trial, bumping the latter back by one month. This suggests that Smellie was keen to get M'Carty's critique of the verdict into the wider circulation that a magazine provided over a newspaper, especially with the *Scots Magazine*'s London readership, an unambiguous indication of his support for the defence, and his willingness (with Henry Dundas's backing) to risk offending Lord Kames, whose behaviour on the Bench was most in question.

Smellie had many run-ins with the authorities throughout his career in journalism, including a notorious series while editing the *Edinburgh Magazine and Review* between 1773 and 1776,[28] and Auld wrote later in November 1765 from Aberdeen chastising Smellie for printing an incendiary piece in Auld's absence about the price of corn that invoked sympathetically the name of one of Edinburgh's chief rioters.[29] Smellie's name only appears in the imprint of the *Weekly Journal* after his contract with the *Scots Magazine* expires in late 1765/early 1766, but he is prominent in the imprint and the advertisements for the monograph about the trial. One further suspects that Auld and Smellie would only have gone so far with M'Carty's opinion had they known all the while that Dundas and his political faction were behind them. And it is equally probable that the surprising leniency shown by the Lord Advocate towards Auld when the latter appeared with his publishing colleagues at the bar on 18 November was also prompted by the long cast of the political shadow of the Dundases.

And just how genuine was Smellie's printing partner's contrition before the high court? Not enough to deter William Auld's *Weekly Journal* from continuing to suggest that Lieutenant Ogilvie's conviction was unsafe. Two days after his rebuke from the

---

[28] See William Zachs, *Without Regard to Good Manners: A Biography of Gilbert Stuart 1743-1786* (Edinburgh, 1992), pp. 63-95.

[29] William Smellie's Manuscript Papers, Book Trade Correspondence: Robert and William Auld.

Lord Advocate, Auld is alone among Edinburgh's newspaper publishers in printing Ogilvie's gallows speech, and he does so (or his editor William Smellie does) in a way seemingly designed to inflame readers and present yet another challenge to a 'paper-war'.[30] On 20 November, the *Weekly Journal* carries, in fact, two death speeches, including one from Paisley, where the truly horrid and self-confessed murderer Alexander Provan had his right hand sliced off before being hanged for slaughtering his wife with a broken bottle. In his dying words, the fifty-six-year-old weaver describes himself as having come from 'credible parents ... who gave me a liberal education' before he 'brought up a numerous family of children' with his first wife 'and was respected by everybody'. But when he married his second wife Elizabeth Bryce, 'a virtuous and loving spouse', he confesses to having 'lived a wicked and ungodly life (entirely my own fault)'.[31] He then admits to being a smuggler and committing two rapes before killing his wife for offering him only eggs and butter for his supper. The *Weekly Journal* next prints in graphic detail Provan's description of the actual murder:

I thrust my hand within the matrix, or private part of her womb, broke her all within with the sole or bottom of a glass bottle, which was forked, and tore out her belly; that, by such force and cruel savage usage, which I now cannot express, my right hand and slieve [*sic*], was found from the top of my shoulder to the end of my fingers, in hot reeking blood.[32]

At this point, Provan's account gets even darker, as he contradicts his claim to having been a good father by admitting 'having a son, a child in a bad state of health, and being in drink, I put the child's arse on the fire, and afterwards put him to bed, where

---

[30] *Scots Magazine*, vol. 27, p. 564.
[31] *Edinburgh Weekly Journal*, 20 November 1765, p. 4.
[32] *Edinburgh Weekly Journal*, 20 November 1765, p. 4.

he continued languishing, about eight days; and I gave out, that the small pox was the cause of his death'.[33] Provan says that a man of such 'wicked passion and ill nature'[34] as himself fully deserves the sentence passed on him, and one suspects that the *Weekly Journal*'s readers would agree, and find Ogilvie's situation poignantly unjust by comparison.

The other dying words in this issue, those of Patrick Ogilvie, are prefaced by two related news items: the first announces that Katharine Nairn, her pregnancy now confirmed by the midwives, has had her sentence delayed until March of the following year; the second, following immediately, says simply: 'We are told, that on Friday last, Dr Alexander Monroe [sic] opened the body of Lieutenant Patrick Ogilvie, and gave a public lecture over it to his Class; after which it was soldered up, and carried off to be buried'.[35] Readers of the *Weekly Journal* were no doubt meant to relate this brief item ironically to the gory details Provan provided about vivisectioning his wife. The editor of the *Journal* then introduces the text of Ogilvie's dying words with this bare observation: 'The following SPEECH in his name was sold about the streets; but we cannot ascertain it to be authentic.'[36]

The entire gallows broadside is then printed, in which Ogilvie eloquently addresses the apparently damning eyewitness accounts of his behaviour, wherein 'civility and possibly folly, are explained into actual guilt'.[37] His words, educated and considered, contrast starkly with those of Provan, and when framed by the reference to Ogilvie's final performance in Monro's anatomy class, the editorial intent can only be to raise sympathy among the *Weekly Journal*'s circulation for the Lieutenant. The juxtapo-

---

[33] *Edinburgh Weekly Journal*, 20 November 1765, p. 4.
[34] *Edinburgh Weekly Journal*, 20 November 1765, p. 4.
[35] *Edinburgh Weekly Journal*, 20 November 1765, p. 3.
[36] *Edinburgh Weekly Journal*, 20 November 1765, p. 3.
[37] *Edinburgh Weekly Journal*, 20 November 1765, p.3.

sitioning of the two gallows speeches in this manner by the *Journal*'s editor is a dramatic tactic that borders on the inflammatory in its manipulation of public opinion. Subsequently, as editor of the *Scots Magazine*, Smellie publishes an extract of Ogilvie's speech in that periodical, contextualized with a succinct account of the Lieutenant's four reprieves, emphasizing the psychological agony of last-minute postponements for those awaiting capital punishment. The *Scots Magazine* next reports that 'a very moving incident occurred at his execution' when the noose slipped, Ogilvie fell to the ground, and then had to be 'turned over' a second time. Before printing his actual dying words, the editor remarks that the Lieutenant 'behaved with decency and resignation'.[38] After the extract, the editor tellingly observes that 'there is not the least mention of his unhappy partner', an oversight he immediately corrects by informing his readers that her pregnancy has preserved her until at least March. Clearly the *Scots Magazine* agrees with the *Weekly Journal* that Ogilvie has suffered a miscarriage of justice, and since William Smellie was still editing the *Magazine*, it is safe to assume that his hand shaped both publications' challenges to the court's verdict.

But if Smellie's nascent Whiggishness inclined him all his life to antagonize Scotland's staid authorities, Auld's was a deeply inbred conservatism, and he would only have allowed Smellie so free a hand if he anticipated a commercially (not politically) beneficial outcome. Smellie's ill ease with Lord Kames's precedent-setting behaviour on the Bench at the Nairn/Ogilvie trial where he became the first Scottish judge to deliberately direct a jury's decision by confining them to his interpretation of the legal facts of a case, would simmer for years and instigate Smellie's interest in the law as a publisher and an author. Their disagreement here no doubt contributed significantly to Kames with-

---

[38] *Scots Magazine*, vol. 27, pp. 556-7.

drawing his support for Smellie whom he had mentored in the early 1760s and whose observations on the *Elements of Criticism* Kames had welcomed when the text was passing through the press. On the other hand, Smellie's promotion of Dundas's position in the *Weekly Journal* and the *Scots Magazine* initiated an on-again-off-again relationship that lasted until Smellie's death and included correspondence with Dundas in the 1790s seeking assistance in finding Smellie's son John a berth as a naval officer.

Still, Smellie never forgot what he perceived to be essential inequities in the criminal justice system in Scotland, especially in the authority judges exercised over juries. He would align himself with Hugo Arnot, printing his legal thesis for the University of Edinburgh and publishing Arnot's *Collection and Abridgement of Celebrated Criminal Trials in Scotland* in 1785. In the previous year, William Creech had published Smellie's own *Address to the People of Scotland on the Nature, Powers, and Privileges of Juries*, which he had designed to 'restore the original intention of trials by Jury...to guard against the partiality and injustice of magistrates and judges'.[39] Smellie goes on to assert that 'the law of Scotland...declares, in positive terms, that jurymen are equally judges of the law, as well as of fact'.[40] Auld, however, was a traditionalist and small-time entrepreneur with a reputation for being a tough, even abusive, master printer[41] who squeezed every penny he could from his operations, and his only objective in apparently blazing a trail around the Nairn/Ogilvie trial was neither political nor legal, but simply the opportunity to print a sterling

---

[39] *An Address to the People of Scotland on the Nature, Powers, and Privileges of Juries* (Edinburgh, 1784), p. 6.

[40] *An Address to the People of Scotland*, p. 12.

[41] Auld was notoriously sued in 1773 by an apprentice, James Murray, for physical and emotional abuse. The apprentice won the case, was freed from his obligation, and his father reimbursed for the cost of the indenture and his legal fees. See National Archives of Scotland, CS 271/41914.

text: *An Account of the Trial of Katharine Nairn and Patrick Ogilvie for the Crimes of Incest and Murder* (Edinburgh, 1765).

The *Account* appeared in September 1765, very probably compiled by Smellie who, as Edinburgh's premier editor at the time, was already under contract to do the same for William Buchan's *Domestic Medicine* and the first edition of the *Encyclopaedia Britannica*.[42] Its publication had been delayed, however, as Auld and Smellie waited to hear the ultimate fate of the temporarily reprieved Lieutenant. But with Katharine pregnant, and Ogilvie receiving yet another reprieve, the book went to press with an unusually open ending for one of its genre. The last page reads:

N.B. *The Conclusion of this **Trial** will be published and given* gratis *to the Purchasers, so soon as the Proceedings of the Court, with regard to Katharine Nairn, are finished.*[43]

But since the 'Proceedings of the Court with regard to Katharine Nairn' were never finished because of her successful prison break, no conclusion appeared, a lapse corrected only in the mid-nineteenth century when the Edinburgh publisher and bookseller James Stillie brought out a two-page ending to Auld and Smellie's work to supplement a cheap reprint of their narrative of the trial.

The *Account* was vigorously advertised for weeks in three of the Edinburgh papers, with regular half-column advertisements in Auld's own *Weekly Journal*. One of the venture's partners, John Balfour, used the opportunity to promote his remaining

---

[42] William Buchan's *Domestic Medicine* came out in 1769 with an Edinburgh imprint bearing the names of Balfour, Auld and Smellie. The *Britannica* was published in numbers between 1768 and 1771. On Smellie's contracts, see Kerr, *Memoirs*, vol. 1, pp. 259, 361.

[43] *An Account of the Trial of Katharine Nairn and Patrick Ogilvie* (Edinburgh, 1765), p. 200.

copies of two other notorious murder trials, those of James Stewart of Appin and James Carnegie of Finhaven, originally published by Balfour in 1753 and 1762, respectively. Both seem to have sold out through this strategy of joint promotion, as they quickly disappear from the advertisements, which continue to announce the Nairn/Ogilvie account into December; in November Auld had begun to offer it together with what would eventually become his best money maker, his *Free Masons Pocket Companion and Song Collection*.[44] The *Account*'s first edition was printed in large character on fine paper and sold at three shillings, obviously intended for the libraries of the better-heeled, and many exist to this day in fine bindings and occasionally together with either or both of the Stewart and the Carnegie. The poorer quality single-shilling second edition is much rarer, and was obviously intended for a popular readership. Some two thousand of the latter were sold.

One Edinburgh newspaper, Donaldson's *Edinburgh Advertiser*, never carried promotions for the *Account*, and also, we may recall, declined to follow Auld in printing the troublesome *Opinion* of M'Carty. Donaldson launched his paper in 1764, printing it on Tuesdays and Thursdays, when the *Courant* and the *Mercury* were silent, and filling the gap left by the 1760 failure of Hamilton, Balfour and Neill's *Edinburgh Chronicle*. Donaldson was not afraid of litigation and was obviously keen to see his newspaper succeed. So why ignore M'Carty's *Opinion*, if his more experienced competitors felt pressure to publish it to appease their readers (and we know that Donaldson's readers complained when he didn't)[45]? The answer may lie in taking

---

[44] See advertisement in the *Edinburgh Weekly Journal*, 20 November 1765, p. 3.

[45] The *Advertiser* for 1 November 1765 carried a curious note from Donaldson himself: 'The epistle signed Criticus of the 24th current, came to hand two days ago. The publisher of the Advertiser thanks him for his well-meant hints, which will be attended to in due time. There were several very

note that during the fortnight when the other three Edinburgh newspapers were promoting M'Carty and filling four columns in doing so, Donaldson's paper was overflowing with advertisements. He simply had no room to spare for M'Carty and was, in fact, undercutting his competition in order to steal away advertisers from them, a tactic that resulted in a 1768 agreement among Edinburgh's newspaper publishers to fix rates and terms of payment for all newspaper adverts in the capital. Donaldson was already rapidly eroding Auld's advertising income; in fact, the *Weekly Journal*, like the *Edinburgh Chronicle* before it, died because its chief competition strategically cut off its revenue from advertisements.[46] And there is good reason to believe that Fleming (the *Courant*) and Ruddiman (the *Mercury*) colluded with Donaldson in undermining Auld. But there is no room to tell that story here; suffice to say that the *Advertiser*'s behaviour with regard to the Nairn/Ogilvie trial has all to do with respect for profits, and not the high court. That Balfour, Smellie and Auld did not promote the *Account of the Trial of Katharine Nairn and Patrick Ogilvie* in the *Advertiser* no doubt reflects this ongoing animosity between their *Weekly Journal* and Donaldson's upstart newspaper.

Criminals are almost as good for the newspaper business as advertisers; both generate sales.[47] Our story ends with an odd foreshadowing in that regard. Just as the clamour surrounding the Nairn/Ogilvie trial was receding in late 1766, despite irregu-

---

good reasons for not inserting Mr McCarty's Opinion in the Advertiser, of which Criticus may be satisfied if he will take the trouble to call upon the publisher' (p. 8).

[46] Stephen W. Brown, 'Wrapping the News: *The Historical Register* and the Use of Blue Paper Cover Wrappers on Eighteenth-Century Scottish Magazines', *The Journal of the Edinburgh Bibliographical Society*, 1 (2006), pp. 49-70.

[47] See John Brewer's discussion of the relationship between journalism and crime in the eighteenth century in *A Sentimental Murder: Love and Madness in the Eighteenth Century* (New York, 2004), pp. 37-62.

lar reports in the London and Edinburgh press of sightings of Katharine, a new joinery firm promoted itself on page four of Auld and Smellie's *Weekly Journal*, accompanied by a handsome engraving, something rarely found in that newspaper:

AT FRANCIS AND WILLIAM BRODIES...Is ready made variety of Cabinet and Upholstery work...They likewise will do all manner of house carpenter and joinery work, and undertake funerals. **N.B.** This advertisement is not to be repeated.[48]

Some twenty years later in 1788, William Smellie would find himself printing a monograph about the only other criminal trial in eighteenth-century Scotland to equal the notoriety of the Nairn/Ogilvie affair: William Creech's *Account of the Trial of William Brodie and George Smith*. But that remarkable piece of Scottish book-trade history is another story.

---

[48] *Edinburgh Weekly Journal*, 21 January 1767, p. 4.

John Ferrar 1742-1804:
Printer, Author and Public Man

JENNIFER MOORE

JOHN FERRAR PLAYED a considerable role in shaping the cultural, social and economic landscape of both eighteenth-century Limerick and Dublin. He was active in Limerick from about 1757 to 1794 where he was a noted poet, historian, printer and newspaper proprietor. Limerick city proved to be an excellent centre for the printing industry in Munster and produced a thriving print trade that exceeded the economic developments of the city during this period. Ferrar moved to Dublin in 1795 and remained there until his death in 1804 where he was known as an author, printer and promoter of education particularly among the lower classes.

Frustratingly, almost no primary sources survive from John Ferrar. But despite the absence of personal diaries or account books, his interests and trade networks may be traced through his association with prominent figures, his many publications, subscriptions to books and charities, through membership of various societies, and a book printed for private circulation by Michael Lloyd Ferrar in 1903.[1] His businesses and personal successes exceeded that of many of his contemporaries. One of the questions raised about Ferrar is why he moved to Dublin at fifty-two years of age when he was an established figure in Limerick. While in

---

[1] Michael Lloyd Ferrar, *The Limerick-Huntingdon Ferrars* (Private circu-lation, 1903). The book was compiled by M. L. Ferrar after he borrowed and annotated the Ferrar Papers from Cambridge University. In this publication, M. L. Ferrar refers to John Ferrar's will, correspondence with his niece, Rose Ferrar and his family bible that listed his twelve children. M. L. Ferrar died shortly after this publication and, unfortunately, these items have not been found since. There is also a Psalter belonging to John Ferrar that was passed to a descendant in recent years, although this has not been found by the author.

Dublin he had a large degree of social standing and was regarded highly in the Association for Discountenancing Vice and Promoting the Practice of Virtue and Religion. This study focuses on the career of John Ferrar in Limerick and Dublin, both printer and public man. The first section examines the era in which Ferrar lived, particularly looking at the growth of Limerick as a city. The second considers his family background, networks and career. The third illustrates his evolving political tendencies and his role in Dublin society towards the end of the century.

Provincial trade in Britain and Ireland

Much work has been carried out on the provincial book trade in Britain. A pioneering study by John Feather illustrated the interaction of printers with other provincial book traders as well as with the printing centre of London.[2] Work on the print trade in the provinces of Ireland is beginning to appear.[3] Useful articles by Máire Kennedy and Hugh Fenning on the book-trade networks in Munster, and substantial bibliographies such as those by E. R. McClintock-Dix and Mary Paul Pollard have detailed the provincial traders and trading in Ireland.[4] Some local bibliog-

---

[2] John Feather, *The Provincial Book Trade in Eighteenth- Century England* (Cambridge, 1985).

[3] Niall Ó Ciosáin, *Print and Popular Culture in Ireland 1750-1850* (London, 1996), p. 52.

[4] Máire Kennedy, 'The distribution of locally produced French periodicals in provincial Ireland; the *Magazin á la Mode*, 1777-1778', *Eighteenth-Century Ireland*, 9 (1994), pp. 83-98; Máire Kennedy, 'Eighteenth-century newspaper publishing in Munster and south Leinster' in *Cork Historical and Archaeological Society*, 103 (1998), pp. 67-88; Máire Kennedy 'Book trade networks in the south of Ireland' in *Branches of Literature and Music: Proceedings of the Thirteenth Seminar on the History of the Provincial Book Trade held in Bristol, 11-13 July 1995*, ed. by M. T. Richardson (Bristol, 2000), pp. 25-46; Hugh Fenning, 'The Catholic press in Munster in the eighteenth century' in *Books Beyond the Pale: Aspects of the Provincial Book Trade in Ireland before 1850*, ed. by Gerard Long, (Dublin, 1999), pp. 19-32; Mary Pollard, *A Dictionary of Members of the Dublin Book Trade, 1550-1800* (London, 2000); Mary Pollard *Dublin's Trade in*

raphers, such as Robert Herbert and Seámus Ó Cassaide, have identified and compiled collections of provincial printers.

As in provincial England, Dublin booksellers were dependent on London for trade and it was centrally manipulated by the leading booksellers of the city who controlled the copyright and distribution of books. In Ireland, Dublin was viewed as the centre of the printing business. When examining the print trade in the context of Britain and Ireland, Limerick was regarded as a sub-province. This may have been the case in general economic terms in the first half of the eighteenth century, but not so for printing and bookselling. The Limerick print trade developed concurrently with that of provincial England, with almost thirty printers, binders and booksellers setting up in business between 1729 and 1800. Many Irish provincial printers and booksellers also travelled to London to purchase books and establish networks.

In order to understand John Ferrar it is necessary to examine the market he worked for and the political climate in which he lived, as his political stance was integral to his success. He came of age at a pivotal point in the history of Limerick city, which was experiencing growth to such an extent that it became the second fastest growing city in Ireland behind Belfast between 1760 and 1820 (see Fig. 1). The city had not developed as had other provincial cities in the early part of the eighteenth century. The lack of development was blamed by some on corporation control and heavy tolls. In an analysis of the growth of Irish cities, David Dickson claimed that even taking into account the more favourable positions of the ports of Cork and Waterford on the eastern and southern coasts, Limerick still lagged behind economically.[5]

Books 1550-1800 (Oxford, 1989); E.R. McClintock-Dix, Irish Printers, Booksellers and Stationers 1726-1775 (Kirkpatrick, 1937); E.R. McClintock-Dix, List of Books, Pamphlets Newspapers etc. Printed in Limerick from the Earliest Period to 1800 Inclusive, 2nd ed. (Limerick, 1912).

[5] David Dickson, 'Large-scale developers and the growth of eighteenth-century cities' in Cities and merchants: French perspectives on urban development

There had been a number of corporation disputes during the century, mainly concerning tolls and taxes, but an especially severe one split the inhabitants of the city in the 1740s and 1750s. The ensuing anti-corporation faction, the Independent Free Citizens, was led by Edmond Sexton Pery, later Speaker of the Irish House of Commons.[6] They were particularly effective and, after a number of petitions and public meetings, they secured a select committee of the House of Commons to investigate the Corporation's affairs in 1761. It found the mayor, Arthur Roche, guilty of the misconduct he was accused of. The subsequent bill for the 'better regulation of the city of Limerick' was passed by the Irish parliament and enacted in December 1760 but it failed to gain approval of the Privy Council at Westminster.[7] Despite this, an amnesty granted a large number of merchants, craftsmen and gentlemen freedom of the city in 1761. A satirical play, *Liberty and Property, or the Downfall of Arbitrary Power*, anonymously published in the same year, celebrated the removal of the oligarchy from power.

Prior to these events, Edmund Sexton Pery, persuasive in promoting the prosperity of the city with the government, attained 'encouragements' for improvements and modernization of

---

1500-1900, ed. by Paul Butel and L.M. Cullen (Dublin, 1986), p. 109.

[6] The anti-corporation faction was inspired by similar protests against the Dublin Corporation by Charles Lucas in the 1740s. For more on this see Jacqueline Hill, *From Patriots to Unionists. Dublin Civic Politics and Irish Protestant Patriotism, 1660-1840* (Oxford, 1997), pp. 79-105.

[7] Maurice Lenihan, *Limerick its History and Antiquities* (reprint, Cork, 1967), p. 353; John Begley, *The Diocese of Limerick from 1691 to the Present Time* (Dublin, 1938), p. 113; Eamon O'Flaherty, 'Urban Politics' in *Eighteenth Century Ireland*, 6 (1991), p. 117-8. Nicholas Smyth and Andrew Shepherd were agents for the Independent Free Citizens and Corporation respectively. Shepherd claimed that contrary to the New Rules, there were over one hundred priests in the city and the bill was influenced by this popish faction. The council concurred and the bill was thrown out.

the city.[8] A plan for a new town was drawn up in the 1760s and named Newtown Pery after its instigator. Pery's new town and the old medieval city existed side by side with separate governing bodies for over twenty years. The population increased dramatically, stimulated by the amenities of the new city and its lower taxes. The various trades benefited, not least those involved in print. With this expansion came an increased consumer base for literary material. John Ferrar capitalized on this growth by providing advertising space, acting as the middle man and supplying the inhabitants with the latest local, national and international news, religious sermons and literary material.

Background, Career and Influences

There have been questions over the origins of the Limerick Ferrars but it is now thought that John Ferrar of Limerick was of a family that originated at Ewood Hall in Halifax. The Ferrars of Ewood Hall were distant cousins of Nicholas and John Ferrar of Little Gidding in Huntingdon who established an Anglican community there in the 1640s.[9] The founder of the Limerick Ferrars was William, born at Ewood Hall in 1647/8. He fought at the Boyne and at the Siege of Limerick in 1691 aligned with William of Orange. Paid off at the Peace of Rhyswick in 1697, William married and settled in the city. His only son, William, born in 1700, started in the book-trade business: paper making, binding and bookselling. He was granted freedom of the city in 1732 and was described as *Bibliopegus,* or bookbinder.[10]

---

[8]   The parliament bounty amounted to £3,500 for a new bridge and £4,500 to make the River Shannon navigable from Limerick to Killaloe. See *Report from the committee appointed to take into consideration the petition of the mayor, sheriffs, and citizens of the city of Limerick, in behalf of themselves and all the Merchants and traders of the said city, 11 November 1761, House of Commons* (vii), appendix lxv.

[9]   The author is grateful to David Ransome for this genealogical information.

[10]   Michael Lloyd Ferrar, *The Limerick-Huntingdon Ferrars*, p. 5.

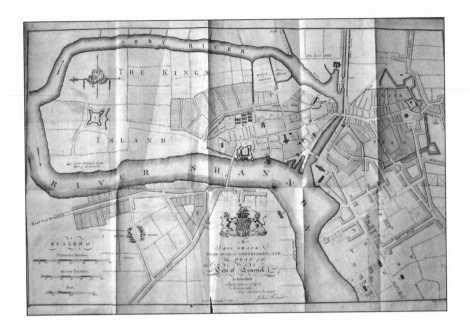

Fig. 1 'The plan of the city of Limerick' showing the medieval town and the expansion of Newtown Pery. This appeared in John Ferrar's *The History of Limerick*...(Limerick, 1787). Courtesy of the Special Collections Department of the Glucksman Library at the University of Limerick.

Another Huntingdon connection was established in 1757 when William's daughter Mary (John's sister), married Hugh Ferrar of Huntingdon when he was stationed as a soldier in Limerick.[11] William, whose surname had a number of variations,[12]

---

[11] M. L. Ferrar, *The Limerick-Huntingdon Ferrars*, p. 6. Son of Hugh Ferrar (d. 1778), Recorder of Huntingdon, he married Mary Ferrar in 1757 and had two children, Hugh (d. 1765) and Rosetta (1761-1841). It appears that Hugh Ferrar was appointed as an officer in a regiment of light infantry to Limerick in 1760. See *Royal Magazine, or Gentleman's Monthly Companion* vol. ii (London, 1760), p. 59. They lived with Rose Ferrar until Hugh Ferrar was sent to the West Indies. Mary followed with the two children to discover that they had left for England. Mary returned to England after Hugh's transport, the *Admiral Pocock*, sank losing all 600 souls on board. She then took the children to Huntingdon where they remained.

[12] These included Farrar, Farrier and Farriar.

was agent for many principal Dublin booksellers and publications, including John Exshaw's *London Magazine* in the 1740s and 1750s.[13] He subscribed to many major publications including William King's *State of the Protestants in Ireland*, G. P. Marna's *Eight Volumes of Letters Writ by a Turkish Spy*, and James Ware's *Works*.[14] His orders for these and other works sometimes exceeded those of eminent Dublin booksellers such as George Faulkner. Together, his subscriptions reveal a high level of readership and interest in Limerick and its hinterland.

When William died in 1754 his son John was twelve years old. It is likely that John was apprenticed to Andrew Welsh, an eminent printer and newspaper proprietor.[15] Welsh seemed to have had a partnership or agreement with William Farrier as they never subscribed to the same Dublin publication but would always subscribe to each other's. John was too young to take over his father's business but a 'Mr Ferrar' continued to subscribe to books, periodicals and work as a distributor for the Dublin University Press[16] until John Ferrar's name appears in the list of subscribers to *Bradstreet's lives* in 1757.[17] It is possible that the

---

[13] Robert Munter, *A Dictionary of the Print Trade in Ireland 1550-1775* (New York, 1968), p. 96.

[14] William King, *The State of the Protestants of Ireland under the Late King James's Government* (Dublin, 1730), printed by S. Powell; Giocanni Paolo Marna, *The Eight Volumes of Letters writ by a Turkish Spy who Liv'd Five and Forty Years undiscover'd at Paris* (Dublin, 1736), printed by S. Powell; James Ware, *The Whole Works of Sir James Ware concerning Ireland Revised and Improved in Three Volumes* (Dublin, 1739), printed by E. Jones.

[15] Andrew Welsh arrived in Limerick in 1739 and became the city's first major printer. He established the first successful newspaper in the city, the *Limerick Journal*, which changed its name to the *Munster Journal* in the 1740s and continued until at least 1761.

[16] *Faulkner's Dublin Journal* 14-18 January 1755. A Mr Ferrar of Limerick was one of the undertakers to print T. Livii *Patavini historiarum ab condita*.

[17] Dudley Bradstreet, *Bradstreet's Lives: Being a Genuine History of Several Gentlemen and Ladies, All Living within these Ten Years Past, Remarkable for*

business was kept going from 1754 to 1757 by another family member, either mother or cousin, or even by Andrew Welsh. John's address in the 1750s and early 1760s was given as 'near the exchange,' possibly in the same building as Welsh until he moved to the New Printing House in Quay Lane about 1768.[18]

John Ferrar had twelve children with his wife Mary who died in 1815. She was daughter of Joseph Johns, a silversmith who was burgess in the Corporation, sheriff in 1755, chamberlain in 1766 and mayor in 1773. In turn, John Ferrar would also become a member of the Corporation, serving as its printer in 1770s and its sheriff in 1780.[19] Joseph Johns was also the treasurer of the Masonic Lodge no. 9, known as the 'Corporation Lodge'. Although no records of Lodge no. 9 are extant, it is probable that Ferrar too became a member during the 1760s, possibly as early as 1762.[20] We owe descriptions of Ferrar to Daniel Beaufort and the blind dramatist John O'Keefe, who wrote:

I knew Mr Ferrar of Limerick, a printer, bookseller, and author; he wrote an excellent history of Limerick, which, a few years ago, I heard read with pleasure. His little shop was at the corner of Quay lane. Ferrar was very deaf, yet had a cheerful animated countenance; thin and of middle size.[21]

The Author and Publisher: 1760s
In Ferrar's first major publication, *Poems on Several Subjects* in 1765, there were 222 subscribers ordering a total of 248 books.

---

their Virtues, or other Vices...with a letter from the River Seine to the Shannon &c. &c. (Dublin, 1757).

[18] Munter, *A Dictionary of the Print Trade in Ireland*, p. 9.

[19] John Ferrar, *The History of the City of Limerick*, pp. 287-9.

[20] It is also possible that John Ferrar was misspelled as 'John Barrar', admitted to Lodge 174 (also known as the 'Boyne Lodge') in Limerick city on 27 December 1762. Taken from the *Membership Registers* in the Grand Lodge, Dublin. The author acknowledges David Fleming for this reference.

[21] *Literary Memoirs of Living Authors of Great Britain* (London, 1798), ii, p. 90.

Subscribers originated largely from the city of Limerick, including twenty-one members of the military. Some were also from Thomastown, Exeter and London. The poetry was composed by Ferrar when he was eighteen and nineteen years old and was described by him as 'flights of youthful fancy, penned as an amusement at the author's vacant hours'.[22] The collection consisted of thirty-two poems and one play. He was aware that the content had to have a wide appeal in order to maintain a high readership. He wisely dedicated poetry to a number of influential families in the city at the time. They included, 'On the Death of Lieut. Gore', 'On the Recovery of Mr. Pery' dedicated to Pery's wife, Jane and 'A Picture of the Assembly' which was 'inscribed to the universally admir'd Ladies of the City of Limerick'. In this poem well known local families such as Perys, Bowens, Greens, Gradys, Westropps, Hickmans, Sextons, Whites and Welshs appeared.[23] Not surprisingly these names are also prominent among the list of subscribers.

In 1767 Ferrar produced the first Irish provincial urban history of a city in it own right. Previous works exist by Charles Smith, the doctor and member of the Physico-Historical Society, on the counties and cities of Waterford and Cork published in 1753 and 1756 respectively. However, these histories examined the cities in the context of their counties and the cities only received two chapters' worth of discussion in the publications. Both of these books were published in Dublin. Ferrar, however, wrote and published two editions of his history of the city in Limerick in 1767, employed Andrew Welsh as printer and obtained the paper from Joseph Sexton.[24] It was based largely on a

---

[22] John Ferrar, *Poems on Several Subjects,* (Limerick, 1765), advertisement.

[23] Ferrar, *Poems on Several Subjects*, pp. 64-9.

[24] Joseph Sexton was the local paper maker. He had a paper mill just outside the city in Annacotty and had two offices in the city; his was the only paper mill in Munster until 1763.

manuscript by Reverend James White and its use distinguished him as 'John the Historian' in the Ferrar family papers.[25] Relatively few provincial urban histories were published in Ireland during the eighteenth century. Rosemary Sweet argues that because there were such divisions and turmoil in seventeenth century Ireland, expressions of communal sentiment, continuity and civic antiquity were difficult to achieve.[26] John Ferrar followed the English model and produced a polite and harmonious image of the city, emphasising peace, tranquillity and amiable citizens despite contentious changes in the Corporation and development of the city. Its inhabitants were split over corruption allegations and over a parliamentary inquiry into the dealings of the Corporation in 1761. Ferrar's *History of the city of Limerick* served as part of a healing process and marked a progressive point for the city. This publication had a much larger list of subscribers than Ferrar's book of poetry. There were 459 individual subscribers with a total order of 823 copies. The list clearly illustrated the local interest in the history of the city.[27] Of those who gave addresses, twelve were from Dublin including bookseller John Exshaw. There were at least ten from Cork of whom William Flyn, prominent bookseller in that city, took fourteen copies. However, it was an itinerant bookseller, John Kennedy,

---

[25] A photostat of the original manuscript, 'The annals of the city and diocese of Limerick' can be found in the National Library of Ireland MS 2714. The original lies in National University of Ireland, Maynooth. There are two known transcripts by Maurice Lenihan of the White manuscript. See British Library, Rev. J. White manuscript, MS 31888; and Royal Irish Academy, Rev. J. White Manuscript, MS 24 D 21.

[26] Rosemary Sweet, 'Provincial culture and urban histories in England and Ireland during the long eighteenth century' in *Provincial Towns in Early Modern England and Ireland; Change, Convergence and Divergence*, ed. by Peter Borsay and Lindsay Proudfoot (Oxford, 2002), p. 234.

[27] As suggested by Rosemary Sweet, *Writings of Urban Histories in Eighteenth-Century England* (London, 1997), p. 186.

who subscribed to the most copies.[28] His request for one hundred indicated the thriving position of the journeyman bookseller.

Ferrar dedicated the book to 'The civic people of Limerick' and to promote civic pride he identified past achievements and former glories. Emphasising its antiquity, he claimed that the city's charter was granted before that of Dublin and London. In the 1767 edition he stated that:

The list of mayors, and whose authenticity I cannot doubt, says that in 1198, the Provost of Limerick, Adam Sarvant, had the title of mayor conferred on him, which was ten years before London.[29]

In the 1787 edition he repeated and reaffirmed this:

Another great proof of the early consequence of Limerick, is, that King Richard, in the 9th year of his reign, 1197, granted a charter to the city, to elect a Mayor, an honour which London did not obtain until ten years after; Dublin, not until the year 1308; Cork, not until the year 1318.[30]

Although historically inaccurate, it is what Ferrar believed and wanted his audience to read and understand of the city. This apparent promotion of antiquity was common in the eighteenth century. Ferrar's focus was Limerick city and its importance on a national scale, particularly when a number of books were sent to London and Dublin. Such attributes, as Sweet has suggested, were key elements in the creation of an urban community.[31]

---

[28] John Ferrar, *An History of the City of Limerick* (Limerick, 1767); all of the above statistics may be calculated from the list of subscribers.

[29] Ferrar, *An History of the City of Limerick*, p. 8.

[30] Ferrar, *An History of the City of Limerick*, p. 4. London's Charter was granted *c*.1131-3.

[31] Sweet, 'Provincial culture and urban histories', p. 224.

Like most authors and printers Ferrar required financial backers to produce his publications. He initially targeted the gentry
in the city and surrounding countryside for subscriptions and patronage. Thus he dedicated much of his work to those on both
sides of the Corporation divide. However, as he became increasingly involved in the Corporation, both personally and profes-
sionally, his writings and publications became more partisan.
The second edition of *An History of the City of Limerick* was published in 1767 (see Fig. 2) and was almost identical to the first.
The only significant difference lay in the preface where the first
edition's homage to Edmond Sexton Pery was removed.

We begin to rival in Trade, our Neighbours at *Corke, Waterford,* &c.
The Plan for still greater Improvements, by the addition of almost a
new City, is struck out, and it is impossible to tell at what Perfection
Limerick may in a short Time arrive, under the Protection of a Patriot
Citizen [Edmond Sexton Pery], endowed by Nature with a Genius to
form, and enabled by an ample Fortune [his family wealth], and yet
greater Influence, [his position as Member of Parliament and owner of
the new land to be developed] to execute the glorious Design.[32]

In the second edition the paragraph ended at 'what perfection
Limerick may in a short time arrive.' Ferrar was possibly advised
by the Corporation to remove this paragraph due to his connection with the Corporation and also Pery's involvement in the
Independent Free Citizen movement and the select committee
established in 1761. The removal of this homage served him well
as he was made a freeman of the city the following year.[33]
Ferrar was also pioneering in the publication of *The Limerick
Directory* in 1769, which he also printed. It was the most comprehensive directory published in provincial Ireland to that date.

[32] Author's interpretation in square brackets. Ferrar, *An History of the City of
Limerick,* first edition, preface.
[33] 'The Freemen of Limerick' in *North Munster Antiquarian Journal* [hereafter
NMAJ] iv (1944-5), p. 109.

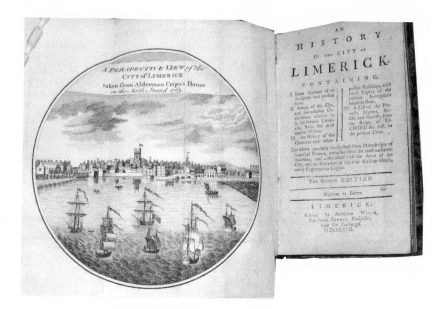

Fig. 2 The very rare second edition of *An History of the City of Limerick*. Here the frontispiece is uniquely 'A perspective view of the city of Limerick' as opposed to the Custom House which usually appears. Courtesy of the Special Collections Department of the Glucksman Library at the University of Limerick.

Wilson's Dublin directory was established by the 1760s; Ferrar followed his model but included more aspects of polite society, namely the merchants, Corporation, clergy, lawyers, guilds and Masonic lodges. Also included was a schedule of the tolls and customs of the city for 1769.[34]

The Printer: 1770s

Ferrar published the first edition of his newspaper, *The Limerick Chronicle,* on 11 August 1768 and retained control of it until Andrew Watson took over on 26 November 1781.[35] It was the major newspaper for the city and surrounding countryside.

---

[34] John Ferrar, *The Limerick Directory* (Limerick, 1769), p. 4.

[35] Until recently, it was thought that the earliest edition of the paper extant was 13 October 1768 with only a further three issues for 1768 and four issues for 1769. However, a bound volume of the *Limerick Chronicle* was acquired

Good networks were essential to the survival and prosperity
of printing and publishing houses. Effective advertising and efficient distribution were especially important.[36] Ferrar maintained
and expanded the networks that his father had established, and
began to do so in the issue dated 15 August 1768. *The Chronicle*
was sold every 'Monday and Thursday by the Widow Green
near John's Church, Mrs Watson opposite the parade and Mr
Gleeson at Thomond Gate'; gentlemen at the Strand and outside
Thomond Gate could get their papers at Mr James Gloster's

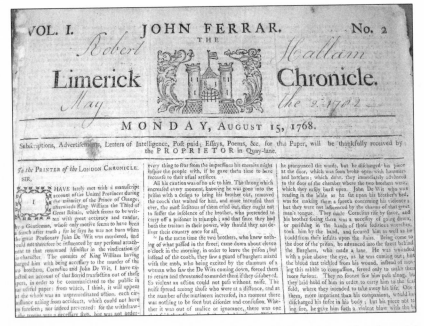

Fig. 3 The earliest known edition extant of *The Limerick Chronicle*.
Courtesy of the Special Collections Department of the Glucksman Library at the University of Limerick.

by the Glucksman Library, University of Limerick that contains upwards of
one hundred issues commencing with number two (see Fig. 3).

[36] Fiona A. Black, 'Book distribution in Scottish and Canadian provinces
1750–1820; examples of methods and availability' in *The Reach of Print: Making, Selling and Using Books*, ed. by Peter Isaac and Barry McKay (Winchester,
1998), p. 104.

shop opposite the end of Thomond Bridge.[37] Ferrar sold lottery tickets in the Belfast scheme at one guinea each, for a prize of £2,500. He advertised for riders 'to carry this paper twice a week to Ennis, Charleville, Tipperary and Newcastle'.[38] Subscriptions and advertisements were taken by a number of men in Sixmile-Bridge, Tipperary and Charleville. The paper cost 5s. 5d. for those who lived in or near Limerick city, and 10s. 10d. for those living in towns such as Tipperary, Nenagh, Charleville or Ennis.

By 1774 the paper was delivered to twenty-two distributors, including apothecaries, booksellers and coffee house owners in the Munster area. The price increased to 16s. 3d. per annum after the implementation of the Stamp Act in 1774.[39] Ferrar was also agent for a number of periodicals including *Exshaw's London and Gentlemen's Magazine*, *The Monthly Review*, Walker's *Hibernian Magazine* and Bingley's *Independent Chronicle*.[40] The success of *The Limerick Chronicle* allowed him to disseminate his ideas and the news he wanted subscribers to read. He travelled to London on a number of occasions to buy books which he reviewed regularly in his newspaper. The revenue generated from the advertisements in the paper allowed Ferrar to dominate the Limerick printing business and its content aided in the emergence of the city's polite urban culture and a growing civic consciousness.[41]

Aside from his newspaper Ferrar published a wide variety of material of different religious persuasions during the 1770s. His titles ranged from *The Work in Verse of Daniel Hayes*, to the priest, Laurence Nihill's, *Rational Self Love* and *Answers to Doc-*

---

[37] Gloster was also listed as a dyer in the Limerick Directory.

[38] *The Limerick Chronicle*, 18 August 1768.

[39] *Limerick Chronicle*, 3 March 1774.

[40] *Hibernian Chronicle*, 26 August 1773.

[41] Ian Jackson, 'The geographies of promotion: a survey of two eighteenth-century English newspapers' in *Printing Places. Locations of Book Production and Distribution since 1500*, ed. by John Hinks and Catherine Armstrong (London, 2005), p. 65.

tor Meaghar's Popish Mass, by Eusebes Mesoprendes. He also printed
sermons, almanacs and freeholder lists. Occasionally he published a catalogue of books held in his bookshop to be distributed to the various coffee houses along the routes he used. Although none of these catalogues are known to be extant he
periodically included large lists of books in *The Limerick Chronicle.* Prominent among them was political and historical literature
as well as over 200 plays.[42] His collection of books, numbering
several thousand, included the latest publications as well as some
of the books his father had subscribed to in the 1730s. He also
distributed English periodicals and the French *Magazin á la
mode.*[43] His principal journeyman was Mathew Eyres until he
left him in February 1771 and moved to Cork.[44] Ferrar was also
a distributor for the Dublin University Press and also sold many
books to masters of ships.[45] Therefore some of his authored
books found their way to English catalogues.[46]

Ferrar swiftly moved up the scale in Limerick's mercantile
elite as he became increasingly involved in civic activities. He
maintained links with the Huntingdon Ferrars and combined
visits to English relatives with trips to London to purchase books
and periodicals.[47] It is evident that his family in Huntingdon

---

[42] *The Limerick Chronicle*, 30 May 1774.

[43] For more on this see Máire Kennedy 'The distribution of a locally produced French periodical in provincial Ireland: the *Magazin á la mode, 1777-
1778,* in *Eighteenth-Century Ireland,* 9 (1994), pp. 83-98.

[44] Robert Herbert, *Limerick Printers and Printing: Part One of the Catalogue of
the Local Collection in the City of Limerick Public Library* (Limerick, 1944),
p. 57.

[45] Vincent Kinane, *A History of Dublin University Press, 1734-1976* (Dublin,
1994), p. 68.

[46] *A Catalogue of the Minerva General Library* (London, 1795); *Catalogue of the
London and Westminster Circulating Library* (London, 1797); and *A Catalogue
of the London Institution* (London, 1843).

[47] On one trip in the 1790s he was recorded as returning on the Dublin-
Holyhead packet with his daughter where she met her future husband, 'The

were also a source of financial support. For example, in May of 1771 Thomas Carryer bequeathed £500 to his niece, Rose Ferrar of Limerick.[48] There was also correspondence with the Huntingdon Ferrars about the christening of John Ferrar's niece, Rosetta. She was born in Limerick in 1761 to John's sister Mary and her husband (and cousin) Hugh Ferrar of Huntingdon and moved back to Huntingdon with her siblings, after the death of her father in 1763.

During the decade Ferrar tightened his grip on the print trade. He was appointed printer to Limerick Corporation and in that capacity published schedules of tolls and other Corporation material. He also sold patent medicines and a variety of lottery tickets. He was churchwarden for St Mary's and regularly appealed for charitable donations to aid the foundlings of the city. He was secretary and treasurer of the city's Annuity Society, formed in 1769 and also member of the Grand Jury and the Market Jury in 1779. In the same year, and as an expansion to his business, he was appointed agent for the Hibernian Insurance Company Against Fire.[49] He reached his climactic position in Limerick civic office when he was appointed Sheriff in 1780.

A move away from printing
By the end of the 1770s support for the patriotic Volunteer movement engulfed much of Ireland when many British troops were withdrawn for duty in the American War of Independence.

Commodore' or William Augustus Minchin of Woodville Co. Wexford. Ferrar, *The Limerick-Huntingdon Ferrars*, p. 8.

[48] *The Limerick Chronicle* 9 May 1771: 'Died: a few days ago at Huntingdon England, Thomas Carryer Esq; who has bequeathed a fortune of 500l to his niece Miss Rose Ferrar of this city.' It is thought that the Carryer, or Carrier connection was through Hugh the Recorder of Huntingdon's third and fourth marriage into the family.

[49] *The Limerick Chronicle*, 15 August 1768; 13 March 1769 & 6 January 1774; 3 May 1779 & 22 July 1779.

Ferrar was a staunch supporter of the volunteers and included many announcements in his paper concerning parades, calls for members, oaths and reports on reviews at Loughmore.[50] He was listed as a member of the Limerick Loyal Volunteers on 26 September 1779 under the command of Colonel Thomas Smyth and other members of the Corporation. In his 1787 edition of *An History of the City of Limerick* he dedicated thirteen pages to the formation, activities, and listed the corps, cavalry, infantry and commanders.[51] He was strongly influenced by the patriot movement and concentrated on the Volunteers for a number of years.

He may have spent some time in London, as a recently catalogued pamphlet of Ferrar's has come to light called, *A Mirror of the Volunteers or; a Sketch of the Present State of that Kingdom by John Ferrar, Citizen of Limerick, and one of the Volunteers of that City*,[52] which is not in the English Short Title Catalogue. It was published in 1783 by Thomas Wilkie of St Paul's Churchyard. In the pamphlet Ferrar wrote passionately of the Volunteers and what they had achieved but realised that if control of the militia fell into the wrong hands licentiousness would arise. He described the Volunteers, with special mention of the Limerick corps, as a 'loyal body of men, many of them are sensible, moderate men; they have promoted the manufactures of the country, they have in a very high degree, preserved the peace and improved the police of the kingdom.'[53] The main objective of the pamphlet was to obtain legislative support for the poor and complete the inland navigation of Ireland.[54] In the same year as

---

[50] *The Limerick Chronicle* 7 January 1779, 11 February 1779, 1 July 1779, 22 July 1779, 2 August 1779, 16 August 1779, 19 August 1779, 26 August 1779, 20 September 1779, 28 August 1780, 25 March 1782, 3 March 1782.

[51] John Ferrar, *An History of the City of Limerick* (Limerick, 1787), pp. 133-46.

[52] This pamphlet is located in the Lady Margaret Hall Library in Oxford, catalogue ref. 941.071 16(8).

[53] John Ferrar, *A Mirror of the Volunteers*, (London, 1783), pp. 13-14.

[54] Ferrar, *A Mirror of the Volunteers*, pp. 15 & 16.

its publication, the Lord Lieutenant, the Duke of Rutland visited the city and Ferrar, as the man of culture and of national recognition, dedicated a poem to Her Grace of Rutland.[55]

The next project we know Ferrar concentrated on was the publication and reworking of the history of Limerick. This was the third and final edition which was extended to incorporate the county and used more elaborate engravings. Carrying on from his pamphlet of 1783 he focused on the promotion of Irish manufacture and the education of poor children in Limerick. His charitable and educational pursuits culminated in 1793 when he established a school for fifty girls and fifty boys of 'every religious persuasion'. In this school all books of religious controversy were excluded and it was recorded that 'The Primer, Spelling-book, and New Testament, only, were used; the children agreed cordially and attended their respective places of worship on Sundays.'[56] The school was honoured by a poem in the *Hibernian Magazine* in 1794 entitled 'Lines addressed to John Ferrar, the patron and friend of 400 poor children, in Limerick'.[57]

Ferrar lived through an era when the power of many institutions he held dear was challenged. Society became increasingly secularised and liberal and traditional forms of governance were challenged. As he grew older Ferrar's own political opinions were tailored to a patriotic Ireland. He was clear that while Ireland should be aligned to the Crown, it should have more autonomy and encourage development and the creation of infrastructure. A conservative, he assumed the duty of promoting the charter of the city and the Corporation throughout his work on Limerick and in his newspaper. His opinions altered and can be

---

[55] *Gentleman's and London Magazine,* (Dublin, 1785), pp. 557-8. The author acknowledges Tim Conway for this reference.

[56] John Ferrar, *The Prosperity of Ireland* (Dublin, 1795), p. 50.

[57] *Hibernian Magazine,* January 1794. This was signed by 'BME'. The author acknowledges Johanna Archbold for this reference.

traced through his publications. Initially he wrote for a universalised civic readership. This can be seen from his early *Poems on Several Subjects* (1765). Ferrar was clear that Ireland's destiny was intertwined with that of Britain. He dedicated a poem to his brother-in-law, Hugh Ferrar of Huntingdon, a captain in the army, when he drowned at sea off Dartmouth.[58] In it he refers to Ireland as 'Britannia'. He elaborates on this point in a footnote by stating:

The author has, as they always should be, ranked the two islands under the name British. It would be unjust to rob the Irish of the honour they have gained in this, and every other enterprise, during the whole war.[59]

Contrary to his later stance, this statement conveyed four ideas. It honoured the Irish army, acknowledged the military strength of Britain, elevated the position of Ireland, and attempted to promote a sense of unified political identity. In later years, particularly during the height of the Volunteer popularity, he frequently referred to Ireland as 'Hibernia' and in the preface to the 1787 edition of the *History of the City and County of Limerick* stated 'the author was desirous to promote the manufacture of his country; the paper, except a few Royal copies, was made in Dublin.'[60]

In England it was common for Corporations to subsidize and encourage the publication of histories, but there is no evidence for this in Ireland. All the same, he favoured the Corporation in his histories by ignoring the dispute of 1749 where the inadequacies of the mayor, Arthur Roche, and his oligarchy were exposed

---

[58] M. L. Ferrar, *The Limerick-Huntingdon Ferrars*, p. 6.

[59] Ferrar, *Poems on Several Subjects*, p. 11.

[60] Ferrar continued 'The Irish will never rival the French in this great article of commerce, until they are enabled to give age to the paper, and until they lay aside the shameful practice of putting too much blue in it.'

in Andrew Welsh's *Munster Journal*. Ferrar's views were more ardent, however, when describing the struggle between the Corporation and the Independent Free Citizens in 1761.

This year on a new election of members to represent the city in parliament, a contest arose between some members of the Corporation, and a number of the freemen, which the latter stiled [*sic*] themselves Independent Free Citizens. This affair is so recent in the memory of persons now living, that I should consider it as an affront to their judgement, either to offer a recital or give my opinion; I therefore leave it to the writer of some distant period, to animadvert on the different causes and effects of this dispute.[61]

By 1787, however, Ferrar felt he had gained sufficient distance to comment:

A violent contest arose in the year 1761...They raised a considerable amount of money, and succeeded so far, that a bill passed the house of commons of Ireland, tending to subvert the charter of the city, and to alter the mode of electing magistrates. But the members of the Corporation defended their rights like men who valued liberty without licentiousness, and the bill was rejected in England...Dispassionate and good men have seen and lamented the direful effects of popular elections, as they not only destroy the public peace, but injure the morals of the people.[62]

Ferrar denounced a mob that in 1774 attacked and threw stones at the mayor, his father-in-law, Joseph Johns. This was a work of 'such wicked and evil minded persons' that he offered twenty pounds for their capture. Ferrar then published an abstract of the Riot Act to remind citizens of the penalties for such behaviour.[63] He was equally dismissive of the agrarian Whiteboys' hostilities and methods of intimidation displayed to the landlords.

---

[61] Ferrar, *An History of the City of Limerick,* p. 68.

[62] Ferrar, *An History of the City of Limerick,* (Limerick, 1787), p. 87.

[63] *The Limerick Chronicle,* 2 May 1774.

Ferrar's opinion of Ireland and Limerick can be viewed in some of the illustrations he used in his publications. In the 1767 and 1787 editions of *An History of the City of Limerick* he included a plate of the recently completed Custom House, another innovation of Edmond Sexton Pery which was designed by Davis Duckart, and was Limerick's finest piece of Palladian architecture. The plate was used as the frontispiece to the 1767 editions. Added to the plate was *Georgio Terto Fel Reg.* This dedication to the king was removed from the plate in the 1787 edition. Of further interest concerning his patriotism was the frontispiece of the 1787 edition of Ferrar's history of Limerick.

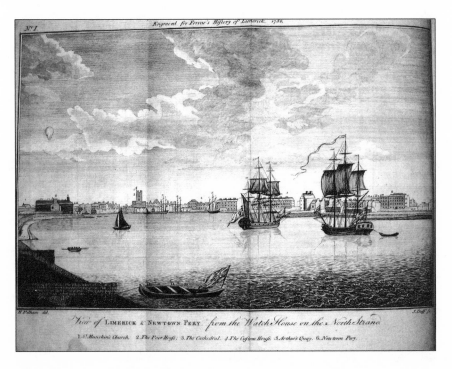

Fig. 4 'A view of Limerick and Newtown Pery, from the Watch House on the North Strand'. Courtesy of the Special Collections Department of the Glucksman Library at the University of Limerick.

This panoramic view 'From the Watch House on the North Strand' of Limerick city from the Clare side of the Shannon was painted by Henry Pelham and indicated a number of key features which Ferrar wanted to include that conveyed a political message.[64] Numbered from right to left were firstly St. Munchin's Church, which represented the oldest parish in Limerick; secondly, the Poor House, which emphasised the charitable nature of the citizens of Limerick; thirdly, St. Mary's Cathedral, built by the O'Brien clan, and representing the antiquity and importance of the city; fourthly, and juxtaposed to the ancient architecture of the Cathedral, was the recently completed Custom House, which was symbolic of the city's revenue and a focal point of trade; fifthly, Arthur's Quay which accentuated the success of the privately-funded quay by the enterprising Arthur family; and sixthly, Newtown Pery, highlighted to show the progress the city made from the 1760s. In addition, and to stress the scientific progress of the city, a hot air balloon was included in the frontispiece. The famous balloonist, Richard Crosbie, took off from Limerick city on 27 April 1786.[65] Even more striking was the purposeful omission of King John's Castle which had so regularly dominated the skyline in drawings of perspectives of the city.[66] But this was patriotic Ferrar and he wanted to portray an independent city with all the elements of progress and Irish antiquity.

Ferrar earned at least £150 according to a visitor to the city in 1790. Pope Pius IV also commended his effort and offered him

---

[64] For more on Henry Pelham see: Peter Harbison 'Henry Pelham (1749-1806), painter, engraver, engineer, map-maker and illustrator of County Clare's antiquities' in *County Clare Studies; Essays in Memory of Gerald O'Connell, Séan Ó Murchadha, Thomas Coffey and Pat Flynn*, ed. by Ciarán Ó Murchadha (Ennis, 2000), pp. 72-100.

[65] Harbison, 'Henry Pelham (1749-1806)', p. 90.

[66] The castle should be located under the hot air balloon behind the Poor House.

help to write a history of Ireland.[67] From the late 1780s it seems that he moved away from the publishing business and increasingly focused on the charitable elements of the city. He was the man of culture in Limerick and had reached the pinnacle of the city's cultural and ecumenical society as a layman. This and his own wealth and the wider attractions of Dublin may be some of the reasons why he moved to the capital.

Ferrar in Dublin

John Ferrar left Limerick for Dublin around 1794. His exact reasons for leaving are not documented, but there are two likely reasons that have materialised through some recently discovered diaries of William Hugh, John's eldest son. William Hugh was a shopkeeper in Limerick but he went bankrupt and had to close his shop in 1794. A number of letters were written to keep the debtors at bay and John pulled some strings to get Hugh a job in Dublin.[68] He moved to Dublin in the same year to work for David La Touche, the banker.[69] Hugh also discussed his mother's and sisters' increased time spent socializing in Dublin in the early 1790s. He noted that, in June of 1794, John's wife Mary and his daughter Rose went to Dublin with the 'intention of taking a house'. For a rent of sixty pounds and a fine of £200 they secured a house on the fashionable Merrion Row just off St Stephen's Green.[70]

---

[67] Charles Etienne Coquebert de Montbret from Rheims made the comments. For more on his visit to Limerick see Sighle Ní Chinnéide 'A Frenchman's perspective of Limerick, town and people, in 1791' in *NMAJ*, 4 (1948), pp. 96-101; and Síghle Ní Chinnéide 'A journey from Cork to Limerick in December 1790' in NMAJ, 14 (1971) pp. 65-74.

[68] Old Library, Magdalene College, Cambridge University. 'Diary of William Hugh Ferrar' 30 December 1793.

[69] M. L. Ferrar, *The Limerick-Huntingdon Ferrars*, p. 80. William Hugh was later appointed Pro-Collector of Customs in Larne, Co. Antrim in 1800.

[70] 'Diary of William Hugh Ferrar', 10 June 1794 and 25 June 1794.

John Ferrar maintained his links with Limerick and his expanding charitable crusade elevated his own social status. He was admitted a member of the Association for Discountenancing Vice and Promoting the Practice of Virtue and Religion on 1 January 1795.[71] The Association maintained close links with the administration in Dublin Castle and frequently petitioned the Lord Lieutenant. Members from Dublin Castle were often guests of honour at charity sermons for the association. Ferrar was regarded highly by his fellow members and appeared at the top of the list of members in the minute books on many occasions and he chaired at least one meeting.[72] He did not, however, attend the meetings year round but tended only to attend in the spring and summer. This could suggest that he either spent the time away from Dublin travelling and researching back in his native Limerick or with other charitable organisations, such as the Stranger's Friend Society where he was a collector of subscriptions.[73] During this time he wrote a number of pamphlets promoting the education of the poor in Dublin and was listed as a subscriber to the Association's fund at charity sermons along with the La Touches and the lord lieutenants of the day. His pamphlets included *A Plan for Clothing and Educating the Destitute Orphans and Poor Children of Soldiers, Labourers and Others* (Dublin, 1795) and *The Prosperity of Ireland Displayed in the State of Fifty-four Charity Schools in Dublin containing 7416 Children* which were printed by the Association. He proposed to the government that a charity school could be maintained on £250 per year. This would have included the rent, salary of the master and

---

[71] Representative Church Body [hereafter RCB] Library, Proceedings of the Association for the Purpose of Discountenancing Vice and Promoting the Practice of Virtue and Religion, 1 January 1795, MS 174/1/1/1.

[72] RCB Library, Proceedings of the Association for the Purpose of Discountenancing Vice...5 April 1798, MS 174/1/1/1.

[73] *The Nature, Design and General Rules of the Stranger's Friend Society as Established in Dublin, 1790* (Dublin, 1790), p. 24.

mistress, and clothing and the education of 'one hundred poor children; – a small sum, when we consider the vast national importance of the object!'[74] Ferrar's interest in education was no doubt influenced by the utilitarian attitudes towards education and manufacture that developed during this time. Increased population in Dublin also saw widespread poverty.

Aside from the material published for the Association he also penned a survey of Dublin and a tourist guidebook to the La Touche's demesne, Bellvue, in 1796. In the same year he published *A Tour from Dublin to London*. These books, probably commissioned by the La Touche family, were some of the earliest guide books written by an Irish author.[75] During the Rebellion year of 1798 membership and meetings of the Association for Discountenancing Vice declined, but Ferrar continued his work with the society until 1801 when an extraordinary general meeting was convened to accept a letter from him asking that his name be removed from membership. This was accepted by those present. While no obvious row was recorded in the minute books, a letter was sent to the lord mayor concerning the resignation and stating that 'any investigation on their part of the business in question, is necessarily precluded.'[76] Despite leaving the Association Ferrar maintained his interest in education and published *Important hints to the Fifty District Committees of the*

---

[74] John Ferrar, *The Prosperity of Ireland Displayed in the State of Fifty-four Charity Schools in Dublin containing 7416 Children* (Dublin, 1796), p. 48.

[75] John Ferrar, *A View of Antient and Modern Dublin with its Improvements to the year 1796. To Which is Added a Tour to Bellvue, the Seat of Peter La Touch, Esq; Knight of the Shire for the County of Leitrim.* (Dublin, 1796); *A Tour from Dublin to London, in 1795, through the Isle of Anglesea, Bangor, Conway* [...] *and Kensington* (Dublin, 1796). A second and posthumous edition of *A View of Antient and Modern Dublin* was published in 1807, edited by Graisberry and Campbell, which described more towns in Dublin.

[76] RCB Library, Proceedings of the Association for the Purpose of Discountenancing Vice..., 30 May 1801, MS 174/1/3.

City of Dublin in 1803. He also maintained his civic duties and in July of 1802 he wrote to Alexander Marsden, Under Secretary in Dublin Castle, reporting a riot that had taken place in College Green.

Many were wounded, if not killed and it was some time before the magistrates or military arrived. Wearing green and orange ribbands is daily productive of quarrels, it would therefore be productive of happy and good effects, if his Excellency...would infuse an order prohibiting men from wearing those ribbands on any part of their dress, under pain of being considered as enemies of the public peace. When these distinctions are abolished, the people will be more united, and our manufacture will flourish.[77]

John Ferrar died at the age of sixty-one on 3 May 1804 and was buried with his three grandchildren in the graveyard of St Ann's church, Dawson Street, Dublin.[78] By this time he had acquired a great deal of property in Limerick as well as the houses on Merrion Row, Andrew Street and Exchequer Street in Dublin.[79] He occupied many roles in provincial and capital life. He extended the borders of the Limerick printing trade which saw him achieve more than most of his contemporaries. His prosperity, connections and publishing enabled him to step outside the tradi-

---

[77] Ferrar to Marsden, 13 July 1802 (NAI, Rebellion Papers, 620/62/27). Marsden (1761-1834) was born in Dublin, educated at Trinity College, Dublin:, BA 1783, LL.B. 1786, Bar 1787. He became under secretary in 1801 in succession to E. Cooke. He had to deal with bribes and promises made at the Union and deal with Emmet's insurrection in 1803. Many of his letters are in *Castlereagh Correspondence* and *Viceroy's postbag*. J. S. Crone, *A Concise Dictionary of Irish Biography,* (Dublin, 1928).

[78] 'Sacred to the memory of John Ferrar, who died 3rd May, 1804, aged 61. Also his three grandchildren, John Ferrar, aged 8, Edward Minchin and Mary Minchin, infants.' RCB Library, Grave inscriptions LXXIV, MS 442. He was later re-interred in Mount Jerome cemetery in Dublin when Saint Anne's cemetery was removed.

[79] Will of John Ferrar, 7 November 1803 (Private collection).

tional role of printer and become an influential figure, both in the province of Munster and in Dublin. His rise as a prominent printer, publisher and author was aided by patrons and perhaps his family in Huntingdon, though it may have owed more to the expanding trade and civic development of Limerick. Commercial ventures and new consumers ensured a substantial advertising income. His publications helped in the formation of an urban mentality in a community trying to establish itself in the wake of the Corporation dispute during the 1760s and 1770s. Limerick developed as an important centre for printing and book distribution in north Munster. His move to Dublin in the 1790s suggests that he had achieved all he could in Limerick and was socially mobile. His focus on charitable and educational issues aligned him with the rising Dublin classes and established him as a man of culture.

As there are few primary sources on Ferrar himself more of the man is yet to be uncovered to allow questions to be conclusively answered. In two of his publications his own choices of phrase are apt in representing aspects of his life. First, in his *Tour from Dublin to London* he described the duties of the travel writer. 'If he observes what may appear trifling, let him remember that trifles light as air often prove entertaining to the traveller and antiquary' and, indeed, the historian.[80] A second example appears on the frontispiece of his 1767 edition of the History of Limerick, *multum in parvo* – or, 'much in little'.

---

[80] John Ferrar, *A Tour from Dublin to London* (Dublin, 1795). p. iv.

William Flyn (1740-1811) and the Readers of Munster in the Second Half of the Eighteenth Century

MÁIRE KENNEDY

I N THE LAST QUARTER of the eighteenth century Cork was Ireland's second city, with a population estimated at about 70,000.[1] Travellers to the city described how busy it was, the streets thronged with people.[2] As early as 1732 Edward Lloyd of London considered Cork the second city of Ireland but the first sea-port for trade.[3] Two decades later Charles Smith encountered the outlines of the medieval city still much in evidence, but he noticed new houses beginning to replace the decayed ones; he described the Spanish-style mansion houses with balcony windows being built along the North and South Main Streets.[4] From the middle of the century the city began to expand beyond its medieval core, channels of the river were culverted, marshy areas were drained and new streets formed.[5] The city was at the centre

---

[1] K.H. Connell, *The Population of Ireland, 1750-1845* (Oxford, 1950). Thomas Campbell, *A Philosophical Survey of the South of Ireland, in a series of letters to John Watkinson, M.D.* (London, 1777), p. 4. (ESTCt84447). Campbell estimates the population of Dublin to be above 160,000. Samuel Derrick, *Letters Written from Leverpoole, Chester, Corke, the lakes of Killarney, Dublin, Tunbridge-Wells, and Bath*, 2 vols (Dublin, 1767), i, p. 34. (ESTCt135402). Arthur Young, *A Tour Through Ireland*, 2 vols (Dublin, 1780), ii, p. 66. (ESTCt78931). Derrick estimates the population of Cork at 80,000 in 1760, while Young puts it at about 67,000, based on hearth tax returns, in 1780. Young's figure is considered the more accurate.

[2] Young, *A Tour*, ii, p. 65.

[3] Edward Lloyd, *A Description of the Flourishing City of Corke* (Cork, 1732). (ESTCt164728).

[4] Charles Smith, *The Antient and Present State of the County and City of Cork* (Dublin, 1750), pp.407-8. (ESTCt97653).

[5] Maurice Hurley, 'Below sea-level in the city of Cork', in *Irish Cities,* ed. by Howard B. Clarke (Cork, 1995), p. 47.

of a wealthy and populous hinterland.[6] Agricultural produce from much of the Munster region was brought to the port of Cork for export and to supply the lucrative provisioning trade for transatlantic shipping, including the vessels of the English navy. Wool was brought from as far afield as Galway and Roscommon for export.[7] Thomas Campbell, in his tour of 1777, echoing the observations of other travellers before him, was impressed with Cork Harbour: 'The harbour called the Cove is one of the best in the world; the entrance is safe; and the whole navy of England may ride in it secure from every wind that blows.'[8] The size and security of the deep-water harbour, in addition to the prime situation of Cork for trade with the West Indies and the Americas, ensured its prosperity throughout the century. Cork merchants became wealthy thanks to the export trade, and many built fine villas on the salubrious hillsides overlooking the harbour, from Blackrock, Glanmire and Tivoli, to Passage and Monkstown.

By the 1760s the city was only beginning to find its place as a cultural centre although the book trade was active from the early years of the century and visiting troupes of actors had been bringing theatrical entertainment in the summer season from the late 1730s.[9] The first newspapers published in the city were short-lived: *The Idler* and *The Cork Intelligence* were published in 1715, the *Cork News-Letter* and a reprint of the *Free-Holder* were issued about 1717, but it was not until the 1750s that regular newspapers could be sustained.[10] In 1750 there were two coffee

---

[6]   For a detailed discussion of Cork's importance as an agricultural centre see David Dickson, *Old World Colony: Cork and South Munster 1630-1830* (Cork, 2005), and for a more succinct account see his 'The South Munster Region in the 1790s', in *The French are in the Bay: the Expedition to Bantry Bay, 1796*, ed. by John A. Murphy (Cork, 1997).

[7]   Young, *A Tour*, ii, p. 68.

[8]   Campbell, *A Philosophical Survey*, p. 191. Lloyd, *Description*, p. 8.

[9]   William Smith Clark, *The Irish Stage in the County Towns 1720-1800* (Oxford, 1965).

[10]   *Newsplan*, ed. by James O'Toole, revised edition (London and Dublin,

houses, the Exchange and English coffee houses, both situated near the Exchange in Castle Street. Here the English and Dublin newspapers could be read. Smith tells us that: 'The better sort are fond of news and politics, and are well versed in public affairs.'[11] Later in the century two new coffee houses were established, the Tontine which opened in 1793 and the Merchants'.[12] By the last quarter of the century the Irish language was still spoken by many of the inhabitants of the city and surrounding areas.[13] The business of the city and port, however, was carried out in English, and virtually all printing work was in English. Many booksellers and stationers worked in the city from the early years of the century, catering for the civil administration and Cork's intellectual elite. Books were distributed from Dublin or imported directly from London. Because of Cork's prime position for trade the road networks were extensive. Local booksellers distributed their printed works to the main towns in Munster using the Post Office network and private couriers to circulate newspapers, periodicals and books.

Of the many successful booksellers working in Cork in the second half of the eighteenth century William Flyn offers an insight into a number of different aspects of the book trade and the cultural life of the region. Flyn was advertising books of Catholic interest from the start of his career, and as printer of *The Hibernian Chronicle* he established a rapport with his readership throughout Munster, offering literary fare through the pages of the paper. William Flyn was born in 1740, possibly in Limerick.[14] His father,

---

1998). Robert Munter, *The History of the Irish Newspaper 1685-1760* (Cambridge, 1967).

[11] Smith, *Antient and Present State*, ii, p. 407.

[12] *Copy of the Deed or Charter entered into by the Associated Society to Raise a Fund for Erecting a Coffee-House...in the City of Cork* (Cork, 1794).

[13] Seán Beecher, *An Gaeilge in Cork City: an Historical Perspective to 1894* (Cork, 1993).

[14] *International Genealogical Index* compiled by the Church of Jesus Christ of Latter Day Saints.

Sylvester, was residing in Engine Alley in Dublin at the time of
his death in 1778.[15] His uncle, Laurence Flin, had a thriving bookselling, bookbinding and book auctioneering business at Castle
Street, Dublin, from the mid-1750s until his death in 1771. He was
warden of the Guild of St Luke the Evangelist, the Guild of Cut-
lers, Painter-stainers and Stationers, and was elected to Dublin's
Common Council. He was succeeded by his nephew, Laurence
Larkin, who took the surname Flin when he took over the business.[16] Edward Flin, printer in Limerick, may also have been a
relative. William was in Cork from at least 1764 and he remained
in the city for the rest of his life. He gave up the bookselling business in 1801 and died a decade later, in December 1811.[17]

William Flyn seems to have been a Catholic; his daughters
and their families were prominent in Catholic circles, although
his Dublin cousins were almost certainly members of the
Church of Ireland, holding high office within the Guild and on
the Common Council. Flyn had at least four daughters, Eliza,
the eldest, married the bookseller James Haly in 1788, Mary
married Francis Hynes, from Galway, a linen draper in 1791;
both sons-in-law had their businesses near the Exchange in
Cork.[18] James and Eliza Haly had six sons and three daughters.
At least three of their sons attended the Jesuit Stonyhurst College in England: their third son, Robert, joined the Jesuit order
and was rector of Clongowes Wood College, Co. Kildare, from
1836 to 1850.[19] James Haly died in 1850, aged 86 years. Mary

---

[15] *Walker's Hibernian Magazine*, VIII (January 1778), p. 64. *Hibernian Chronicle*, 12 January 1778.

[16] M. Pollard, *A Dictionary of Members of the Dublin Book Trade 1550-1800*
(London, 2000).

[17] *Cork Mercantile Chronicle*, 20 December 1811.

[18] *Cork Evening Post*, 17 June 1788; 29 August 1791.

[19] Rev. Henry Browne, S.J., 'Father Robert Haly, S.J. (1796-1882)' in *A Roll
of Honour: Irish Prelates and Priests in the Last Century*, with preface by Most
Rev. John Healy, D.D. (Dublin, 1905), pp. 247-94. I am very grateful to

and Francis Hynes lost their eldest son, William, in 1807; he died in his thirteenth year while attending Carlow College, a leading Catholic school.[20] In 1822 their son Timothy was taken into partnership with his father in the linen and silk drapery business.[21] Mary Hynes died in 1827 leaving a large family.[22] Another daughter, Charlotte, married John A. Pearce, merchant and grocer, in 1800.[23] Flyn's eleven-year-old daughter, Lelia Sophia, died after a long illness in 1795 and his wife died in 1799.[24] William Flyn died at his home on George's Quay on 20 December 1811, aged 71 years.[25]

James Haly, Flyn's son-in-law and himself a successful bookseller, took over the printing of *The Hibernian Chronicle* in 1801, changing the name to *Flyn's Hibernian Chronicle*. Haly also specialised in Catholic publications, one of his earliest being *An Humble Remonstrance*, published in 1789, in which the author argues for Catholic participation in the commercial life of Cork. An Irish language catechism, *An Teagusg Criesdeegh*, was published by Haly and Thomas White in 1792. According to his son Robert, James Haly kept a classical school in which he provided instruction for boys who wished to become priests.[26] Haly's business seemed to thrive, but in 1812, one year after Flyn's death, he got into serious difficulties.[27] He was guaranteed to the sum of £7,000 by his brother-in-law, Francis Hynes. When he failed to recover Hynes withdrew support, turned him out of his

---

Penny Woods, Librarian at the Russell Library, Maynooth, for this reference.
[20] *Cork Advertiser*, 21 April 1807.
[21] *The Constitution*, 15 July 1822.
[22] *The Constitution*, 8 March 1827.
[23] *Hibernian Chronicle*, 3 November 1800.
[24] *Cork Evening Post*, 10 December 1795; 23 May 1799.
[25] *Cork Mercantile Chronicle*, 20 December 1811.
[26] Browne, 'Father Robert Haly', pp. 248-49.
[27] *Cork Advertiser*, 14 April 1812.

bookshop and handed it over to Jeremiah Geary, also a printer of Catholic books. Eliza Haly later described her ejection from her home, with nothing but 'a slop bowl of raspers'.[28]

William Flyn worked as a printer, bookseller, stationer and newspaper proprietor at the 'Sign of Shakespeare' in Cork for nearly forty years. He had his bookshop in the heart of the old city at Castle Street, close to the civil and legal administration.[29]

The earliest reference to Flyn is in 1764 when his name appears on the imprint of John Dryden's *The Hind and the Panther*, printed by Thomas Meighan the younger in Drury Lane, London,

Fig. 1 The Exchange, Charles Smith, *The Ancient and Present State of the County and City of Cork*, second edition (Dublin, 1774), Plate X. (Dublin City Library and Archive).

---

[28] Séamus Ó Casaide, *A History of the Periodical Literature of Cork from the Beginning up to A.D. 1900*, typescript, National Library of Ireland (Ir 6551 C2).

[29] Máire Kennedy, 'At the Exchange: the eighteenth-century book trade in Cork', in *That Woman! Studies in Irish Bibliography: a Festschrift for Mary 'Paul' Pollard*, ed. by Charles Benson and Siobhán Fitzpatrick (Dublin, 2005), pp. 139-61.

and sold by William Flyn, bookseller in Cork.[30] The verso of the final leaf carries advertisements for Flyn's stock of works of Catholic interest. The imprint is tantalising and presents two main possibilities. The twenty-four-year-old Flyn, newly in business, may have printed this classic work himself, but lacking confidence in the market or fearing danger due to the subject matter, decided to give it a London imprint. Thomas Meighan's name would have been an obvious choice to use as a false imprint, and it is interesting to note that his surname is misspelt as Meaghan. Thomas Meighan the elder was a Catholic, overtly dealing in books of Catholic interest from about 1715 to 1753. His high-profile stance on political matters relating to Catholic affairs would have made his name known. His son, Thomas, continued to publish and sell Catholic books, thus keeping the name alive in Catholic circles. The second possibility suggests a reciprocal arrangement with Meighan, in which Flyn tapped the Irish market for the sale of the book and Meighan printed Flyn's advertisement at the end of the publication. Meighan would certainly have been one of Flyn's main suppliers of Catholic works. In either case Flyn chose to place himself at the centre of Catholic book production and distribution by associating himself with one of the chief London printers supplying the market in Catholic books.

The books advertised at the end of *The Hind and the Panther*, twenty-two in all, are Catholic works, and set the tone for Flyn's future business. The list included a five-volume Bible, works by Challenor and Blyth, *An Introduction to a Devout Life* by St Francis de Sales, *The Catholic Christian Instructed* and Scupoli's *The Spiritual Combat*. No publication details are given and there are

---

[30] John Dryden, *The Hind and the Panther* (London, printed by T. Meaghan in Drury Lane, and sold by William Flyn, bookseller in Cork, 1764). (ESTCt221936). For a valuable list of Catholic publications see Hugh Fenning, OP, 'Cork imprints of Catholic historical interest, 1723-1804' and 'Cork imprints of Catholic historical interest, 1805-1830' in *Journal of the Cork Historical and Archaeological Society*, 100 (1995) and 101 (1996).

no surviving examples of any of the titles printed by Flyn at this time, although he did print an edition of *The Spiritual Combat* in 1772. An examination of editions published in or before 1764 indicates that many could have been Dublin imprints, issued by Bartholomew Gorman, Eleanor Kelly or, after 1755, by the executors of Eleanor Kelly. Two titles, *The Evening-Office of the Church in Latin and English* and Challoner's *The Garden of the Soul,* could have come from the press of Thomas Meighan, the first published in 1759, the second in 1751 and again in 1764. *The Evening-Office* was also printed by Eleanor Kelly in 1754, and *The Garden of the Soul* printed for her executors in 1759. Flyn set out his business plan at the end of the volume: intending 'to keep himself well supplied with all sorts of books fit for the closet or school', offering money for libraries or parcels of books, offering a binding service, and willing to 'write for books by commission'.[31]

Flyn continued to print and sell works of Catholic interest. His imprint on the publication of *An Abstract of the Doway Catechism* in 1774 read 'where may be had the greatest variety of Catholick books by wholesale and retail'.[32] [In it he advertised a 'variety of Catholic books and school books, printed and sold by William Flyn'. He noted two titles 'just published' by him: Challoner's *Considerations upon Christian Truths* in two volumes, selling at 5s. 5d. bound, which he printed the previous year, and *The Spiritual Combat,* a new edition printed in 1772 in large type and on fine paper, priced at 1s. 7½ d.[33]

Flyn had advertised proposals for printing Challoner's *Considerations* by subscription in January 1772. His subscription agents

---

[31]   Dryden, *The Hind and the Panther.*

[32]   *An Abstract of the Doway Catechism. For the Use of Children, and Ignorant People* (Cork, printed by William Flyn, 1774). ESTCt183672.

[33]   *The Spiritual Combat...Also Twelve Advantages Arising from the Contemplation of Death* (Cork, printed by William Flyn, 1772). (ESTCt82143). Richard Challoner, *Considerations upon Christian Truths* (Cork, printed by William Flyn, 1773). (ESTCT221720: ESTC wrongly gives date of [1780?]).

were Richard Fitzsimons and Thomas Walker in Dublin, Hugh and James Ramsey in Waterford, Edmund Finn in Kilkenny, and Catherine Long in Limerick. Volume one was completed in February 1773, with volume two due to follow shortly.[34] He printed the single sheet prospectus for the new Augustinian school, the Brunswick Street Academy, established in 1783.[35] Flyn was involved with the Catholic Committee as they sought relief for Catholics from civil and legal restrictions. He is noted as secretary to the committee in an advertisement placed in *The Hibernian Chronicle* in October 1792 announcing a meeting of the Roman Catholics of the county and city of Cork 'for the purpose of signing a declaration of their sentiments'.[36] He printed a single-sheet account of this general meeting, chaired by Dr Justin McCarthy, which was also printed on the front page of the *Chronicle* on 18 October 1792.[37]

Throughout his career Flyn juggled the various strands of the business of provincial bookseller. Disaster struck in October 1770 when a large chimney stack fell through the roof of his printing office, breaking three floors and burying the printing materials in the ruins. Fortunately his journeymen and apprentices were at breakfast and nobody was injured.[38] He put this setback behind him and his business was resumed. Flyn continued to offer money for libraries, advertised second-hand books for sale, and held a diverse stock of printed materials and stationery, including printed forms, parchment, processes, wafers, music, and stamped paper. He stocked the monthly magazines

[34] *Hibernian Chronicle*, 13 January 1772; 4 February 1773.
[35] William D. O'Connell, 'An Eighteenth Century Cork Manuscript. The Augustinian Academy at Brunswick Street, 1783-1787', *Journal of the Cork Historical and Archaeological Society*, XLV no.161 (January-June 1940), pp. 33-7.
[36] *Hibernian Chronicle*, 8 October 1792.
[37] *At a General Meeting of the Roman Catholics of the County and City of Cork...held at the Cork Tavern, the 15th October, 1792* [Cork, Mr Flyn, printer, 1792]. (ESTCN033349). *Hibernian Chronicle*, 18 October 1792.
[38] *Hibernian Chronicle*, 4 October 1770. *Freeman's Journal* 9-11 October 1770.

Exshaw's *Gentleman's and London Magazine* and the *Gentleman's Magazine*. He imported paper and in 1773 he received Post, Propatria, Demi, Royal and Imperial papers made by the 'noted Sterlings of Rotterdam'.[39] Flyn co-operated with other booksellers in Cork, especially with Thomas Lord and Thomas White, and acted as subscription agent for books published by Dublin and Limerick printers, subscribing to multiple copies. Publishing books of local interest, often by subscription, he used his Dublin and Limerick contacts to sell these works. In 1773 he opened up a 'correspondence with a principal bookseller in Holland' for the importation of books, he kept a catalogue at his shop and readers wanting books in any language would be supplied on reasonable terms.[40] As part of his second-hand stock he carried books in French, and it is likely that his customers sought continental publications which could be supplied from the Netherlands.[41] He sold part-books and specialized in the sale of children's books, some of which were imported from Newbery in London.[42] He issued sale catalogues for libraries which were sold by auction, including the libraries of Dr Joseph Fenn Sleigh and Rev. Dr Marmaduke Phillips in 1770 and Sir Richard Cox in 1772.[43] He was a lottery agent and purveyor of patent medicines. As the printer of a successful newspaper he established contacts throughout the Munster region for the sale of his publications.

---

[39] *Hibernian Chronicle*, 11 February 1773.

[40] *Hibernian Chronicle*, 25 October 1773.

[41] In 1769 he advertized a two-volume *Bible* in French, St. Francis de Sales in French, as well as grammars, works of history and philosophy. *Hibernian Chronicle*, 25 December 1769.

[42] *Hibernian Chronicle*, 20 August 1770; 2 January 1772; 16 April 1772; 24 December 1772.

[43] *Hibernian Chronicle* 12 July 1770; 23 August 1770; 30 October 1770. *A Catalogue of a Valuable Library, Collected by the late Chancellor Cox, Sir Richard Cox, and the Rev. Sir Michael Cox, Bart....which will be sold by auction...at Mr Zachery Morris's Great Room...* (Cork, printed by William Flyn, 1772). (ESTCt162448).

Flyn managed to span the religious divide in a city whose administration was Protestant-dominated at this period. In 1773, together with Thomas White, he advertized a catechism written by the Church of Ireland Bishop of Cork and Ross, Dr Isaac Mann, and a Bible for children, offering a discount to 'the benevolent to buy parcels to bestow'.[44] He carried out printing work for Cork Corporation and other bodies in the city. The former paid a total of over £762 for printing work and advertisements in *The Hibernian Chronicle* from 1777 to 1799, averaging just under £35 per annum for twenty-two years.[45] Showing a humane and charitable face Flyn was one of the founding mem-bers of the Society for the Relief and Discharge of Persons Confined for Small Debts, to which he acted as secretary for thirty years.[46] This society was a model of religious co-operation as can be seen by the make-up of its committees, and he printed the accounts of the society from 1774.[47]

The Hibernian Chronicle was established by Flyn in October 1769. He printed two thousand proposals in September, and when he had attracted 'a respectable number of ladies and gentlemen' as subscribers he launched the venture.[48] The paper was published twice a week, on Mondays and Thursdays, at the price of one penny per issue, or five British shillings per annum to town subscribers, and a half-guinea per annum to country sub-

---

[44] *A Familiar Exposition of the Church Catechism* by Dr Isaac Mann, Bishop of Cork and Ross, and *The Children's Bible* by an eminent divine of the Church of England. *Hibernian Chronicle*, 20 April 1772.

[45] Richard Caulfield, *The Council Book of the Corporation of the City of Cork* (Guilford, Surrey, 1876), pp.915, 985, 1009, 1015, 1021, 1042, 1078, 1097, 1107, 1117, 1127, 1132.

[46] *Cork Mercantile Chronicle*, 20 December 1811.

[47] *A Short Account of the Institution, Rules, and Proceedings of the Cork Society for the Relief and Discharge of Persons Confined for Small Debts;* accounts have survived for 1774, 1777, 1783, 1784, 1787 and 1797.

[48] *Hibernian Chronicle*, 23 October 1769.

scribers; for this sum Flyn included a title page and index at the end of the year.[49] His customers were encouraged to settle their accounts at the assizes in Cork.[50] In May 1770 Flyn informed his readers that he had 'at a great expense purchased a complete collection of quite new types, which shall appear in his paper before the 20th of the month'.[51] The newspaper was distributed widely using the Post Office network and by employing couriers, whom Flyn paid quarterly.[52] By early 1770 agents were in place in the major Cork towns: Youghal, Cloyne, Midleton, Castlemartyr, Mallow and Kinsale. By the middle of the year he had an agent in Killarney, Co. Kerry.

These agents were not booksellers but an innholder, a merchant, an apothecary, a cooper, two post-masters, and a teacher.[53] By 1772

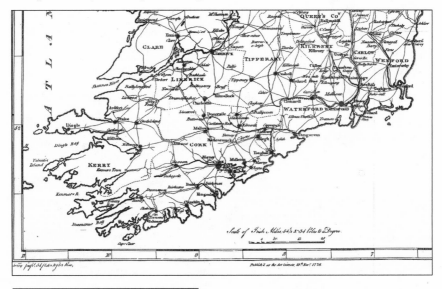

---

[49] *Hibernian Chronicle*, 31 December 1770; 2 January 1772.

[50] *Hibernian Chronicle*, 30 March 1772.

[51] *Hibernian Chronicle*, 31 May 1770.

[52] *Hibernian Chronicle*, 16 July 1772.

[53] Thomas Shea, cooper, Youghal; John Scanlan, teacher and land surveyor, Cloyne; Mr Barry, innkeeper, Midleton; William Hamilton, Midleton; Robert O'Brien, apothecary, Castlemartyr; John Furzer, post-master, Kinsale; Kennedy Hayes, post-master, Mallow; James Craswell, merchant, Killarney.

The Hibernian Chronicle was circulated by couriers to twenty-six towns in Cork, Limerick, Waterford and Kerry, 'besides a great number to the different post-offices in the kingdom'.[54] At Flyn's retirement from publication of the paper in April 1802 his successors, who included James Haly, renamed it *The Cork Mercantile Chronicle* and increased its publication to three times a week.[55]

A provincial newspaper created a network by which books and periodicals could be distributed to the smaller towns and country places. The regular delivery of a paper ensured a constant audience for the advertisements carried in its pages. The agents for the newspaper took in subscriptions and orders for books advertised. For example James Craswell, a merchant in Killarney, was agent for *The Hibernian Chronicle*, and *The Corke Journal* printed by Eugene Swiney, and when William Bingley came to Ireland in 1773 was one of Bingley's Irish agents for the *Independent Chronicle* and *Bingley's London Journal*.[56] He acted as subscription agent for *John Brenn's Book-keeping* in 1767, and when Flyn published Poulson's *Moral and Divine Observations* by subscription in 1775 James Craswell was on the subscription list.[57] John Furzer, post-master in Kinsale, and with his sisters, linen draper, hosier, haberdasher, and distributor of stamps, was agent for *The Hibernian Chronicle*. He subscribed to Temple's *History of the General Rebellion*, published in Cork in 1766, and to Fitzgerald's *Cork Remembrancer* in 1783.[58]

---

[54] Kinsale, Bandon, Bantry, Skibereen, Clonakilty, Rosscarbery, Berehaven, Skull, Mallow, Buttevant, Charleville, Limerick, Youghal, Midleton, Cloyne, Castlemartyr, Lismore, Tallow, Cobh, Passage, Macroom, Killarney, Shanagh, Castleisland, Tralee and Dingle. *Hibernian Chronicle*, 2 January 1772.

[55] *Hibernian Chronicle*, 25 March 1802. *Cork Mercantile Chronicle*, 26 April 1802. *Newsplan*, 1998.

[56] *Hibernian Chronicle*, 18 June 1770. *Corke Journal*, 2 April 1770. *Hibernian Chronicle*, 6 September 1773. *Freeman's Journal*, 19-21 October 1773.

[57] *Finn's Leinster Journal*,7-11 March 1767. James Poulson, *Moral and Divine Observations* (Cork, printed for the author, and sold by William Flyn and Thomas White, 1775). (ESTCt170104).

[58] Richard Lucas, *The Cork Directory* (Cork, printed for the author by J. Cro-

Mrs Furzer became agent for *The Waterford Herald* in 1792, subscribed to Dodd's *Essays and Poems* in 1770, and was agent for *The
Cork Mercantile Chronicle* in 1802.[59]

Not only did *The Hibernian Chronicle* provide the news of the
day and carry the advertisements necessary to make it a viable
venture, but Flyn sought to make it a literary vehicle, inviting
readers of both sexes to contribute to its pages: a first, he
claimed, for a Cork paper.[60] Its stated aim was to provide 'a
compleat reservoir of politics, history, poetry, literature, agriculture, commerce...and everything relative to the fair sex'.[61] The
provision of an annual title page and index suggests that Flyn
saw it less as an ephemeral news sheet which would be passed
around to other readers but more as something to be kept for
ongoing consultation. The leading article of each number was an
essay, signed only with an initial or pseudonym. In addition to
original essays, *The Hibernian Chronicle* reprinted literary and
scientific pieces. An extract was printed from Voltaire's *Questions sur l'Encyclopédie* in November 1772, an account of
Voltaire's new play, *Jean Hennuyer, Evêque de Liseux*, taken from
The Critical Review, in February 1773, and the 'Character of
Voltaire' by the King of Prussia in March of the same year.[62]

In 1802, when he handed over full control of the *Hibernian
Chronicle* to his successors, Flyn thanked the public for their

---

nin, 1787). (ESTCt230034). *Hibernian Chronicle* 14 May 1770. John Temple,
History of the General Rebellion in Ireland (Cork, printed by Phineas and
George Bagnell), 1766. (ESTCt127399). John Fitzgerald, *Cork Remembrancer*
(Cork, printed by J. Sullivan, 1783). (ESTCt204654).

[59] *Waterford Herald*, 4 February 1792. J.S. Dodd, *Essays and Poems* (Cork,
printed by Eugene Swiney, for the author, 1770). (ESTCt64210). *A Catalogue
of the Bradshaw Collection of Irish Books in the University Library Cambridge*, 3
vols (Cambridge, 1916), ii, p. 873.

[60] *Hibernian Chronicle*, 2 January 1772.

[61] *Hibernian Chronicle*, 2 January 1772.

[62] *Hibernian Chronicle*, 26 November 1772; 18 February 1773;29 March 1773.

support over thirty-three years and paid tribute to 'the great talents which first brought it to its maturity'.[63] Nearly a decade later his obituary stated that the paper was set up 'under the auspices and support of the first literary characters in this city'.[64] Flyn had as his editor Henry Sheares, an eminent banker in Cork, and M.P. for Clonakilty, who guided the literary content of the paper from the beginning until his death in December 1775.[65] Sheares was also one of the founding members of the Society for the Relief and Discharge of Persons Confined for Small Debts. He was very influential in the cultural life of Cork at the period and gathered around him a coterie of men and women who made regular contributions to the pages of the *Chronicle*. Very much part of the endeavour was Flyn's daughter, Eliza Haly, a cultured woman heavily involved in literary pursuits. A selection of these literary essays was gathered together and reprinted in a book entitled *The Modern Monitor; or, Flyn's Speculations*.[66] Several copies of this volume have contemporary annotations identifying the authors, including one copy belonging to the Countess of Shannon.[67]

The main regular contributors were the editor, Henry Sheares, who often used the signature William Flyn or any of the letters W.F.L.Y.N., Mrs Sheares, Dr John Longfield, Mrs Elizabeth Gray, Dr Richard William Stack of London, Mrs Stack, Miss Waterhouse, Mrs Therry, Mr Comerford and Dr Joseph Fenn Sleigh.[68]

---

[63] *Hibernian Chronicle*, 22 March 1802.

[64] *Cork Mercantile Chronicle*, 20 December 1811.

[65] Richard Robert Madden, *The History of Irish Periodical Literature*, 2 vols (London, 1867), ii, pp. 172-78. *Hibernian Chronicle*, 30 November - 4 December 1775; 4 - 7 December 1775.

[66] *The Modern Monitor, or Flyn's Speculations* (Cork, printed by William Flyn, 1771). (ESTCt147019). *Hibernian Chronicle*, 30 July 1770.

[67] Dublin City Library and Archive: Dix Collection 082.

[68] Madden, *History of Irish Periodical Literature*, pp. 172-78. Charles G. Doran,

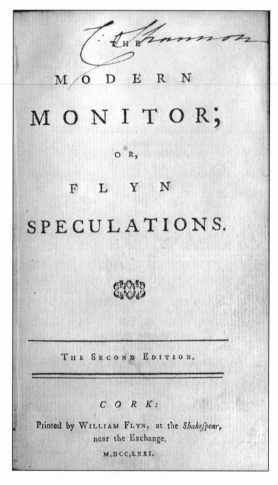

Fig. 2 The Modern Monitor; or, Flyn Speculations (Cork, 1771). (Dublin City Library and Archive. This variant has 'Flyn Speculations' as its subtitle).

In July 1770 Flyn issued proposals for printing the first volume of *The Modern Monitor*, priced at a British half crown, bound and lettered.[69] He clearly had the intention of producing further volumes. Even though proposals were issued in July 1770, which corresponds with the imprint date of 1771, it seems

---

'The Lough of Cork', *Journal of the Cork Historical and Archaeological Society*, II, no. 24 (December 1893), pp. 238-40.
[69] *Hibernian Chronicle*, 30 July 1770.

not to have appeared until 1774.[70] All surviving copies are from the second edition, the first being published in the *Hibernian Chronicle*.[71] Subscriptions were taken by James Williams and Thomas Walker in Dublin, Hugh and James Ramsey in Waterford, John Ferrar and Catherine Long in Limerick, and at all country places where the *Hibernian Chronicle* was circulated in 1770.[72] The subscription list is quite small, comprising 102 names, including most of the contributors, some of whom subscribed to multiple copies.[73]

By using subscription lists to his publications a broad profile of Flyn's customers can be drawn. A cross-section of readers and potential readers can be glimpsed in Cork and the surrounding counties at this period. An examination of five subscription lists for works printed by Flyn between 1768 and 1775 reveals 1,460 subscribers ranged over six counties: Cork, Kerry, Tipperary, Clare, Waterford and Limerick.[74] The spread of subscribers closely mirrors the distribution patterns of *The Hibernian Chronicle*, although other factors would also have been at work in gathering the subscription lists. The subject matter of the different works determined their particular support: *The History of*

---

[70] Seamus Ó Casaide, *History of the Periodical Literature of Cork*, NLI typescript.

[71] I am grateful to Dr Charles Benson for confirming the significance of the second edition.

[72] *Hibernian Chronicle*, 30 July 1770.

[73] Mrs Gray, 6 books; Dr Stack, 6 books; Miss Waterhouse, 3 books; and one each for Dr Longfield, Henry Sheares, Mrs Sheares, and Mrs Stack. Dr Sleigh had died on 10 May 1770 and therefore was not a subscriber.

[74] *The History of Hypolitus, Earl of Douglas* (Cork, printed by William Flyn, 1768). (ESTCt8723). *The Works of the Late Rev. George Russel* (Cork, printed for the benefit of the author's widow and children, by William Flyn, 1769). (ESTCt179710). *The Modern Monitor, or Flyn's Speculations* (Cork, printed by William Flyn, 1771). (ESTCt147019). Richard Challoner, *Considerations upon Christian Truths* (Cork, printed by William Flyn, 1773). (ESTCt221720). James Poulson, *Moral and Divine Observations* (Cork, printed for the author, and sold by William Flyn and Thomas White, 1775). (ESTCt170104).

Hypolitus translated from the French by local teacher, Peter Guitton, appealed to a literary audience, francophiles, and members of the Huguenot congregation including Rev. John Madras, minister of the Huguenot church in Cork, and Peter Ardouin, a prominent Huguenot merchant, who took twenty books. *The Modern Monitor* also appealed to literary subscribers. *The Works of Rev. George Russel* attracted large support from members and clergy of the Church of Ireland. Challoner's *Considerations* was supported by Catholic individuals and families. Only volume two has survived, the main subscription list is missing and only the names which arrived late are printed. A large proportion are from Co. Kerry, including the Catholic bishop Rev. John Madgett, who took 80 sets. Poulson's *Moral and Divine Observations* was a religious work by a local author and contains the largest subscription list, with 614 subscribers taking 732 copies of the book. It was printed for the author and sold by William Flyn and Thomas White, who took twenty and fifty copies respectively.

Analysis of subscription lists gives only tentative results as most do not provide occupations or addresses, so these categories are under-represented. Those subscribers who have a title (Rev., Capt., Mrs/Miss) are most easily categorised. Women account for just over fourteen per cent of subscribers.[75] Members of the professions are well represented: clergy (just under ten per cent), the military (over five per cent), legal, political and administrative (under four per cent), and medical (over two per cent). In 110 cases one customer subscribed to two of the five publications, and in a further eleven cases one subscriber took three titles. Thomas White, bookseller in Cork, subscribed to four of the five publications.

Many names which appear on the lists are known as book collectors. Dr John Longfield, one of the contributors to *The*

---

[75] These figures take into account multiple entries for each subscriber.

Hibernian Chronicle, subscribed to three of the five publications, and is known to have subscribed to a range of publications coming from Cork, Dublin and London presses. From a distinguished North Cork family, he practised medicine at Patrick Street, Cork, having qualified at Edinburgh.[76] He had a keen interest in the sciences, particularly astronomy and mathematics, corresponding with the Astronomer Royal; letters from 1773, 1774 and 1779, on the subject of his observations for determining the latitude and longitude of Cork, were published in *The Philosophical Transactions of the Royal Society*.[77] He subscribed to such works as Dr John Rutty's *Natural History of the County of Dublin* (Dublin, 1772), Joseph Priestley's *History of Vision, Light and Colours* (London, 1772), Thomas Sheridan's *General Dictionary of the English Language* (Dublin, 1784), John Hellens' *Mathematical Essays* (London, 1788), Michael Taylor's *Tables of Logarithms* (London, 1792) and Beaufort's *Memoir of a Map of Ireland* (London, 1792). His interests also included poetry, as seen from his subscription to J. S. Dodd's *Essays and Poems*, and James De la Cour's *A Prospect of Poetry*, both published in Cork in 1770, the first by Eugene Swiney and the second by Thomas Lord, and John Leslie's *Killarney, a Poem*, published in London in 1772.

Henry Sheares, editor of *The Hibernian Chronicle*, his wife Jane Anne, and sons Henry and John, were frequent subscribers to literary works published in Cork and Dublin. Henry senior supported several Cork publications, subscribing to James Eyre Weekes' *Poems on Several Occasions* in 1743, Charles Smith's *Antient and Present State of the County and City of Cork* in 1750, David Fordyce's *Dialogues Concerning Education* in 1755 and J. S. Dodd's *Essays and Poems* in 1770. Lieutenant, later General,

---

[76] John Longfield, *Dissertatio medica inauguralis, de febre hectica: quam...pro gradu doctoratus...*(Edinburgi, 1759). (ESTCt54656).
[77] John Lecky, 'The Longfield Family', *Journal of the Cork Historic and Archaeological Society*, XXIII (1917), pp. 173-74.

Charles Vallancey, the antiquary and Irish language enthusiast, subscribed to Poulson's *Moral and Divine Observations*. His library of over one thousand lots was sold by auction after his death in 1812.[78] An army engineer, Vallancey came to Ireland with Lord Townshend to assist in a military survey, designed the plans for Queen's Bridge in Dublin and was responsible for fortifications on Spike Island in Cork harbour. He translated two works from French, *Essay on Fortification* (Dublin, 1757) and *The Field Engineer* by De Clairac (Dublin, 1760). Another subscriber, Barry Yelverton, later Lord Avonmore, also collected an extensive library in his lifetime.[79] When he subscribed to *The History of Hypolitus* in 1768 he is listed as barrister-at-law, and went on to become Attorney General for Ireland in 1782, and Chief Baron of the Exchequer in 1784.

Several well-known county families are in evidence across the lists: Richard and Catherine Boyle, Earl and Countess of Shannon, the leading Protestant family in the county with their seat at Castlemartyr, were subscribers. The Earl subscribed to *The History of Hypolitus* in 1768, and both Earl and Countess supported *The Works of the Late Rev. George Russel* in 1769, this last certainly to support the cause of the rector's widow and children. They did not subscribe to *The Modern Monitor* yet an annotated copy that belonged to the Countess has survived. Lord and Lady Midleton, the Countess of Tyrone, Lord and Lady Blayney, Lord and Lady Kinsale, and Lord Mountcashel represented the aristocracy. Henry Cole Bowen built up a renowned library at his country house, Bowenscourt. He and his wife contributed money for *The Works of the Late Rev. George Russel*, and he had also subscribed to John

---

[78] *Catalogue of a Valuable Collection of Books, Manuscripts and Irish History, the Library of the Late Celebrated Irish Historian General Charles Vallancey* (Dublin, Thomas Jones, 18 February [1813]).

[79] *Catalogue of Scarce and Valuable Books, being the Miscellaneous Part of the Library of the Late Lord Avonmore* (Dublin, James Vallance, 11 February 1807).

Rutty's *Essay towards a...History of the Mineral Waters of Ireland* in 1757 and William Temple's *History of the General Rebellion in Ireland* in 1766. The local administration included the Honourable St John Jefferyes, M.P., Lieutenant Governor of Cork; the Honourable Joseph Lysaght, M.P., Collector of Cork; John Travers, Mayor of Cork; Hugh Carleton, Recorder of Cork; Thomas Brown, Register of Cork; Aldermen John Harding, Philips, Westropp, and Samuel Maylor of Cork; John Newman, Collector of Kinsale; Matthew Pennefeather, Mayor of Cashel; Nicholas Stout, Mayor of Youghal; Richard Harte, Mayor of Limerick; Robert Hallam, Town Clerk of Limerick; and Thomas Dixon, Under-Sheriff of Limerick. In all, the lists represent the professional people, local administration, merchants and tradesmen, the middling and higher clergy, country gentry and members of the local aristocracy. There is evidence of cross-confessional support for these publications consistent with their subject matter.

William Flyn represented a typical printer and bookseller of the late eighteenth century. The range and scope of his business activities are comparable to those of booksellers in other Irish towns and British provincial booksellers. Flyn's specialization in books of Catholic interest from the beginning of his career is noteworthy, but his publishing output and book sales were not targeted solely at this religious grouping. In a city that was much divided along religious lines in the second half of the eighteenth century, Flyn seems to have moved easily through the religious divides, and to cater for all sections of the population. His work for Cork Corporation for over two decades and his involvement with the Society for the Relief and Discharge of Persons Confined for Small Debts exemplify his non-sectarian stance.

Of particular interest are Flyn's contributions to the literary and cultural life of his sphere of influence. *The Hibernian Chronicle* introduced literary fare to readers in six Munster counties and made the distribution of books and other printed matter easy to

achieve through its networks. His encouragement of local authors through the pages of the *Chronicle* was important in fost-
ering participation in this cultural milieu. Flyn was well connected in literary and administrative circles, and the subscription
lists to his publications afford us a view of his customer base.
They show a cross-section of the literate market. Support for his
publications came from clergy and congregations of several de-
nominations, officers of the English army stationed in Cork,
local landed gentry and aristocracy, and local officials from the
major cities and towns in the region.

Humble Pie: *John Fletcher, Business, Politics and the* Chester Chronicle

VICTORIA GARDNER

IN 1816, A VISITOR to Chester purchased a new guidebook there, appropriately named *A Stranger to Chester*. He was so enchanted with the volume that he decided to call on its printer in order to congratulate him.

> We went to a Mr Fletcher, the printer of this book...expecting to find a dwelling house and shop where the printing business [was] carried on; we were however agreeably surprised on ascending several steps cut out of the solid rock to find ourselves in the most beautiful garden...From the side of his house projected a hot-house...On entering the [main] house a very handsome carpet covered the floor of the room, filled with good furniture... [and] the most extensive library of books, [all of which] induced me to apologise for my intrusion, naturally conceiving our director had made a mistake.[1]

The visitor had made no such error. The large and elegantly filled home was that of John Fletcher, printer and proprietor of the *Chester Chronicle* from 1783 to 1835.[2] The visitor's surprise was somewhat misplaced, for some provincial printers and proprietors were financially successful enough to own such a property by the later eighteenth century.[3] Even so, John

---

[1] J. H. Hanshall, *Stranger of Chester* (Chester, 1816), unpaginated (MS notes, Cheshire and Chester Archives edition).

[2] On John Fletcher, see also C. R. Hand, 'John Fletcher and the Stranger in Chester', *Transactions of the Society of Lancashire and Cheshire* 76 (1924), pp. 219-39; H. Hughes, *Chronicle of Chester: The 200 Years, 1775-1975* (London, 1975), pp. 32-89.

[3] Benjamin Collins of the *Salisbury Journal* was one of the most financially successful of eighteenth-century provincial newspaper proprietors and at the

Fletcher was no ordinary printer, but also a surveyor and engineer, for whom his *Chester Chronicle* fulfilled two roles. First it constituted a profitable section of his business portfolio. Second, and most importantly, the *Chronicle* enabled Fletcher to engage in the politics of Chester town. This essay focuses on an unexamined *Chester Chronicle* account book, dating from the first three years of Fletcher's ownership (1783–6).[4] The account book provides fresh evidence on the business of late eighteenth-century provincial newspaper production, furnishing a more detailed breakdown of the weekly business of a provincial newspaper than similar extant account books.[5] Moreover, in providing data on Fletcher's seminal years of ownership, this chapter shows how an enterprising businessman used his expertise to turn an ailing newspaper into a prosperous venture and, in the process, gain entry into Chester's political arena.

I

The *Chester Chronicle*, launched on 2 May 1775, was Chester's second newspaper. The town's first paper, the *Chester Courant*, had been established over forty years earlier, in 1732. As was usual for most pioneering provincial newspapers, the *Courant* followed the town's prevailing politics, in Chester's case, Tory. The new *Chester Chronicle* opposed it and the town Corporation. Its arrival was indeed timely. By the later eight-

---

time of his death, was worth between £85,000 and £100,000: C. Y. Ferdinand, *Benjamin Collins and the Provincial Newspaper Trade in the Eighteenth Century* (Oxford, 1997), p. 59.

[4]   Cheshire and Chester Archives, D3876 (Account Book of John Fletcher of the *Chester Chronicle*), hereafter CRO/D3876.

[5]   Hannah Barker has examined the financial records of the *Salopian Journal* (Shropshire Archives, MS 1923), the *Chelmsford Chronicle* (Essex Record Office, Acc. 5197, D/F, 66/1) and the *Hampshire Chronicle* (National Archives E140/90-1), the latter of which were located and first explored by Ferdinand: H. Barker, *Newspapers, Politics and Public Opinion* (Oxford, 1998), pp. 98-105, 119-22; Ferdinand, *Benjamin Collins*, pp. 3-4, 63-4, 75-8, 115-17.

eenth century, Chester was a regional capital and leisure resort for the gentry of the surrounding region, with a population of around 14,000. Moreover, the war in America was just beginning and newspapers were appearing in response to growing public interest.[6]

The two newspapers fought for the first year over market share, engaging in the usual rows between competing newspapers over which day to publish. The row was intensified by the involvement of the town Corporation, led by Chester's MPs, Richard, Lord (and from 1784, Earl) Grosvenor and his son, Robert, who, apparently concerned over the appearance of a Whig newspaper that actively disagreed with them and the American war, sought to put the *Chronicle* out of business. Whatever the initial troubles, they do not appear to have continued for long. The row between the rival papers died down after a year, the two evidently receiving enough market share to survive.[7] The American war also neutralised the perceived threat of the *Chronicle* to the ruling Corporation, for while the paper remained critical of Lord North's administration, it now shared in the Corporation's dissatisfaction with the war policy.[8] In August 1783, however, the *Chester Chronicle* was struggling and John Poole decided to discontinue it, explaining in his last issue as proprietor that 'finding the printing of...[the *Chester Chronicle*] to be a losing concern, on several counts, he is determined to discontinue the publication of it from this day.'[9]

Before a week had passed, John Fletcher purchased Poole's stock-in-trade and became the new owner-editor of the *Chester Chronicle*.

---

[6] K. Wilson, *Sense of the People: Politics, Culture and Imperialism in England 1715-1785* (Cambridge, 1995).

[7] Hughes, *Chronicle of Chester*, pp. 8-9.

[8] Hughes, *Chronicle of Chester*, p. 9.

[9] *Chester Chronicle*, 8 August 1783.

II

John Fletcher was born in Halton, Cheshire, in 1756, the eldest son of Thomas Fletcher, a reasonably prosperous yeoman. Little is known of John's early years, but by the late 1770s, he was working as a surveyor and engineer.[10] In 1783 he became the proprietor of the *Chester Chronicle*, which he owned for fifty-two years until his death in 1835. Fletcher was aware of the paper's political potential from the outset and under him the *Chronicle* became one of a number of radical provincial titles that argued for urgent parliamentary reform.[11] Assisted by several financial backers, Fletcher purchased the *Chronicle* shortly before the Chester elections of 1784, in which he supported the independent candidate John Crewe in the first such contest with the town's two MPs since 1747.[12] In the event, Crewe lost the elections and both the Grosvenors were re-elected. In October, at the Assembly elections, the Grosvenors disregarded charters that empowered a select body of men to elect the Mayor and Corporation officers and instead chose them arbitrarily. Incensed, Fletcher wrote an article in the *Chester Chronicle* condemning the Recorder of Chester, Robert Townsend, for his role in the affair. For specifically targeting and naming Townsend, Fletcher

---

[10] It has been alleged that Fletcher was working as a schoolmaster in Chester for several years: D. Nuttall, *A History of Printing in Chester From 1688 to 1965* (Chester, 1969), p. 27. The present author has uncovered no such evidence. There is no record of him as a registered member of the clergy (required by law for village and town school masters). It is possible that the confusion arose because Fletcher's nephew, also Thomas Fletcher, who inherited the *Chester Chronicle* in 1835 was a schoolmaster in Halton by 1822.

[11] H. Barker, *Newspapers, Politics and English Society* (Harlow, 2000), pp. 171-95. On the press and politics of the period, see also H. Barker, *Newspapers, Politics and Public Opinion, passim*; H. T. Dickinson, *The Politics of the People in Eighteenth Century Britain* (Oxford, 1995); B. Harris, *Politics and the Rise of the Press. Britain and France, 1620-1800* (London and New York, 1996).

[12] C. P. Lewis and A. T. Thacker, *A History of the County of Chester* (2003), p. 8.

was prosecuted with libel.

Despite profuse apologies in print, paying the Recorder's costs and a donation to Chester General Infirmary, Fletcher was convicted of libel on 17 November 1785, ordered to pay a fine of £50 and sentenced to six months' imprisonment. Whilst residing at the King's Bench prison, he received a festive parcel. Sent from a house on the Grosvenors' estate, the 24-pound pie consisted of umbles, or animal innards, including

three domestic rabbits devoid of brains and equally remarkable for having each of them...a bladder of gall preternaturally large, with ears so unusually capacious that, were we inclined to speak ludicrously, they might be deemed a new species of trap to catch the artless words of poor, inoffensive printers; also a goose without a heart which, were it not for spoiling the pie, we could heartily have wished had been an old gander. [13]

Fletcher declined to eat his humble pie. Instead, he sent his thanks to the donor through the *Chronicle*, expressing his disappointment at its weight, for John Wilkes had received one weighing forty-five pounds. [14]

For the business at least, Fletcher's incarceration was beneficial, for it meant that Fletcher engaged William Cowdroy, an editor with considerable expertise in the trade, to manage and edit the paper while he was in prison. Whether Fletcher had fired his first manager, a Mr Ogden, for some reason relating to the libel, or the libel had simply highlighted to Fletcher that he needed an experienced editor to pen his editorials, is unknown. Regardless, Cowdroy was an excellent choice. He had worked in the Chester newspaper trade for twenty years, having been bound to Fletcher's rival, John Monk senior, in 1764, becoming his journeyman compositor on his freedom in 1777 and taking

---

[13] *Chester Chronicle*, 23 December 1785.

[14] *Chester Chronicle*, 23 December 1785.

on a greater editorial role at the paper.[15] Cowdroy was also an accomplished writer who had instigated a war of words with John Poole in 1782 and who was later described in his role as owner of the *Manchester Gazette* (1795-1814), 'a poet, a wit, a facetious companion...[whose] light punning paragraphs had no equal'.[16] The relationship that Cowdroy and Fletcher struck up, moreover, was one that would last throughout their careers in the newspaper trade.

The *Chester Chronicle* remained committed to reform, but the failure of the independent cause in Chester and the dearth of candidates contesting the Grosvenors between 1790 and 1806 (and probably Fletcher's experience of prison) meant that the paper became far less vocal about local politics. It continued to comment on parliamentary reform at national level throughout the 1790s (initially approving of the French Revolution) but by the turn of the nineteenth century, its radical stance was waning. In 1807, however, the *Chester Chronicle* again became immersed in Chester politics. One of the parliamentary seats was left vacant by the Grosvenors and the independent John Egerton was returned unopposed.[17] Fletcher now turned his support to the Corporation, forcing his rival *Courant* to take an opposing position.[18]

---

[15] Nuttall, *History of Printing in Chester*, pp. 28-9; I. Maxted, 'The British Book Trades 1710-1777: an Index of Masters and Apprentices. Apprentices: C', *Exeter Working Papers in the British Book Trade* (Exeter, 2001), online at http://www.devon.gov.uk/etched?_IXP_=1&_IXR=121778.

[16] C. H. Timperley, *Encyclopaedia of Literary and Typographical Anecdote; Being a Chronological Digest of the Most Interesting Facts Illustrative of the History of Literature and Printing From the Earliest Period to the Present Time* (London, 1842), p. 854.

[17] Lewis and Thacker, *History of the County of Chester*, *passim*, p. 9.

[18] A war of words thus again erupted between the two Chester papers, collated in *Compilation of all the Authorised Papers Relating to the Election for City Officers in 1809*, ed. by J. Monk (Chester, 1810).

Fletcher's about-turn in his newspaper's politics meant that he now engaged fully in Chester's political life. On 15 March 1810 he was admitted a freeman and by 1813 he was an alderman. From this time, Fletcher was heavily involved in town politics and civic administration. He masterminded the 1818 elections and was mayor twice, in 1825 and 1832.[19] Fletcher's *Chester Chronicle*, initially purchased in order to provide him with a voice in popular politics, had provided a springboard for his public political career. Indeed, such was Fletcher's belief in the power of the newspaper press that he was one of the trustees for subscribers to the Commercial News Room, which opened in 1806. The News Room initially took over the public library in Bolland's Entry, but later moved to Fletcher's *Chronicle* buildings, where his portrait hung in the main reading room.[20] Fletcher therefore transferred his opinions and beliefs not only from the political action of the local community into the newspaper world, but reinforced his belief in the power of the newspaper press by entrenching it in physical form in the urban social and cultural sphere.

John Fletcher's achievements in the Chester newspaper and political world were assisted by, and replicated in, his successful surveying and engineering career. Fletcher was involved at the conceptual stages of the Chester-Nantwich canal as early as 1779. By 1790 he was one of the guarantors of a loan for £9,000 raised for the purchase of William Egerton's mortgage and interest on the Chester Canal. In 1791 Fletcher published a pamphlet by the architect and engineer Charles Turner, promoting the linking of the Severn, the Dee and the Mersey.[21] By 1793 the canal extension was underway, under the engineer, and Fletcher's friend, Thomas Telford, who allegedly shared Fletcher's office during

---

[19] Hand, 'John Fletcher', p. 226; Hughes, *Chronicle of Chester*, p. 83–7.

[20] Hughes, *Chronicle of Chester*, p. 76.

[21] Hughes, *Chronicle of Chester*, pp. 88-95.

this time. During this period, Fletcher was a shareholder in the Chester Canal Navigation Company and later the Ellesmere Canal Company and worked as a sub-contractor and engineer with his partner John Simpson, cutting the route of the canal along Chirk, Llanymynech and Weston.[22] In 1795 he launched the 'Passage Boat' on the Ellesmere Port in the New Canal and used the Chronicle to promote it, both with advertisements and a glowing report on the launch. The boat, readers were told, could take over 100 passengers, providing 'A cheap, pleasant, swift and easy intercourse with Liverpool...the boat made two trips the same day'.[23] Beyond the waterways, Fletcher was involved in the construction of the road from Wrexham, through Llangollen to Ruthin, the planning and creation of Chester Roodee racecourse and the building of the Grand Stand there.[24]

On 7 January 1835 John Fletcher died in his eightieth year, leaving just under £20,000 in personal estate and effects (including the *Chester Chronicle*) to his nephew, Thomas.[25] His obituary considered the breadth of his achievements:

He was an architect of his own fortune, and rose by the force of his genius and talent alone to considerable eminence among scientific men...The history of his life is curious and instructive and furnishes a practical lesson of the value of temperance, prudence, persevering industry, unsullied probity, and uncompromising integrity in all the relations of social life...His servants have lost a liberal and considerate master, his fellow citizens an upright and intelligent magistrate, the cause of public and private charity a munificent benefactor, and the community among whom he lived a kind-hearted and benevolent man.[26]

---

[22] Hughes, *Chronicle of Chester*, pp. 88-95.

[23] *Chester Chronicle*, 5 June 1795.

[24] Hand, *Stranger in Chester*, p. 226.

[25] Cheshire and Chester Archives, WS 1835 (Will of John Fletcher).

[26] *Chester Chronicle*, 9 January 1835.

III

The account book, covering 1783-6, the earliest years of Fletcher's ownership, provides detailed and previously unknown evidence about the day-to-day running of a provincial newspaper business. It also underlines that, even in a period of growing prosperity for provincial newspapers, the business demanded considerable skill in order to negotiate successfully the eighteenth-century culture of credit and produce a profit.[27]

Fletcher's new business consisted of the *Chester Chronicle* newspaper and an allied printing business. With his purchase, he inherited responsibility for the rent of the building in Hop-pole Yard, off Foregate street; the men in his office (one manager, one journeyman and three apprentices); the newsmen who delivered the paper (whom, to ensure their initial cooperation, he 'encourage[d]...by a Treat in Ale') and around 750 readers, scattered across Cheshire, Lancashire and North Wales.[28] The newspaper, still published on a Friday, contained the usual blend of international and national news, mostly taken from the London papers that arrived by express coach from Birmingham. The printing business mainly dealt with jobbing printing, consisting chiefly of cards, handbills, bonds, summonses and the like. The business was therefore not one of the largest provincial printing houses and the paper's circulation was modest. Nevertheless, it had the potential to make a profit.

The account book of John Fletcher's *Chester Chronicle* and allied printing business were located by the present author in the Chester archives. Mention is made of them stored in the *Chester Chronicle* office (the paper is still in publication) in 1975, in Hughes's history of the paper, *Chronicle of Chester*, although that

---

[27] M. Finn, *The Character of Credit: Personal Debt in English Culture, 1740-1914* (Cambridge, 2003); C. Muldrew *The Economy of Obligation: The Culture of Credit and Social Relations in Early Modern England* (New York, 1998).

[28] CRO/D3876, 15 August 1783.

author did not examine them beyond the first page.[29] The folio
book runs from Fletcher's first day of ownership, 15 August
1783, to 17 February 1786. Within it, one week's accounts is
provided per opening, the left-hand page detailing the week's expenditure and the right-hand page detailing income transactions.
On each page there are three columns, the first detailing each
transaction (London papers, advertising and so on), the second
listing money paid and the third listing money owed. Thus, on
the left-hand page, the first column itemizes each expenditure
made at the office that week, such as for wages, distribution and
the London papers; the second column shows the total amount
owed by the business for each item; the third shows how much
was actually paid out per item. At the end of the page, each
week's total monies owed and still owing are calculated. Usually
there was significantly less paid out than was owed. Wages were
immediately settled, as well as, initially at least, money for the
London papers and paper for print jobs. The right-hand page
itemizes all income from advertisements and print jobs, with the
second column showing the amount owed to the business per
item and the third showing what was actually immediately settled. At the end of that page, the week's total monies paid and
payable by debtors to the business are also calculated. There was
again considerable disparity between the two, with many advertisers in particular not settling their debts immediately.

It is more than likely that the account books were only one
part of a set of Fletcher's financial records. If Fletcher followed
John Clay of Daventry's 'typical' accounting practices, 'once a
month or so all credit purchases listed in the daybooks but not
yet paid [would have been] posted to each individual customer's
account in a ledger', whilst another probably listed Fletcher's
own outstanding debts to his creditors.[30] Delayed payment was

---

[29] Hughes, *Chronicle of Chester*, p. 34.

[30] J. Fergus and R. Portner, 'Provincial Bookselling in Eighteenth-Century

indeed expected in a credit-based society, with most businesses settling debts within a quarterly or half-yearly timeframe. While the incomplete nature of Fletcher's accounts thus frustrates absolute conclusions as to the *Chronicle*'s income and expenditure over the period, they also underline how the mechanism of floating capital demanded significant skill in order to balance satisfying a business's own creditors with the expectation of payment from debtors.

Figure 1 shows the profitability of the newspaper and printing business, supposing that all monies owed by the business were paid and all the monies owed to the business were paid. Over the first five months, the business should have made a profit of £46. Net profits for 1783, therefore, have been estimated at £121. In 1785 the business should have made a profit of £181: a 50 per cent increase in profits in just one year. Estimated total profit for 1786, the final year in the accounts, stands at £246, calculated from the account book's extant weeks, which saw a remarkable £33 profit in the first seven weeks of the year. Figure 2, however, underlines the complex nature of credit in the eighteenth century, and exposes potentially significant cash-flow problems. The black again represents the potential profits that could have been made by the business if all monies were paid. The grey represents the actual monies paid out by Fletcher and the actual income he received, as recorded in the account book, that is, the floating, or rolling capital of the business. However, this does not account for the monies that Fletcher himself owed on credit and would have had to have paid to sustain the business's reputation long-term. The white, therefore, shows just how much the business could be losing if Fletcher paid all of his bills but received no additional income, aside from those monies already paid to him in the weekly accounts.

England: the Case of John Clay Reconsidered', *Studies in Bibliography* 40 (1987), pp. 147-63.

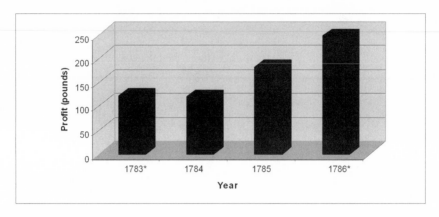

Fig. 1 Potential Annual Net Profit, John Fletcher's Chester Printing and Newspaper Business, 1783-6.[*]

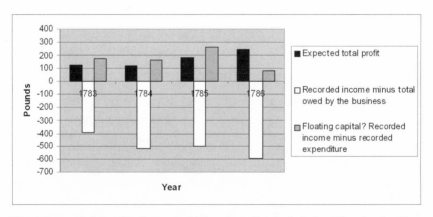

Fig. 2 Potential Profit, Loss and Floating Capital, John Fletcher's Chester Printing and Newspaper Business, 1783-6.

---

[*] Due to the incomplete nature of the accounts for the years 1783 and 1786, annual profits for these years are estimated by dividing the total profit of the extant weeks by the number of extant weeks and multiplying by 52.

The biggest problem for the business, therefore, was that of bad debt. This would certainly account for Poole's decision to sell the business, which he declared to be a 'losing concern on several accounts'.[31] Fletcher did try to deal with the issue of delayed payment in his very first issue as proprietor. In it, he requested payment for 'Advertisements at the time of insertion; and...payment for papers sent into the country...quarterly in Chester'.[32]

Payment for the overwhelming majority of newspapers and advertisements, however, was not fulfilled immediately, a problem that was all too common for eighteenth-century newspaper proprietors.[33] Nevertheless, the only subscribers list (placed at the back of the accounts), that for Chester subscribers, indicates that under Fletcher's ownership, most customers were timely with their payments, paying 1s. 6d as requested, at quarterly intervals, although a few continued to pay their accounts half-yearly.[34] That Fletcher was probably successful in recovering the debts owed him is indicated in his declaration in March 1785, less than two years after he first purchased the *Chronicle*, that he was now the sole owner of the paper, for he would have surely been unwilling to continue the business if it was making heavy losses.[35] Moreover, Fletcher went on to own the paper for another half a century. In view of the probable – and usual – mechanism of floating capital employed in eighteenth-century businesses, coupled with Fletcher's long-term prosperity, the re-

---

[31] *Chester Chronicle*, 8 August 1783.

[32] *Chester Chronicle*, 15 August 1783.

[33] See, for example, announcement in the *Norwich Mercury*, 23 June 1780, '*Ready Money for Advertisements*, being affixed at the front of their papers, the Printers of the *Norwich Mercury* and *Norfolk Chronicle* hope nothing further was necessary to remind the public; *That all advertisements should be paid for when sent*: but unluckily the very reverse happens to be the case...'

[34] CRO/D3876 'Subscribers in and around Chester'.

[35] *Chester Chronicle*, 18 March 1785.

mainder of this chapter presumes that Fletcher did pay all his debts and recovered those owed to the business. In doing so, this chapter can thus focus more fully on the variation between the different types of expenditure and income that were typical of a provincial newspaper office.

IV

Costs at the *Chronicle* can be divided into two categories, those that were relatively fixed (rent, labour and the London newspapers) and those that varied, depending on sales (paper for printing jobs, stamped paper and advertising duty). The variable costs will be examined later, alongside the income that they each produced.

As Figure 3 shows, 'fixed' costs came to just over one quarter of Fletcher's annual expenditure. Rent for the printing office in the Hop-pole Inn Yard, came to between five and six shillings per week. Staff costs came to around £2 10s. per week. Mr Ogden, the office manager, was paid one guinea per week and the journeyman printer, Mr Spence, twelve shillings. Fletcher's three apprentices received incremental wages depending on the stage of their apprenticeship, starting at one shilling and working up to 7s. 6d. In addition to the men in the office, Fletcher employed seven newsmen who delivered the *Chester Chronicle* on horseback across the North-West and two boys who delivered the paper locally around Chester. Around a quarter of subscribers received their newspapers through the post. This was more than any single newsman delivered, the practice saving Fletcher money, for there is no evidence that he paid the postage, probably exploiting parliamentary privilege instead (also explaining his gift of Christmas boxes to the Post Office and postman every December).[36] Indeed, Fletcher appears to have been a benevolent (and shrewd) employer. He also gave Christmas boxes to his

---

[36] CRO/D3876, 9 January 1784.

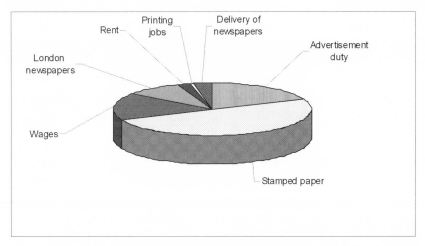

Fig. 3 Average Weekly Distribution of Expenditure, John Fletcher's
Chester Printing and Newspaper Business, 1783-6.

manager, journeyman, apprentices and the delivery boys. He
provided ale for the men in the office on a regular basis (probably on a Thursday, in order to lubricate the long printing
process) and he occasionally rewarded the printing office staff
with a cash bonus. On 7 May 1784, for example, all the men's
wages were increased for that week, by between one and three
shillings. The bonuses arrived shortly after the second most profitable period in the accounts, the result of a significant increase in
advertising and print output, thanks to the elections of 1784
(Fletcher printing for John Crewe) and were, no doubt, in gratitude for the extra hours that his staff must have worked.[37]

In terms of newspaper personnel, Fletcher's most significant
and long-lasting decision was not overtly financial, but rather, in
the choice of his new editor, William Cowdroy. Although
Fletcher was forced to employ an editor so that the paper was
left in a competent pair of hands during his imprisonment, the
move proved crucial to the future direction of Fletcher's newspaper and wider career. In the immediate aftermath of Fletcher's

---

[37] For example CRO/D3876, 5 April 1784; 12 April 1784.

libel, it was critical that he employed an experienced professional who would avoid repeating the same mistake. The long-term effects were even more significant, for Fletcher introduced an experienced hand who could run the paper, leaving him to pursue alternative business interests and, later still, to become increasingly involved in the town's political and civic processes. The experience of Cowdroy's editorship was so successful that Fletcher went on to employ four more editors in his lifetime.[38]

After personnel, the London newspapers, which provided the majority of the *Chronicle*'s news, represented the second largest outlay. The average combined cost of the London papers and their delivery over the period 1783-6 was one pound per week. In 1783 Fletcher initially paid four shillings for his London papers, rising to seven shillings in the October, and dropping again to around four shillings in 1786, seemingly experimenting with the number of London newspapers that might provide adequate content for the *Chester Chronicle*. The express coach delivering the papers initially cost 16s. 6d per week, although here too, the account books reveal how Fletcher trialled different ways of reducing costs. Initially, he appears to have operated within a network of newspaper proprietors who shared the cost of the carriage of the London papers, the papers first being sent to Miles Swinney at the *Birmingham Chronicle*, from thence to Fletcher's *Chester Chronicle* and then to John Gore of the *Liverpool General Advertiser*.[39] These supply chains were attempted elsewhere in the country and were typical of the experimental nature of the later eighteenth-century newspaper trade. In 1780, William Blanchard, owner of the *York Chronicle*, for example, proposed a similar scheme to Thomas Slack of the *Newcastle Chronicle*.[40] Unfortunately for the

[38] Hughes, *Chronicle of Chester*, pp. 95–6.

[39] See for example CRO/D3876, 31 October 1783; 7 November 1783.

[40] William Blanchard to Thomas Slack, 23 November 1780, British Library Add. MS 50240 (Hodgson Papers).

Chester Chronicle, the practice was problematic. With the express from Birmingham frequently delayed, Fletcher often had to hire a rider of his own, resulting in extra cost and probably a frantic few hours at the newspaper office whilst the type was set in order to meet the publication deadline. Repeated mention of the problem is made in the account books and by January 1784 Fletcher began to anticipate the delay, gloomily noting that 'Apprehensive of a Disappointment (as usual) with the Express, sent a Boy and Horse...to wait its Arrival'.[41] The additional horse and rider usually cost upwards of one pound per week. The total cost of the London papers and their delivery therefore equalled the workforce's combined weekly wage bill. Unsurprisingly, on 10 July 1785 Fletcher noted that the troublesome express had been discontinued.[42]

V

Figure 4 shows the different areas of income produced by John Fletcher's newspaper and printing business, alongside the achievable overall profits. Broadly speaking, newspaper sales rose gradually over the period, whereas advertising and printing sales both dropped in late 1784 and then commenced an upward trend from early 1785. Newspapers would have brought in the highest regular and reliable income over the period. 775 newspapers were printed for Fletcher's first publication of 15 August 1783, and the following week, sales rose to 786 newspapers, the number of papers adjusted weekly depending on the previous week's sales. Precision was important, for newspapers were printed on pre-stamped, and therefore pre-paid, paper but Fletcher swiftly found a novel way of reducing waste. He sold off any remaining papers a few days after publication, for the cost of the stamped paper, 1½d. instead of the usual 2½d. This was important, for as

---

[41] CRO/D3876, 16 January 1784.
[42] CRO/D3876, 10 July 1785.

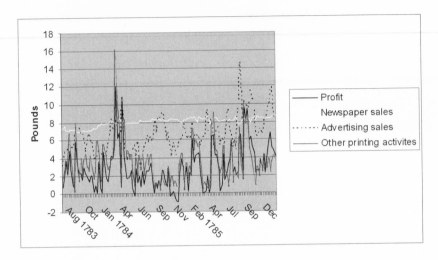

Fig. 4 Sources of Profit, John Fletcher's Chester Newspaper and Printing Business, 1783-6.

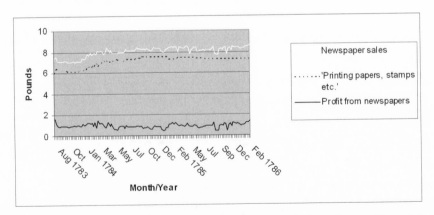

Fig. 5 Income, Expenditure and Profit on Sales of the *Chester Chronicle*, 1783-6.

Figure 5 shows, although newspapers brought in the highest income of any areas of Fletcher's business, the cost of the stamped
paper meant that the sale of newspapers produced the lowest return, their total sale each week making a profit of around one
pound, before Fletcher had paid out the printing office wages,
the newsmen's wages, postal delivery fees, and the cost of the
London papers. Moreover, with the cost of the stamped paper so
high, even with the concessions on bulk orders allowed by the
government (and amounting to 0.1d. per newspaper), selling
more newspapers made little, if any, difference. Proprietors
therefore frequently identified advertising income as the source
of profits for a newspaper. As Joseph Harrop put it, 'from advertisements, the sole profit of a Newspaper arises', a sentiment that
was echoed by London and provincial proprietors alike.[43] It was
in this respect that circulation mattered the most, for advertisers
were attracted to the papers with the widest geographical circulation, combined with reader numbers.

Placing an advertisement in the *Chester Chronicle* cost between
four shillings and five shillings, depending on length, although
column-long advertisements cost 7s. 6d. Advertisement duty had
been raised in 1780 and stood at 2s. 6d. per advertisement. Fletcher
therefore made at least 1s. 6d. per advertisement (the equivalent
profit made on the sale of twenty-six newspapers) and, as Figure 6
shows, this amounted to a weekly profit of between two and four
pounds. In terms of profitability, advertisements were therefore
critical in the success of a newspaper.

Such was the importance of advertising that provincial papers
were commonly sent to other provincial offices in order to maxi-

---

[43] *Harrop's Manchester Mercury*, 27 June 1797. See also the *Reading Mercury*,
'The Profits of a Newspaper arise *only* from Advertisements', *Reading Mercury*, 10 July 1797. On the financial importance of advertising, see I. Asquith,
'Advertising and the Press in the Late Eighteenth and Early Nineteenth Centuries: James Perry and the *Morning Chronicle* 1790-1821', *Historical Journal*,
18 (1975), pp. 703-24.

mise potential custom. Agents' names that appear in the accounts include John Gore of Liverpool, Charles Wheeler and Joseph Harrop of Manchester and Thomas Wood at Shrewsbury, all newspaper proprietors.[44] Even Fletcher's Chester rival, John Monk forwarded advertisements to the *Chronicle* office, as Fletcher did to the *Courant*. The level of dependence on advertising meant that not only did newspaper proprietors have to ensure a wide circulation and maintain good relations with their provincial and London trade contacts, but they had to ensure that their reputation and that of the newspaper was acceptable to advertisers. While most newspapers were not entirely politically partisan, most confessed to no political allegiance at all for fear of losing custom. This was not the case at the pro-reform *Chronicle*, although supporters of John Crewe's cause mostly came from the trade and manufacturing groups in the town, who made up the majority of the *Chronicle*'s advertisers. Unsurprisingly, however, Fletcher was not favoured with Corporation advertisements until 1807, when he switched allegiance to the Grosvenors. This type of economic favouritism founded on political allegiance was common in the period, providing towns with an (albeit limited) commercial lever to influence the press.

This chapter, based on the account book of John Fletcher at the *Chester Chronicle*, has offered new, detailed information about the weekly business and finances of a 'typical' provincial newspaper. In particular, it has underlined how the business knowledge and strategic abilities of a proprietor were critical to the success of his or her newspaper, which in Fletcher's case, were inextricably entwined with his political aspirations. Fletcher's surveying and engineering work probably gave him crucial business experience, as well as access to the town's social and cultural sphere, which in turn enabled him to successfully

---

[44] For example CRO/D3876, 15 October 1784; 22 October 1784; 16 September 1785.

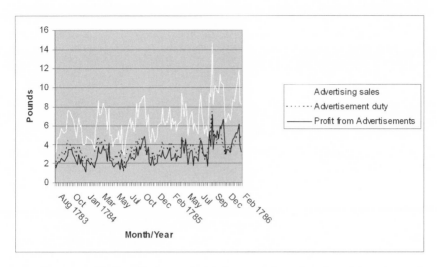

Fig. 6 Income, Expenditure and Profit on Sales of Advertising Space in the *Chester Chronicle*, 1783-6.

negotiate the period's culture of credit to produce a prosperous newspaper, gain a public voice and penetrate Chester's urban political sphere.

As Figure 6 shows, however, there was a noticeable drop in the levels of advertising in the *Chronicle* following Fletcher's libel in November 1784. In the issue of 5 November, the week after the libel, advertising sales dropped by nearly two pounds, to £5 17s., the lowest in seven months, with the low run of advertising sales ensuing until the end of the year. Advertising, therefore, traditionally considered central to press freedom from political control, worked as an effective commercial check on politics. Crucially, however, only two months after Fletcher's libel, advertising levels in the *Chester Chronicle* began to improve and continued to do so over the remainder of the accounts. Sales particularly peaked after Cowdroy's defection to the *Chronicle* towards the end of 1785. The move by an experienced and well-connected editor no doubt assisted in the creation of new trade contacts with London booksellers and brought in fresh interest from local advertisers who usually dealt with Cowdroy.

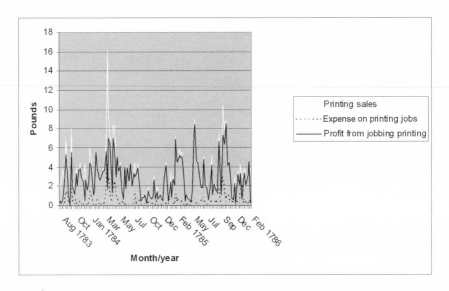

Fig. 7 Income, Expenditure and Profit on Printing Jobs Undertaken at John Fletcher's Chester Printing and Newspaper Business, 1783-6.

In terms of printing jobs, Figure 7 shows that the income derived from printing was the most variable element over the period covered by these accounts. Jobbing printing was crucial to the vitality of the business. With the initial outlay required for jobs extremely low in comparison with newspapers or advertising duties, the profits gained usually exceeded that of the newspaper and, more often than not, equalled the net profit gained in advertising sales.

Along with the advertising in the paper, the amount of jobbing printing also declined around Fletcher's 1784 libel, indicating that it was not simply the newspaper that local businesses sought to distance themselves from, but Fletcher himself. On the other hand, political partisanship gave Fletcher access to lucrative printing. Fletcher was the chief printer for John Crewe in the 1784 elections, printing a total of 26,690 notices, letters, handbills, cards, addresses, and songs, amounting to £16 0s. 6d. Presumably, from the time of Fletcher's political change in 1807, he would have been granted the Grosvenors' printing: an even more profitable venture, for their election campaigns were noted for their opulence. For the majority of the period of the accounts, however, Fletcher continued to produce small print jobs rather than attempt his hand at more prestigious publications, such as pamphlets and books (Chester authors would have sent their works to the *Chester Courant* office to be printed). Such an enterprise would have proved impossible, for not only did Fletcher have no experience in the field, but until William Cowdroy joined the office, his employees were similarly inexperienced.

The arrival of William Cowdroy at Fletcher's office changed the direction of the printing business. Whilst most of the period 1783-6 saw the continuation of jobbing printing, in December 1785 a commission was undertaken by Cowdroy to publish Thomas Baldwin's *Airopaidia...Containing the Narrative of a Balloon Excursion from Chester*, an octavo volume that consisted of 361 pages and included maps, tables, and drawings of the first ever aerial views to be published in England.[45] In 1785 Baldwin had made a solo flight from Chester Castle in a balloon lent to him by the famous aeronaut Vincent Lunardi. The resulting book was published during Fletcher's incarceration but it is plausible that he may have had a hand in gaining the commission from a fellow engineer. The book however would never have been published at Fletcher's office without the expertise of Cowdroy. Only the first ten weeks of the book's painstaking production are revealed in the last ten weeks of the accounts. Cowdroy worked on at most one sheet per week, for the maps and drawings would have required fine print work and minute adjustments. On 10 February 1786, for example, Cowdroy charged Baldwin £1 8s. for '1 sheet Airopaidia & 12 Hours Cor-

---

[45] T. Baldwin, *Airopaidia: Containing the Narrative of a Balloon Excursion from Chester, the Eighth of September 1785...To Which is Subjoined, Mensuration of Heights by the Barometer, Made Plain* (Chester, 1786).

rections'.[46] The volume was published later in 1786 and represented a new direction for the printing office. From the late 1780s, it became the foremost printing house in Chester and one of its next major undertakings was William Cowdroy's own *Directory and Guide for the City and County of Chester* in 1789.[47] Indeed, under Cowdroy, the office entered a period of prolific book production. Once he left the *Chronicle* in 1795, this level of printing output declined, although each of Fletcher's later editors was probably chosen for his literary skills. In particular, the role of newspaper proprietors as printers of local history and antiquities was taken over by the editors at the *Chester Chronicle*. In 1819, James Hanshall completed *A Stranger to Chester* and in 1823, the *History of the County Palatine of Chester*. Joseph Hemingway likewise wrote the *History of Chester*, published in two volumes in 1831.[48] The introduction of designated editors, often from literary backgrounds, was a benchmark in the evolution of the trade from that of a manual occupation based on scissors and paste journalism, to a self-defined literary profession.

---

[46] CRO/D3876, 10 February 1786.

[47] W. Cowdroy, *The Directory and Guide for the City and County of Chester* (Chester, 1789).

[48] Hughes, *Chronicle of Chester*, p. 95.

Sarah Hodgson and the Business of Print, 1800-1822

RIA SNOWDON

S TUDIES OF WOMEN in the business of print have come a long way since one of the earliest researchers on this topic, Frances Hamill, felt compelled to apologise for 'so many feminine trumpetings' in her 1950s article on female printers and booksellers of the eighteenth century.[1] But the volume of work on women's involvement as independent economic agents is still regrettably small when we consider that the print trade was 'one of the most notable commercial successes' of the Georgian period.[2] Research has tended to focus too narrowly on women of a lower social status, as Margaret Hunt states: the 'Hawkers, Bawlers and Mercuries'.[3] Middling businesswomen are overlooked despite the fact that five per cent of all businesses in urban areas may have been female-owned and -run.[4] The work of Hannah Barker, and Paula McDowell is starting to overcome this neglect

---

[1] F. Hamill, 'Some Unconventional Women Before 1800: Printers, Booksellers and Collectors', *Papers of the Bibliographical Society of America* (1955), 49, p. 314.

[2] H. Barker, 'Women, Work and the Industrial Revolution: Female Involvement in the English Printing Trades, c. 1700-1840', in *Gender in the Eighteenth-Century England: Roles, Representations and Responsibilities*, ed. by H. Barker and E. Chalus (London and New York, 1997), p. 85.

[3] M. Hunt, 'Hawkers, Bawlers and Mercuries: Women and the London Press in the Early Enlightenment' in *Women and the Enlightenment*, ed. by M. Hunt (New York, 1984), pp. 41-68.

[4] C. Wiskin, 'Urban Businesswomen in Eighteenth-Century England', in *Women and Urban Life in Eighteenth-Century England: 'On the Town'*, ed. by R. Sweet and P. Lane (Hampshire, 2003), p. 91; H. Barker, *The Business of Women: Female Urban Development in Northern England, 1760-1830* (Oxford, 2006), p. 9.

by opening up the study of the provincial press and women in business in the eighteenth century. They demonstrate that women's work was not limited to 'feminine' professions as the growing print trade not only employed but was directed by a substantial minority of women from the middling classes.[5]

What this revised agenda lacks is detailed and individual case studies of middling women in the provincial print trade. This essay seeks to redress this imbalance by presenting a new overview of the little-known life and career of Sarah Hodgson; an influential printer and bookseller who broke new ground in typography, owned commanding shares in some of the northeast's most infamous work and was proprietor of one of England's most important provincial weekly newspapers, the *Newcastle Chronicle*. New questions on women's networks, professional relationships and influence are posited through this detailed exposition of an individual in light of recent macro histories on women in business and the print trade.

As we live in an age obsessed by borrowing, plastic credit and electronic money, studies on credit and reputation in the early modern period and beyond become all the more pertinent.[6] Of particular interest are those that explore the nexus between credit, social relationships and trade networks. Craig Muldrew and Margot Finn, among others, argue that customers and traders were often friends and neighbours embroiled in networks of mutual reciprocity and economic and social dependency.[7] While

---

[5] Barker, 'Women, Work and the Industrial Revolution'; P. McDowell, 'Women and the Business of Print', in *Women and Literature in Britain, 1700-1800*, ed. by V. Jones (Cambridge, 2000); P. McDowell, *Women of Grub Street* (Oxford, 1998).

[6] R. McGowen, 'Review: Credit and Culture in Early Modern England', *Journal of British Studies*, 41:1 (January, 2002), p. 131.

[7] M. Finn, *The Character of Credit: Personal Debt in English Culture, 1740–1914* (Cambridge, 2003) and C. Muldrew, *The Economy of Obligation: The Culture of Credit and Social Relations in Early Modern England* (New

they disagree over the end date of this interplay (with Finn look-ing to the Edwardian period and Muldrew to 1800), they agree that reputation was increasingly significant in a consumer culture based on credit. Muldrew's revisionist claims, however, set him apart from the current historiography as he portrays a society in which credit was a virtuous, levelling force. He argues it spread a spirit of mutuality and equality across class lines and may have been more important than the Poor Laws as a major form of charity as many of the poor died owing considerable amounts of money that were often forgotten.[8] Whatever the veracity of these bold assertions, where the social and economic entwined so intricately checks and balances needed to be in place to maintain order in people's personal and professional lives. Shani D'Cruze explores the role of 'community brokers', 'active middling indi-viduals who had a heightened public role and were in contact with multiple groups of people', to facilitate and mediate in these complex networks. Or, as D'Cruze drily states, 'In eighteenth-century terminology, these were one's friends'.[9] A picture emerges whereby 'one's friends' take on a social and economic significance and maintaining one's reputation is paramount.

This essay will in part be an endorsement of this view and will explore Sarah Hodgson's print networks and the lengths to which she went to maintain her reputation in her social, spiritual and business circles that were often inextricably interwoven. The term 'friend', unless otherwise stated, will encompass D'Cruze's

---

York, 1998). For reviews of these works, see B. Griffin, 'Review: "The Character of Credit"', *Institute of Historical Research* (February, 2004) < http://www.history.ac.uk/reviews/paper/griffin.html > and McGowan, 'Review: Credit and Culture'.

[8]   McGowan, 'Review: Credit and Culture', p. 129.

[9]   S. D'Cruze, 'The Middling Sort in Eighteenth-Century Colchester: Inde-pendence, Social elations and the Community Broker', in *The Middling Sort of People: Culture, Society and Politics in England, 1550-1800*, ed. by J. Barry and C. Brooks (Hampshire, 1994), p. 182.

'community brokers', useful socio-economic links and contacts, as well as 'friends' in a more modern sense. The key role these 'friends' played in mediating disputes and ensuring the production of key texts in Hodgson's shop will also be examined. What underpins this discussion is the recognition that the business of print and in particular the newspaper business could not fit neatly within this schema of friendly interdependence: friends could be expedient but they also had their limitations. Newspaper proprietors had to negotiate a fine line between their 'friends' aiding them with production by acting as intermediaries or links in their complex social and economic networks and informing or restricting what they produced.

Glowing commendations of Hodgson abound from her contemporaries: eulogies written by her competitors attest to a woman with 'talents of a superior order'; diaries of local dignitaries recall her 'strong and vigorous understanding' of printing and her 'great ability and success' in conducting the *Newcastle Chronicle* for many years.[10] Posthumous representations of Hodgson, however, are sparse in the secondary literature, and occur in the occasional footnote rather than the main narrative. Where cited, impressionistic views of her predominate, offering brief anecdotes of Solomon Hodgson's 'formidable widow'.[11]

Evidence of Sarah's bad press can be found in a famous contemporary, Thomas Bewick. Bewick, the acclaimed Newcastle wood-engraver, wrote an autobiographical memoir in the 1820s: over a decade earlier, he had argued bitterly with Sarah over a discrepancy in his bill for printing. He recounted in his *Memoir* that following this falling-out, which amounted to scores of letters, expensive litigation and public accusations in the *Annual*

---

[10] *Durham Chronicle*, 14 September 1822 and 'The Diaries and Correspondence of James Losh: vol. 1, Diary 1811-1823', ed. by E. Hughes, The Surtees Society (1956), pp. 170-1.

[11] P. Issac, *William Lubbock and Other Newcastle Bookbinders* (Wylam, 1997).

Review and *Monthly Magazine*, he 'could not go on pleasantly with Mrs Hodgson'.[12] Bewick's opinion of Sarah diminished further when she refused to sell him her share in his *General History of Quadrupeds* and instead sold it from under him to Longman's in London.[13] Unfortunately for her memory, Bewick's *Memoirs* were printed in 1862 and became a minor classic, the latest edition published as recently as 1998: when noticed at all, she is recorded as Bewick's difficult businesswoman.

This is unfortunate when we consider that Bewick was renowned for falling out with everyone with whom he had dealings, including printers, partners and apprentices. In business his imperious manner, inability to admit when he was wrong and general willingness to give 'his suspicions the benefit of the doubt' are well documented.[14] But many biographers have delved into every area of his life so that these negative qualities become one aspect of a multi-faceted personality. By contrast, all we have of Hodgson is superficial and lacks depth because until now there has been no comprehensive analysis of the primary material available.

Hodgson's poor and scant historical reputation is exacerbated further when we consider those of her father, Thomas Slack and husband, Solomon Hodgson. In 1764 Thomas Slack established his weekly newspaper the *Newcastle Chronicle* and his printing and bookselling businesses at his shop, 'The Printing Press',

---

[12] S. Roscoe, *Thomas Bewick: A Bibliography Raisonné of Editions of the 'General History of Quadrupeds', 'The History of British Birds' and 'The Fables of Aesop' Issued in his Lifetime* (London, 1953), pp. 1-2; *A Memoir of Thomas Bewick Written by Himself,* ed. by I. A. Bain (Oxford, 1979), p. 125.

[13] Bain, *A Memoir of Thomas Bewick,* p. 125. This is also exhibited in Bewick's correspondence to Hodgson: see letter from Bewick to Sarah Hodgson, 7 April 1802, British Library, Add. MS 50242, f. 25.

[14] A. V. Gill, 'The Beilby and Bewick Workshop', in *Bewick and After: Wood-Engraving in the Northeast,* ed. by P. Isaac (Newcastle-upon-Tyne, 1990), pp. 1-2, 4.

which quickly rose to be one of the most eminent printing houses in the north. He was proprietor until his death in 1784 when Sarah inherited the business but she quickly married Solomon, her late father's apprentice, who officially assumed control in 1785. Both Thomas and Solomon are remembered in a generous assessment, prompted by the historian Richard Welford at the turn of the twentieth century, as the founders of this illustrious institution that stayed in the family for almost a century and continued to influence public opinion until it ceased publication in 1953.[15]

A simple calculation, however, shows that Thomas, Sarah's father, ran the business for twenty years; whilst Solomon, Sarah's husband, died in 1800 after a fifteen-year tenure. Hodgson, on the other hand, continued to run the business as a widow successfully for twenty-two years, longer than either her father or husband. This is a fact barely registered in the literature.

Within the national context Hodgson's situation was not unusual as most female businesses during this period were predicated on inheritance. Widows' economic power, in particular, was set to increase over the Georgian period as remarriage rates amongst widows dropped. There is, however, a need to dispel an implicit binary that exists so far in the historiography that women who inherited businesses maintained either a healthy trade built up by their male predecessors or failed because they lacked the necessary skills to succeed. The fortunes of failing businesses could actually be improved under these female benefactors.

Sarah exemplifies this suggestion: the story of the Hodgson 'Printing Press' is not that of a business that went from strength

---

[15] R. Welford, 'James and Thomas Hodgson, and Solomon Hodgson their Father: The Hodgsons of "The Chronicle"', in his *Men of Mark 'twixt Tyne and Tweed* (London: Walter Scott, 1895), pp. 543-54; R. Welford, 'Early Newcastle Typography, 1693-1800', *Archaeologica Aehana*, 3:3 (1907), pp. 1-134.

to strength but more of a roller-coaster ride, experiencing a dip during Solomon's proprietorship when he was forced to sell off the bookselling and stationery business and borrow large sums of money from Sarah's sisters.[16] A handwritten note on the back of the loan agreement shows that Sarah was still making repayments on this loan as late as 1807.

It was Sarah Hodgson who in 1800, recently widowed, aged forty and with a large young family, turned the print business's fortunes around. With the *Newcastle Chronicle* as her foundation, she built the firm back up and became Newcastle's most important printer, bookseller and newspaper proprietor over the next two decades, surpassing even her father's success. This was not an incremental process but an immediate intervention: seven days after the death of her husband, Sarah placed this advert in the *Newcastle Chronicle* to reassure her readership:

SARAH HODGSON
WIDOW AND EXECUTRIX OF THE LATE SOLOMON HODGSON,
RETURNS Thanks to the numerous Friends of her late Husband, and the Public in general; and respectfully informs them, that she intends to carry on the PRINTING BUSINESS in all its Branches, and to publish THE NEWCASTLE CHRONICLE as usual.[17]

Within two months of Solomon's death Hodgson had also made substantial moves to reclaim the bookshop her husband had sold and to rebuild the business: in June 1800, she gave John Bell formal notice to quit the bookshop which Solomon had leased to him six years earlier:

---

[16] Bond of Solomon Hodgson for the sum of one thousand two hundred pounds payable to Elizabeth and Hannah Slack on the condition of the repayment of six hundred pounds interest, 15 March 1786, Tyne and Wear Archives, 13/35.

[17] *Newcastle Chronicle*, 11 April 1800.

Sir, Previous to my Receiving of your Letter it was my intention to take the Shop into my own hands at the end of the Lease. I can observe nothing in what you say to induce me to alter my determination, as every Person has a right to do the best he can for himself – therefore you will take this notice to quit the Shop at the end of the Lease.[18]

This confidence attests to the fact that Sarah was not a novice when she assumed full control of the business in 1800. When we consider that she was a daughter, then wife, of consecutive proprietors this is not surprising but, like most married women or daughters in this period, any informal apprenticeship served, partnership or work role performed has often been hidden from the record.[19] Hodgson's mother, Ann Slack (née Fisher), was unusual in this respect in that her partnership with her husband in business matters was well documented:

Mr Slack is at London, & has been for some time, on which account I have been too much hurried with business to be so punctual in my correspondence as I cou'd have wished.[20]

Her correspondence with her friend, the poet John Cunningham, shows that Ann was also technically proficient in printing: 'I have two binding in the most elegant taste...ye longer time they have to dry before bound the better'; therefore, Ann was able to take a practical or supervisory role in the business.[21] As a

---

[18] Letter from Sarah to John Bell, 28 June 1800, in Thomas Bell, *Memorabilia Relating to the Booksellers and Printers etc of Newcastle*, Robinson Special Collections, Newcastle University, Bell MSS, fol. RB 942.82 BEL.

[19] For a discussion of women's activities being overshadowed in the historical record by those of men, see Maureen Bell, 'Women in the English Book Trade 1557-1700', *Leipziger Jahrbuch zur Buchgeschichte*, 6 (1996), p. 16.

[20] Letter from Ann Slack to John Cunningham, 17 September 1771, quoted in J. Hodgson, the younger, 'John Cunningham, Pastoral Poet, 1729-1773: Recollections and Some Original Letters', *Archaeologia Aeliana*, 18 (1921), p. 94.

[21] Letter from Ann Slack to John Cunningham, 5 November 1771, quoted in Hodgson, 'John Cunningham', p. 96.

distinguished author of school textbooks, first female grammarian and a capable businesswoman in her own right, the death of
Ann was commemorated with typically strong rhetoric in correspondence to her husband:

I heartily sympathise with you, dear Sir, in the loss you have sustained
of an amiable and affectionate Partner and with your kind Daughters,
who are unhappily deprived of an indulgent Parent...In her, the literary Republic has lost one of its brightest female armaments...Her
distinguished Character will be revered and held sacred by all the Sons
and Daughters of Science; and she shall be respectfully mentioned to
all succeeding Generations.[22]

Hodgson proactively sought to establish a reputation built on
her own work, recognising that the reputations of her mother,
father and husband, while initially helpful, would not provide
for longevity in an industry based on personal credit and reputation. Her success in establishing this independence is exhibited in
her fall-out with the Newcastle wood-engraver, Thomas Bewick.
Their relationship began to falter when Bewick claimed in 1801
that he had been charged for two hundred and forty-six books he
had not received when the *History of Birds* was published in 1797,
claiming 'the affair had a villainous, black appearance'.[23] Initially,
Sarah strove to prove that this was done during Solomon's in-
cumbency, ostensibly defending her husband's reputation but
ultimately safeguarding her own by placing the blame with the
deceased:

---

[22] Letter from Mr. J. Teasdale to Thomas Slack, 5 May 1778, Tyne and Wear
Archives, 13/11/4. For more information on Ann Slack, see M. Rodriguez-
Gil, 'Ann Fisher: First Female Grammarian', *Historical Sociolinguistics and
Sociohistorical Linguistics*, 2 (2002) < http://www.let.leidenuniv.nl/hsl_shl/
rodriguez-gil.htm >.

[23] Letter from Sarah Hodgson to Bewick, 24 January 1802, British Library,
Add. 50242, ff. 14-15. This extract is taken from a passage where Hodgson
quotes a recent conversation with Bewick.

if an Action be bad, the villainy and treachery of that action must at-
tach solely and absolutely to the Person who committed that Action:
therefore your attempting to shift this action (which happened five
years ago) on to my shoulders...is too shallow a subterfuge to require a
reply. Had you found fault with any Action of my own, or said, I had
cheated you out of part of the Number of the Book I had printed for
you, I could have born it...but when you affixed the term of villainy to
an action of Solomon Hodgson, then you roused me...If a mistake did
appear on the face of the Account, was it <u>respectful</u>, nay was it even
<u>delicate</u> to fix it to the only Person, who could not answer for him-
self.[24]

Once Sarah was able to prove the allegation was bogus, however, she copied all correspondence between her and Bewick,
interspersing the letters at regular intervals with her thoughts,
sub-titled 'Notes', eager to maintain her innocence for the record
in anticipation that the case might go to court. While petty
squabbles continued, a derogatory off-hand remark from Bewick
inadvertently shows that she was ultimately successful in establishing herself in her own right and drawing a line between
herself and her husband: 'do not mistake yourself it is not him I
have a bad opinion of it is you'.[25]

Hodgson existed on the cusp of the Victorian era, pervasively
portrayed as a period that witnessed the withdrawal of middling
women from public life as prevailing gender norms became inextricably entwined with a rising middle-class identity. In light of
recent debates on this separation of gender spheres, was Sarah
fully integrated into the business community or did her gender
mean that she had to operate on its periphery?[26]

---

[24] Sarah's emphasis in the letter from Sarah Hodgson to Bewick, 25 January
1802, British Library, Add. 50242, f. 15.

[25] Letter from Bewick to Sarah Hodgson, 22 January 1802, British Library,
Add. 50242, f. 12.

[26] L. Davidoff and C. Hall, *Family Fortunes: Men and Women of the English
Middle Class 1780-1850* (London, 2002); R. Shoemaker, *Gender in English Soci-*

Keen purveyors of the didactic literature would suggest that Hodgson's initial success operating in the masculine print trade was because she was seen as a 'temporary caretaker' of business rather than a permanent fixture. Daniel Defoe's business guide *The Complete English Tradesman* advised women to learn their husband's trade during his lifetime in case of his early demise.[27] Widows' authority was, however, normally seen as transitory until a male heir was eligible. During the late eighteenth and early nineteenth century in England, there were additional pressures on widowed businesswomen to be expeditious in their withdrawal from the public world of work.[28] It has been argued by historians such as Leonore Davidoff and Catherine Hall that between 1780 and 1850 the emerging middle-class identity in England rested on the ideology of domesticity and separate gender spheres.[29] Whilst most scholars now acknowledge that this separation could never be absolute there is still an erroneous and persistent claim, warn historians such as Amanda Vickery, 'that negotiating this ideology was a central middle class concern'.[30]

The Newcastle Booksellers Association existed from 1801 to 1822 and represents one of the few examples of Hodgson encountering resistance within her trade.[31] The Association began

ety, 1650-1850: The Emergence of Separate Spheres? (London, 1998); A. Vickery, 'Golden Age to Separate Spheres? A Review of the Categories and Chronology of English Women's History', *The Historical Journal*, 36:2 (1993), pp. 383-414.

[27] D. Defoe, *The Complete English Tradesman* (Gloucester, 1987; first edn. 1726).

[28] B. J. Todd, 'The Remarrying Widow: A Stereotype Reconsidered', in *Women and Literature in Britain, 1700-1800*, ed. by V. Jones (Cambridge, 2000), pp. 54-83.

[29] Davidoff and Hall, *Family Fortunes*.

[30] Vickery, 'Golden Age to Separate Spheres?', p. 400.

[31] Minute Book of the Booksellers' Association of Newcastle, Northumberland County Archives, SANT/GUI/NCL/2/1.

as an influential cartel and met monthly to regulate the prices of the most commonly sold books to prevent discounting and price-cutting. The minute books show that while the eight male members represented themselves, either a male employee or one of her sons represented Sarah at the meetings. If this was requisite then it shows that she was sidelined in some business matters. However, examining the Association a little more deeply an alternative explanation seems more likely. Attendance at the meetings was so erratic that the Association was forced to introduce fines for non-attenders; their coffers grew to such an extent that they funded their annual dinners and drinks at the local public house, which is where meetings often re-convened if only two members were in attendance. The Association's members, including Hodgson, obviously did not consider this body to be a significant enough concern to attend regularly. It may, therefore, be considered that Sarah was not excluded as a woman but sent a representative, while other members failed to attend and accrued hefty penalties.

Hodgson evidently felt no real pressure to hand over the control of her business: when a wealthy businessman ten years her junior sent her a proposal of marriage, Sarah spurned her suitor in this candid reply: 'I assure you that it is my determination never to change my life...this principle is fixed in my Mind'.[32] When two of her sons, whom she had apprenticed, came of age in 1806 and 1814 Sarah gave them additional responsibility but made it clear that they were 'to be an assistant to me'.[33] There is no archival evidence to suggest that she understood her power to be provisional. The evidence in fact suggests that she was fully integrated into the business community. A conservative estimate

---

[32] Letter from Sarah Hodgson to unknown (suitor), 27 March 1815, British Library, Add. 50240 ff. 120-1.

[33] Letter from Sarah Hodgson to James Hodgson, 3 June 1812, Tyne and Wear Archives, 13/13/10.

suggests that the *Newcastle Chronicle* sold to a readership of over three thousand, so Hodgson's businesses were sound and expanding middling enterprises.[34] Ascertaining her exact worth at the time of her death is difficult because Sarah's will is not a quantifiable statement of what she owned but rather a plan of how she would like her 'Estate and Effects' proportionally divided.[35] Sarah's household inventory, however, does show her extensive acquisition of material goods amounting to £163: the businesses therefore generated enough disposable income for her to be a part of the 'consumer revolution', a must for the aspiring middle class.[36] Most importantly, her shops were at the heart of Newcastle's commercial districts; relocation was only ever warranted due to expansion or demolition of the premises, not exclusionary tactics by male competitors or patrons.[37]

The status of widowhood legitimized a woman's pursuance of a career where she had inherited the means to do so. Her trade was thriving and her network of friends was extensive. She understood the importance of reputation and a network of friends in the print community and beyond on a local and national level to ensure her integration and success. Interestingly, Sarah's spirituality played a key role.

Hodgson attended the Unitarian Chapel at Hanover Square, Newcastle, a congregation composed of some of the town's leading middle-class professionals – solicitors, merchants, publishers and doctors – the increasingly influential bourgeoisie.[38] This congregation exhibits the complex networks within which Sarah

[34] M. Milne, 'The *Tyne Mercury* and Parliamentary Reform, 1802-1846', *Northern History*, 14 (1978), p. 229.

[35] Sarah Hodgson's Will, 27 December 1812, British Library, Add. Ch. 75498.

[36] Valuations of Sarah Hodgson's Furniture, 10 September 1822, Tyne and Wear Archives, 13/40/1.

[37] Wiskin, 'Urban Businesswomen', p. 92.

[38] A. Moffat and G. Rosie, *Tyneside: A History of Newcastle and Gateshead from Earliest Times* (Edinburgh and London, 2006), pp. 215-6.

operated and the implicit links between her social, economic and religious circles. Records for the Church of the Divine Unity hold detailed, if incomplete, members' books.[39] Attendees included rival bookseller William Charnley.[40] He acted as an intermediary in Sarah's trade disputes to ensure the production of profitable texts in her shop and even published in joint ventures with her. Their mutual religious convictions overrode competitive impulses between their businesses and helped to bridge an alliance. Many more Unitarian connections overlap with her business concerns, including Sarah's barrister James Losh, who represented her interests when her business relationship with the Society for the Propagation of Christian Knowledge collapsed, and William Preston, who helped edit and publish the *Newcastle Chronicle* until 1808.[41]

The Reverend William Turner who headed the Unitarian congregation also played his part in Sarah's success. As founder of the Newcastle Literary and Philosophical Society he was not only an influential figure on Tyneside but also Sarah's close friend. When Sarah died in 1822, in language typical of funeral sermons, he lamented her loss:

It is not my general custom, as you well know, to enlarge upon characters of deceased Friends...But there are occasions, on which this general rule may properly be dispensed with; and few in which it may be done with greater propriety than that which makes us this day a congregation of mourners.[42]

During Sarah's lifetime Turner directed much of his printing to

---

[39] Records of the (Unitarian) Church of the Divine Unity, Tyne and Wear Archives, C. NC. 66.

[40] *Ibid.*, C. NC. 66/12.

[41] *Ibid.*, C. NC. 66/12.

[42] Sarah Hodgson's Funeral Sermon given by William Turner, 15 September 1822, Tyne and Wear Archives, 13/55/3.

her shop. The jobbing materials she printed, including handbills, pamphlets and posters show that Turner was responsible for over a third of the surviving ephemera that she printed, thirty-seven out of a total of ninety-seven items. Jobbing printing was the mainstay of most printers and therefore the importance of Turner's business to Sarah should not be underestimated.[43]

So Charnley, Losh, Preston and Turner, among others from Sarah's Unitarian congregation, aided production of news, books and other ephemera in Sarah's shop, 'The Printing Press'. Importantly, she cultivated these trade contacts through her own association with the Unitarians; she had converted in the 1790s whilst her husband continued as a Baptist. Even by non-conformists' standards, as non-Trinitarians, the Unitarians were a fringe religious community; this bold decision shows that these links in Hodgson's network were maintained on the strength of her own reputation and were not inherited from her father or husband's time in the print trade.

Aside from those who aided Sarah's print business were those who informed or restricted what she was able or felt able to produce. The marriage notices in her weekly newspaper, the *Newcastle Chronicle*, were indicative of this. At a time when much of the news was selected from the national papers, the marriage notices were a uniquely local and provincial feature and allow an insight into reputations Sarah felt she could and could not call into question. These notices were, for the most part, modest and brief in content, as we can see by this example: 'The 12th instant, at Alston, Mr Ralph Wandles, to Miss Mary Walton'.[44] Occasionally when a couple were particularly mis-matched a deprecating remark would be included: 'Tuesday

---

[43] For a discussion of the importance of jobbing printing, see R. A. J. Potts, 'Early Cornish Printers: 1740-1850', *Journal of the Royal Institution of Cornwall*, 4:3 (1963), pp. 278-281.

[44] *Newcastle Chronicle*, 23 May 1812.

se'nnight at Stilton, Mr Odam aged 77, to Miss Gaunt, aged 22. The Bridegroom had grand children older than the wife'.[45] Even when Sarah had help with the editing and publishing of the paper, whoever penned the articles or features would have been aware that she would read the newspaper: according to one scholar 'Indeed, she was *the* reader above all others'.[46] It is therefore safe to say that she supported the contents: where Sarah was not directly responsible she was certainly aware of these commentaries.

Interestingly, when it came to the marriages of the sons and daughters of her peers in the Unitarian congregation Sarah was courteous in her coverage as she was towards the Watts' daughter: 'The 24th February, at the Cape of Good Hope, by the Rev. Mr M. A. Parker, Officiating Minister, Alexander McDonald, Esq. merchant, to Jane, eldest daughter of William Watt, Esq.'[47]

In a letter to her son James, who was apprenticed to a London bookseller, Hodgson revealed that she only included news of the latter in the paper because Mr Watt, Jane's father, had placed the announcement himself in the *Morning Chronicle*; therefore, she would not incite his displeasure. In the privacy of this personal correspondence she was free to air her unbridled disapproval of these 'imprudent connections amongst the young Folks of our acquaintance' and referred to the Jane Watt and Bell Falla marriages as 'equally ridiculous', 'I don't know which of the Marriages has the worste prospect'.[48] Bell Falla received the butt of Sarah's condemnation after eloping to Scotland with a Captain

---

[45] *Newcastle Chronicle*, 14 July 1804.

[46] P. Lucas, 'The Regional Roots of Feminism: A Victorian Woman Newspaper Owner', *Transactions of the Cumberland & Westmorland Antiquarian & Archaeological Society*, 3:2 (2002), p. 282.

[47] *Newcastle Chronicle*, 23 May 1812.

[48] Letter from Sarah Hodgson to James Hodgson, 16 November 1811, December 1811 and 18 April 1812, Tyne and Wear Archives, 13/13/5-7.

Clark, seventeen years her senior, and in her words, 'so weather beaten by having been so long at Sea that he looks much older'.[49]

Hodgson had four sons and her letters to James are full of anecdotes from the congregation to serve as warnings to him against unsatisfactory matches; she writes, 'be on your guard and never enter into an engagement hastily...your Brothers have had amorous advances made to them and I do not think you are less likely – so mind yourself'.[50] These letters provide insight to an unguarded Sarah. Alternatively, the marriage notices show her fear of upsetting the delicate balance of her print network composed of some dissenting affiliates and friends whose goodwill was important to her business. This was at a time when Hodgson wanted to expand the *Newcastle Chronicle* and '[procure] for it the greatest variety of important local information as possible'. Thus, the impact of Sarah's 'friends' on the *Chronicle*'s proliferating local news and information sections is something to consider in future work.[51]

This is not to imply that Sarah was sycophantic when it came to these networks of 'friends', especially when her reputation was at stake. One of Sarah's greatest achievements was the production of the Arabic Bible, one of the earliest works printed in Arabic type in England outside of London and the two university towns. Dr Geoffrey Roper, a specialist in Middle-Eastern printing and publishing, called it 'a major feat of Arabic typography, on a scale scarcely attempted before in this country, and all the more remarkable for being the product of a provincial printer with very little experience in such work'.[52] But the furore

---

[49] Letter from Sarah to James Hodgson, December 1811, Tyne and Wear Archives, 13/13/6.

[50] Letter from Sarah to James Hodgson, 16 November 1811, Tyne and Wear Archives, 13/13/5.

[51] Letter from Sarah to the Duke of Northumberland, 23 October 1802, British Library, Add. 50240, f. 61.

[52] G. Roper, 'Arabic Printing and Publishing in England Before 1820', *British*

that surrounded it almost prevented its publication. When the Reverend J. C. Carlyle, vicar of Newcastle, died in 1805 he left the unfinished project, which, as former Professor of Arabic at Cambridge, he had initiated on behalf of the Society for the Propagation of Christian Knowledge and had enlisted Hodgson to print. Whilst the contract had been drawn up, Carlyle died before ever signing it.[53] Without Carlyle to assist in the publication the Bishop of Durham, representing SPCK, transferred the work to an experienced Oxford printer so that a professor of Arabic from the local university could correct the press.[54] By 1811, however, eight years after its inception, it was Sarah who completed publication of this pivotal text.

Sarah took on the establishment of clergymen and scholars, appealed to William Wilberforce, a member of SPCK, went to the Chancery Court to plead her case, and brought this landmark publication back to her provincial print shop from the grasp of the Oxford printing oligarchy.[55] Sarah's fierce determination was not only fuelled by financial gain but the potential damage this episode could do to her reputation whereby an Oxford printer was seen as more capable than she.[56]

Hodgson did not do this without support. Losh, her barrister from the Unitarian chapel, worked tirelessly on her behalf; a list she gave to him of some London friends should he need accom-

---

Society for Middle Eastern Studies Bulletin, 12 (1985), p. 23.

[53] Letter from Sarah Hodgson to James Losh, 16 August 1804, British Library, Add. 50243, ff. 26-7.

[54] Sarah Hodgson's 'Notes' on the Arabic Bible dispute, [n.d.], British Library, Add. 50243, ff. 24-5.

[55] Sarah Hodgson 'Notes' entitled 'Conclusion' on the Arabic Bible dispute, [n.d.], British Library, Add. 50243, f. 170. Agreement in Chancery between the Bishop of Durham and Sarah Hodgson, 12 December 1807, British Library, Add. 50243, f. 178.

[56] Sarah Hodgson's 'Notes' on the Arabic Bible dispute, [n.d.], British Library, Add. 50243, ff. 24-5.

panying to meetings when at the capital on her behalf gives a unique insight into the scale of her national network: 'if you require a second person, either Mr Goulding No. 76, St James's Street; Mr Mawman, or Mr Hamilton will assist you'.[57] Her careful local and national networking was essential as deployment of these contacts or friends ensured her success.

As a woman in the business of print, Hodgson relied heavily on her trade in news through her weekly paper, the *Newcastle Chronicle*, but her dependence on friends throughout all spheres of her active life meant that there were certain subjects and certain perspectives from which she dare not publish for fear of a ripple effect in her vast intertwined network. But Sarah was also a pragmatic businesswoman, shown in her dogged handling of the Arabic Bible dispute, where she was willing to risk her network's delicate balance for personal gain. She problematizes the historian's notion of a separate spheres ideology among the middle class in the late eighteenth and nineteenth centuries. She reached a readership of over three thousand and therefore had the potential to be more inspiring as a female print business magnate operating in a 'masculine' trade than a conduct manual ever could be.[58]

---

[57] Letter from Sarah Hodgson to James Losh, 22 January 1805, British Library, Add. 50243, f. 91.

[58] Milne, 'The *Tyne Mercury*', p. 135.

Latter Struggles in the Life of a Provincial Bookseller and Printer: George Miller of Dunbar, Scotland

GRAHAM HOGG

EORGE MILLER WAS a provincial bookseller and printer living in Dunbar, a small town in the south-east of Scotland. Over 170 years ago he wrote a detailed autobiography of the latter half of his life,[1] the raw material for which survives in two manuscript volumes held by the National Library of Scotland (NLS) and by East Lothian Council (ELC). The volumes also contain copies of correspondence and numerous examples of printed ephemera from his own press. One of the volumes was also used for a history of the Miller family published over ninety years ago.[2] There appears to be no other Scottish provincial bookseller of the hand-press era whose life, with all its many trials and tribulations, is so well documented. Moreover, the printed ephemera from Miller's jobbing press, which are pasted into the volumes, are particularly interesting, as

---

[1] G. Miller, *Latter Struggles in the Journey of Life; or, The Afternoon of my Days* (Edinburgh, 1833).

[2] W. J. Couper, *The Millers of Haddington, Dunbar and Dunfermline* (London, 1914). William James Couper (1866-1938), United Free Church minister and bibliographer, is best known for his work on the early Edinburgh periodical press. The book was sponsored and published by Thomas Fisher Unwin, a descendant of George Miller's family. Unwin also submitted a brief bibliography of the output of Miller's presses along with biographical information to *Notes and Queries* s.10-XII (288) 1909, pp. 1-3 & (290), p. 42. Unwin cites as an authority a manuscript 'Notes on the Miller family' by F. M. Gladstone, but I have been unable to trace this manuscript. Couper does not mention it in the preface to his book.

Fig. 1 (Permission of East Lothian Council Museums Service).

this is the kind of material that has often not survived in library and archive collections.

At 3 am on 4 January 1831, George Miller celebrated his sixtieth birthday by sitting down to compile an autobiography or 'retrospections' based on what he called his 'retrospects' – the yearly accounts of his life that he had written every January – and on all the papers and documents he had methodically kept throughout his life.[3] He seems to have kept working on his autobiography at intervals throughout 1831, before business matters and personal problems apparently forced him to stop writing at the end of the year. The manuscript volume of retrospects held in the NLS covers the years 1803 to 1818.[4] Some letters to Miller from family and acquaintances are inserted in the volume, as well as the aforementioned printed ephemera, prospectuses and subscription agreements. The volume formerly belonged to Miller's biographer, W. J. Couper, who refers in the preface to his book on the Millers to the fact that two manuscript volumes of autobiography covering Miller's life to 1819, and extending to over 1700 pages, came unexpectedly into his hands during the course of his research.[5] The NLS volume is just over 700 pages long (i.e. 359 leaves). It is missing the first eighty pages and possibly a few pages at the end, which leads me to conclude that what the Library now has is the second of the two volumes Couper refers to and that there was an earlier volume for the years before 1803, which has disappeared since Couper's death; hopefully one day it will turn up somewhere.

A second surviving manuscript volume, which was apparently unknown to Couper, was recently acquired by ELC and is now held at their Library and Museums HQ.[6] It begins roughly

---

[3] Miller, *Latter Struggles*, pp. 66-67.
[4] National Library of Scotland MS. 5409.
[5] Couper, *The Millers of Haddington*, p. 10.
[6] MS. EL.102/1. Thanks are due to staff of East Lothian Council: Sheila

where the NLS volume finishes, starting with spring 1819 and ending with December 1831. The first leaf has a title: 'The Evening of Life or Retrospections of a Sexagenarian' and appears to incorporate volumes three and four of Miller's retrospections. Like the NLS manuscript, this volume also has numerous items of printed ephemera pasted into it.

Unfortunately Miller's handwriting is very difficult to decipher. This article is therefore not based on a methodical examination of the two surviving volumes; rather, printed sources, pasted-in correspondence and printed ephemera in the volumes have been used to piece together Miller's life. The manuscript autobiography is of course not purely concerned with Miller's bookselling and printing activities. Miller had several interests and was a 'village worthy' in the truest sense of the word. He was behind a campaign to acquire a lifeboat for his home town of Dunbar,[7] was a key mover in a local society for abolishing the slave trade, appears to have been the initiator of various charitable projects that never got off the ground, and he was involved with the Dunbar Mechanics Institute when it was started in the 1820s. He also had a large and sometimes problematic family to deal with and write about. As Couper notes in his biography, Miller's manuscript volumes are 'filled with much irrelevant matter' as well as valuable information.[8]

The key printed source in uncovering George Miller's life is his published autobiography, *Latter Struggles in the Journey of Life*. The *c*.400 words of the title page are a portent for the con-

Millar, Senior Librarian, Local History & Promotions, for alerting me to the existence of this manuscript; Siân Collins, Records Manager, for arranging access to it; and David Anderson of East Lothian Museums who produced an invaluable listing of this manuscript and passed on additional information about George Miller.

[7]   D. Anderson, 'The Dunbar Lifeboat', *Transactions of the East Lothian Antiquarian and Field Naturalists' Society*, 25 (2002), pp. 89-113.

[8]   Couper, *The Millers of Haddington*, p. 10.

tent of the book. It is long-winded, rambling, self-pitying and infuriatingly indirect, glossing over some of the more difficult and troubling incidents of this time. The book covers only the years 1815 to 1832, with occasional references to events in his early career. Miller chose to skip his early, relatively successful years as a bookseller and general merchant, and to concentrate instead on his later financial hardships caused by a succession of business disasters. The book is largely written as a defence of his conduct and business dealings over this period. It also covers in detail the various ailments he suffered, and highlights the conduct of the numerous people he believes have injured him commercially and personally throughout his career. Prudence, however, overrules any self-righteous anger and the names of most of the key players in his book are left as blanks, which makes it challenging to trace his friends and business acquaintances.

The pre-1819 manuscript volumes and *Latter Struggles in the Journey of Life* were later used by William Couper to write his book, *The Millers of Haddington, Dunbar and Dunfermline*. Apart from a brief mention in his preface, Couper does not give his sources, so it is not easy to verify some of the facts in his biography. It remains nevertheless a valuable guide to Miller's career, not least because Couper seems to have taken the trouble to wade through *Latter Struggles in the Journey of Life*, and to decipher some of Miller's manuscript retrospects. He also had the advantage of being able to talk to Dunbar people who had personally known the Miller family.

The town of Dunbar itself is roughly equidistant between Edinburgh and Berwick-upon-Tweed, about twenty-eight miles east of Edinburgh on the North Sea coast. As well as being a port, it was also on the main eastern coach route from England to Edinburgh. In his account of the parish of Dunbar in volume five of the first *Statistical Account of Scotland*, written when George Miller was just starting out in business, the Rev. George Bruce noted that the population was 3700.[9] Despite Dunbar's coastal location, the number of people being employed in fishing was relatively small, and the herring fishery in particular was deemed by Bruce to be 'precarious and uncertain'.[10] Agriculture, due to the fertile soil of the area, provided the most employment: a male day-labourer earned one shilling a day, and a woman working in the fields earned sixpence. Skilled labourers and craftsmen could earn more, as could servants in domestic service; but a considerable number of the local inhabitants lived below the poverty line, particularly the families of seamen lost at sea. The impression one forms is that Dunbar offered little in the way of advantages for anyone wanting to start a thriving bookselling and printing business. The locals seemingly lacked the means to purchase books, and travellers on their way to Edinburgh could easily wait until they reached their eventual destination, which had sufficient well-stocked bookshops to meet their needs. But this is where George Miller built up his business, which thrived for the first twenty or so years of its existence.

George Miller himself was born in 1771, the son of a general merchant in Dunbar. He was educated locally and developed a passion for books and for the sea at an early age. The safer life of books prevailed when it came to a career choice. An Edinburgh bookseller and bookbinder, Alexander Smart, had set up in business in Dunbar in 1780, and five years later, aged fourteen, Miller began a four-year apprenticeship with him. On the face of it this was hardly a great career move. Miller later described Smart's premises as small and wretched, his book and stationery stock as poor even for a country bookseller.[11] Business was barely suffi-

---

[9]   *The Statistical Account of Scotland. Drawn up from the Communications of the Ministers of the Different Parishes...Volume Fifth*, ed. by Sir J. Sinclair (Edinburgh, 1793), p. 477.

[10]   *The Statistical Account of Scotland*, p. 480.

[11]   Couper, *The Millers of Haddington*, pp. 37-8.

cient to make ends meet, but Miller, with his father's encouragement, probably had his eye on the long-term goal of taking over Smart's business, once he had served his apprenticeship and Smart had moved on. Events did not go quite as planned, as Smart decided to close his business at the end of 1787, less than two years into the apprenticeship, and to move back to Edinburgh. Miller decided to follow him to Edinburgh the following year, but after a few months it was mutually agreed to cancel his indenture. He then briefly ran his father's business together with his older brother James. When the two brothers had a falling out, George went south in 1789 to learn more of the rudiments of bookselling and bookbinding. He stayed with his old master Alexander Smart in South Shields, where the latter was working as a journeyman printer, and picked up the basics of setting type and operating a press; but his stay in England was cut short by the news that his father was dying. Returning to Dunbar, George was reconciled with his older brother and, when his father died a few weeks later, the two young men took over the family business. This time, thanks to George, they sold books, offered a bookbinding service and set up a circulating library.

Despite his less than ideal apprenticeship,[12] George Miller seems to have had the ideas, energy and entrepreneurial spirit necessary to succeed where his master, Alexander Smart, had failed. The circulating library grew quickly, as did the bookbinding business, but it soon became clear that the two brothers could not work harmoniously together. In 1791 they split the business, sold most of the contents of the circulating library, and went their separate ways. James settled down to a life of modest prosperity as a grocer, while George concentrated on bookselling and bookbinding, as well as selling stationery and groceries to

---

[12] Miller had completed less than two years of a planned apprenticeship of four years. In England apprenticeships for booksellers could last up to seven years.

make ends meet. He also began selling books at auctions in local villages, a practice he continued throughout his bookselling career, in later years employing regular auctioneers to carry out the work. He rented his first premises on Dunbar High Street in 1792, and set about re-establishing a circulating library which soon contained over 1000 volumes. Although Couper records that Miller found the library to be unprofitable and troublesome, he realised that it was essential for attracting potential customers to his shop and consolidating his new business.[13] The earliest appearance of him in an imprint as a bookseller is a fourth edition of a seaman's guide in 1792;[14] a logical choice of book to be associated with for a bookseller working in a port on the east coast of Scotland.

Business went sufficiently well for him to take his next big step, purchasing a small printing press from the Berwick-upon-Tweed printer John Taylor in 1795. He had been offered a larger printing press five years earlier, when still in partnership with his brother, but had not been able to afford it. Now he was in the position to do so and he thus became the first known printer in East Lothian.[15] After his purchase of the press he did jobbing printing on demand, before he started printing chapbooks in around 1798. To begin with Miller had to work both as compositor and pressman before his younger brother John and apprentices could take over. He was able not only to sell the

---

[13] Couper, *The Millers of Haddington*, pp. 59-60 & pp. 62-3. The circulating library benefited from the Napoleonic Wars, due to the large number of armed forces staying in the vicinity to guard Dunbar's harbour, who required a regular supply of reading material.

[14] J. H. Moore, *The Coaster's Companion : containing Sailing Directions for the East Coast of England, from London to the Shetland Isles*, 4th ed. (London, 1792). Miller's name appears in the imprint as 'Millar'.

[15] The English Short Title Catalogue (ESTC) records the possible earlier existence of a printer in Haddington in the 1720s, but there is no proof that any printing was done in the town before Miller moved his presses there.

products of his press to chapmen, but could also exchange them for chapbooks printed by other provincial printers, thus increasing the stock in his shop.

Miller was able to purchase a second press in 1801, and to attempt more ambitious works like an edition of *Robinson Crusoe*. Shortly afterwards he appears to have abandoned printing chapbooks in favour of moral tracts. Miller was a man of great piety and he fretted about the influence of chapbooks on the morals of the nation's youth, with their bawdy ballads and witty jests. Behind the profit motive in purchasing his printing presses, there appears to have been an underlying one, which is reminiscent of his fellow Scot Lord Reith's mantra at the BBC over 100 years later: educate, inform and entertain. Between 1802 and 1804, he produced in large numbers his 'Cheap Tracts', pamphlets on morality which were designed to supersede the trash of the hawker's basket. By this stage Miller was not only selling his books wholesale across most of southern Scotland, he even went on one occasion so far as to sell some of his stock at auction to booksellers in Edinburgh, what he called carrying his 'attack into the great literary citadel of the country'.[16]

Further changes were afoot in Miller's personal and business life during this period. His first wife died in 1802, leaving him with six children to take care of; but, despite this tragedy, he moved his presses in 1804 to the county town of Haddington, eleven miles west of Dunbar. Haddington was in some respects a more promising place to launch a bookselling and printing business. As the county town of what was then known as Haddingtonshire (now East Lothian), it was slightly larger than Dunbar in terms of population and was the site of the county courts, which offered a potential source of work for a jobbing printer. Miller's motives for moving are not entirely clear, but it is likely

---

[16] Couper, *The Millers of Haddington*, p. 91.

that he saw an opportunity which was in danger of being taken by a business competitor.[17] The difficulties of maintaining two establishments in two towns, in the days of poor transport links, became all too apparent; these were exacerbated by the decision of his younger brother John in 1805 to move to Dunfermline and set up his own business. Miller accordingly set up a new home with his second wife and family in Haddington, leaving his shop in Dunbar to the care of relatives. The following year, however, problems in Dunbar made him move back there, and he took with him one of his printing presses. He left his eldest son James, who was still in his mid teens, in charge of the Haddington press and its staff. Miller used his press in Dunbar for jobbing work, and concentrated on running his grocery shop which was now grandly named the India Tea Warehouse, whilst the Haddington press, known as the East Lothian Printing Office, also mostly did jobbing work and a few small-scale publications.[18] By 1810 Miller was earning £300 from his Haddington press alone through jobbing work.[19] In 1812 his oldest son James, having served his apprenticeship, became a fully-fledged business partner.

An indication of how settled Miller was feeling in the book trade was his decision to print and publish a monthly magazine of an improving nature, which would be distributed nationally. *The Cheap Magazine or Poor man's Fireside Companion* was in-

---

[17] He was not the first to sell books in Haddington. Archibald Neill, a member of the famous Neill printing family of Edinburgh, had a shop selling books and general merchandize there from the late 1760s to *c.*1800, and it may have been the closure of the Neill establishment which led to Miller moving to Haddington.

[18] A list of publications printed by the Millers appears in the bibliography of Couper's *The Millers of Haddington*, pp. 263-300. This is an expanded version of the list that Thomas Fisher Unwin supplied to *Notes and Queries* (see footnote 2).

[19] Couper, *The Millers of Haddington*, p. 110.

tended, according to the promotional literature for it, to 'promote the interests of religion, virtue and humanity, and to dispel the shades of ignorance, prejudice and error among the lower classes of mankind'.[20] Miller's preparations for the publication were meticulous and well thought out. A prospectus was printed in 1812, nearly six months before the actual publication, and sent out to church ministers in Scotland asking for their support and encouragement for his project. This is a prime example of targeted marketing long before the term was ever dreamt up. Miller also printed a separate prospectus for schoolmasters encouraging them to stock the new magazine at discounted rates. Notices were also sent out to agents to encourage them to sell as many copies as possible, offering them financial incentives if they did so. This procedure of sending out targeted prospectuses in advance to attract subscribers and printed instructions for would-be agents was continued by Miller for his future publications. For a bookseller in a large urban centre such practices may have been normal, but for a small provincial bookseller and printer it may have seemed excessively ambitious.

The Cheap Magazine was printed at Miller's Haddington press. It was launched on his birthday, 14 January 1813, which was appropriate as he was the editor and the main contributor. The magazine was indeed cheap in price, costing four pence for forty-eight pages of simple moralizing didactic prose, some of the articles rehashing his 'Cheap Tracts' of ten years previously. The magazine was targeted at what Miller called in his promotional literature the 'humbler classes of society', who would not have found august literary journals like the *Edinburgh Review* to their taste or within their price range. Whatever its literary merits, *The Cheap Magazine* was initially a great success, selling very well; but, perhaps aware that such enterprises could only have a small

---

[20] The prospectuses for *The Cheap Magazine* and related printed ephemera are preserved in the NLS MS.5409.

life-span, Miller stopped it at the end of 1814 and replaced it with a new title.

The Monthly Monitor and Philanthropic Museum continued in the same vein as *The Cheap Magazine* but with perhaps greater literary pretensions and a higher price of sixpence an issue to match. It had an even shorter lifespan than its predecessor, lasting only a year, an indication that Miller as chief contributor had exhausted his fund of moralizing articles and that the novelty of such a publication had worn off among the reading public. Being relatively close to Edinburgh, it was also difficult for Miller's small business to compete against the publishers based there. Moreover, in 1815 Miller was distracted by a new business venture which would be the cause of his 'latter struggles'.

George Miller's life was changed forever by his decision to launch a nationwide book canvassing scheme. This is the point where his book *Latter Struggles in the Journey of Life* really begins, albeit after ninety-seven pages of digressions and sermonizing. On 11 April 1815 a stranger, who turned out to be William Gracie, a well-known bookseller and printer from Berwick-upon-Tweed, turned up at his shop in Dunbar. Miller notes in his book that the visit was probably planned and was less of a coincidence than Gracie claimed it to be. Inevitably the two men talked shop; Gracie mentioned in passing the book canvassing scheme he was using to sell books and wondered whether Miller would be interested in taking part. The method of selling was hardly anything new; it involved selling books in weekly numbers door to door, using a network of travelling 'canvassers', i.e. door-to-door salesmen, under the direction of a county or district agent. It seemed to offer a regular source of income and a direct and better way of selling books than relying on people to visit shops or holding auctions; moreover, it also appealed to Miller's zealous proselytizing nature as a way of ensuring that the 'humbler classes' had access to improving works of literature. Miller, of course, already knew of such selling methods, but he says in his book he may never have actually considered undertaking something like this himself had Gracie not visited and talked so eloquently of the benefits of such a scheme. He became in his own words a 'whole, instead of a half convert' to a scheme which 'held out such bright and golden prospects'.[21] The extent of Miller's conversion can be gauged by the finances he committed to buying books from Gracie for his canvassing scheme. By July that year he had committed a hefty £1400 to buying books, the first being Alexander Cruden's *Bible Concordance*, a bestseller since its first edition appeared in 1737. Printed by Gracie, it was to be sold in thirty-four parts at the price of one shilling a part. Miller admits in his book that his readers may wonder at his temerity, but he writes that at the time his credit was good and that his weekly receipts showed that he was making the money that he had paid out for the canvassing scheme in two to three months through sales to the public; in emergencies he could also organize wholesale sales to the trade.[22]

By October of 1815 Miller already had agents working throughout Scotland, as far north as Thurso, the most northerly town on the Scottish mainland. He had, as ever, meticulously organized everything and printed directions, including a canvassing engagement which canvassers were expected to sign, and a flyer for Sunday school teachers, collectors for bible societies and respectable private characters.[23] In the meantime he was able to celebrate successful book sales in Edinburgh that netted him over £800, and a sale in Glasgow which brought in over £300; he also became an honorary member of the Glasgow Stationers Company. After more than twenty years of hard graft it seemed that Miller had transcended his status as a lowly country bookseller

---

[21] Miller, *Latter Struggles*, p. 118.

[22] Miller, *Latter Struggles*, p. 119.

[23] The relevant documents are preserved in NLS MS.5409.

and grocer and was on the verge of real prosperity. In fact the reverse was about to happen. The ending of the Napoleonic Wars
in 1815 triggered a prolonged economic depression throughout
Europe and it hit agriculture and the rural communities that depended on it – in other words Miller's prime customers – particularly badly. Miller could not have launched his book canvassing
scheme at a worse time.

By the start of 1816 disaster already seemed to be looming. He
was taking in less and less money in his shop, his own creditors
in the trade were refusing or were no longer able to pay off
debts, the canvassers were reporting poor returns and his finances were starting to look shaky. Miller regarded his forty-
fifth birthday in January 1816 as something of a watershed. 'Joy,
indeed, with me on this birth day, was out of the question', he
writes and he sees his real sorrows, in the afternoon of his life, as
beginning at that point.[24]

The appointment of a new agent in Inverness, and the hope
that the far north of Scotland had escaped the ravages of the depression, briefly raised Miller's spirits in the summer of 1816, but
by September he had to bow to the inevitable and call a meeting
of his creditors to reveal the poor state of his finances. The meeting took place on 7 September.[25] Most of the creditors were men
in the publishing trade, including notable firms such as William
Cadell & Co., Oliver & Boyd and Archibald Constable, as well
as the unwitting agent of his downfall William Gracie; he also
owed money to wholesalers for his India Tea Warehouse shop in
Dunbar. Miller began the meeting with a humble admission that
he was effectively bankrupt and had to place all of his stock and
belongings at the disposal of his creditors. After his speech he
writes, 'I found myself so overpowered by a sense of my cheer-

---

[24] Miller, *Latter Struggles*, p. 129.

[25] A printed record of the meeting, the substance of which also appears in
Miller's *Latter Struggles*, is preserved in NLS MS. 5409.

less and humiliating situation, that I had to retire for a few minutes into another room, to recompose myself'.[26] Fortunately for him, all bar one of them, whom Miller does not name in his book, were sympathetic and encouraging. Miller himself optimistically valued his assets at over £10,500, an astonishing figure, having already written off over £1000 of bad debts, and his liabilities at just over £9500; his creditors however realised that Miller was saddled with a large and, in the current economic climate, practically unsaleable amount of books.

Miller's offer to pay back sixteen shillings in the pound over the next two years in instalments was accepted. He now embarked on an attempt to claw back as much of his money as quickly as he could, starting a series of what were effectively fire-sales through auctions, and by calling in as many debts as he could. His efforts to restore his finances lasted more than two years, in fact the rest of Miller's active life turned out to be a valiant but losing battle to pay off his debts. After his meeting he transferred his main printing operation back to Dunbar to save money, but it was already clear to him by March 1817 that he could not stick to the bargain that he had made with his creditors. Miller had presumed he could still raise the same prices at auction as he made in 1815, before the economic depression had really begun to bite, and in doing so had, in his own words, committed 'a most egregious error' when making his debt repayment arrangements.[27] He soldiered on in the midst of further misfortunes, such as the loss at sea of some of his stock on the way to the Orkney Islands. In the meantime he was hard at work arranging for travelling auctioneers to hold sales of his stock throughout the country, at special sales or country fairs.[28]

---

[26] Miller, *Latter Struggles*, p. 162.

[27] Miller, *Latter Struggles*, p. 169.

[28] Although not directly related to the downturn in his fortunes, the fate of Miller's circulating library, begun in the early 1790s in Dunbar, was sympto-

As can be seen from the numerous handbills for Miller's book sales that survive pasted in to the two manuscript volumes, the main auction season for the rural areas started in the late autumn, around October, presumably after the last of the harvest was gathered in, and sales were held in any convenient indoor location, which was often the village school. Auctions were usually held about 6 pm and the season seems to have lasted until January or even into February. The flyers frequently state that the moonlight 'will be favourable for county purchasers'; in other words, the fullness of the moon played a key role in attracting potential purchasers to venture out of their homes on to unlit country roads on winter evenings. Such predictions of good moonlight must have been rendered meaningless by the heavy cloud cover that is all too frequent in Scotland in winter. Miller's son William did a lot of the work for his father, but Miller also employed a whole network of auctioneers throughout Scotland. There were plenty of bargains on offer, and the public was getting the chance to buy cut-price books: what Miller termed an 'eligible opportunity of laying in a cheap supply of mental food'.[29] The results, however, were almost always disappointing. The people who Miller called his 'literary friends among the working classes'[30] had more pressing financial priorities in these

---

matic of the tide of events going against him. He had transferred his library of over 2,500 volumes to Haddington in 1814, on the understandable grounds that his Dunbar library members had by now been through most of the books in it. Unfortunately for him the library was not a success in its new location. When Samuel Brown of Haddington introduced 'itinerating libraries' in 1817, which were sent in boxes from parish to parish and allowed readers cheaper access to books, he was forced to disperse his own collection.

[29] The phrase occurs in a printed bill for a sale in Tweedmouth, Berwick-upon-Tweed, in August 1822, which is preserved in ELC MS. EL.102/1.

[30] The phrase occurs in a printed bill for a sale in Dunbar 23 October 1820, which is preserved in MS. EL.102/1, 'G. Miller has reason to believe that purchases, numerous as they were, would have been still more so, had money

desperate times and there was no way Miller could recoup what he had originally paid for the books himself.

By February 1818 he was already proposing to his creditors that he pay only fourteen shillings in the pound, which tried the patience of some of them, but they had little option but to agree. However badly Miller had miscalculated the worth of his stock, no one could fault him for his efforts to dispose of it. He placed his hopes on developing his canvassing scheme in the north of Scotland, travelling to Inverness, only to find out he could not find any reliable agents to coordinate the sales. To make matters worse, he also discovered that other booksellers were trying to start operations in this previously virgin territory, including, horror of all horrors, his creditor and now apparently his nemesis, William Gracie. In 1819 came a further meeting with creditors where he estimated his assets and debts at just over £6000, and reckoned that he had in recent years lost £1700 pounds alone through his book sales. A new arrangement of eight shillings in the pound to be spread over a number of years was made. Miller allowed himself some optimism and employed better auctioneers to hold sales at more suitable times. Meanwhile, Miller's oldest son, James, had set up his own printing business in Haddington now called the East Lothian Press and was thus freed from his father's financial entanglements. Miller also took a pragmatic decision to cut his losses and close down his canvassing operation in the far north in 1820.[31]

Miller appears to have been happier with his lot in this period, despite the appearance of a rival bookseller and bookbinder in

---

been plentier among his literary friends among the working classes'. He is thus holding one more sale to 'give them time to recruit their finances'.

[31] Stopping operations there proved to be less straightforward than he expected. It took Miller a couple of years to disentangle himself from his various commitments.

Dunbar.[32] Indeed, life for a few years in the 1820s seems to have proceeded relatively smoothly for him. He continued to run his shop in Dunbar and his book sales, gradually scaling back his operations to Edinburgh and south-east Scotland. He even found time to publish in instalments two books of his own, *The Affecting History of Tom Bragwell*,[33] a morality tale of juvenile delinquency and its consequences, and *Popular Philosophy*,[34] a creationist view of nature and the earth. Both publications were accompanied as usual with detailed printed instructions to the trade on how to proceed with obtaining subscriptions and maximize sales.[35]

He was still casting about for new ways to make ends meet. A few years previously he had lost in a shipwreck a consignment of books worth £200 which were destined for an auctioneer in Aberdeen. Despite this setback, Miller decided in 1822 to send ten boxes of books to America. The books were to be sold in New York by his former agent in the north of Scotland, Thomas Cochrane, who was emigrating there.[36] Unfortunately, Miller would receive only one trivial sum of money the following year from his American venture.[37] The ELC manuscript volume also preserves a printed sale catalogue of 1822 directed at 'friends at a

---

[32] John Clinkscales set up a bookbinding business in Dunbar in *c.*1820; a printed flyer of 1823 preserved in MS. EL.102/1 records that he was now expanding his business.

[33] G. Miller, *The Affecting History of Tom Bragwell* (Dunbar & Haddington, 1821), which had previously been serialized in *The Cheap Magazine*.

[34] G. Miller, *Popular Philosophy; or, The Book of Nature laid open upon Christian Principles* (Dunbar, 1826).

[35] The relevant documents are preserved in MS. EL.102/1.

[36] A printed bill survives in MS. EL.102/1 which announces Cochrane's arrival to the citizens of New York and lists some of the titles he 'is enabled to dispose of upon very reasonable terms', including Miller's *Cheap Magazine*, *Monthly Monitor*, and *Tom Bragwell*.

[37] Miller, *Latter Struggles*, pp. 276-7, p. 279, pp. 284-5.

distance' and managers of subscription and parish libraries, giving them the opportunity of buying the remainder of his stock for prices offered at fifty per cent or less of the retail price. He was still pursuing his targeted marketing, albeit in an increasingly desperate fashion.

Another example of his desperation or initiative, depending on how one looks at it, can be seen in a printed proposal of 1825 concerning the establishment of a 'select library' to enable 'literary friends' to read the Waverley novels and the works of other celebrated novelists, starting with the eagerly awaited *Tales of the Crusaders*.[38] It is not known whether this scheme came to anything, but it probably did not. Debts still needed to be paid off and income was still not sufficient. A printed circular of 6 December 1827 survives; it was sent out to his creditors calling for a meeting in Haddington.[39] This appears to have been the first formal meeting since 1819. Miller writes in his retrospect for that year that he was 'compelled to give up the contest' in view of the heavy losses incurred in selling off his large book stock. Debts were still running at over £3000 and his assets were now only worth about £1000. A further settlement, this time initiated by the creditors, was agreed, but by now age and a series of deaths in the family, including that of his son Robert, were weakening the health and spirits of Miller. There were further sales of what was left of his book stock in 1828, and in May of that year he had to sell some of his furniture. He appears to have given up

---

[38] A printed bill for the scheme is preserved in MS. EL.102/1. Miller proposed to order copies of the book hot from the press and loan them out to people: first-class readers wishing early perusal of the books within the first three months would be charged four pence for each volume for two nights' access to the books (arrangements could be made if other members of the family also wanted to read the books); second class readers would have the chance to look at the book between three-six months for three pence for two nights; after six months other readers would pay two pence for two nights.

[39] The printed circular is preserved in MS. EL.102/1.

book sales and jobbing printing in that year, his name ceasing to appear in imprints of books printed by his son James. He probably entrusted the sale of what was left of his stock to his sons: to James in Haddington, and to William, who had taken over his father's role in Dunbar and opened his own shop, working as a bookseller and jobbing printer.

Miller continued to run his India Tea Warehouse, selling groceries and spirits, as well as acting as agent for the local coach to Edinburgh; but in December 1831, where his manuscript volume ends, he was contemplating giving up his business.[40] A further meeting of creditors was called in 1832, where he placed all his belongings in their hands. That same year he started to sell off his own private library which he had built up since the 1790s. It is not clear when he closed his shop but he appears to have stopped acting as a coach agent in 1832. *Latter Struggles in the Journey of Life* appeared in the following year as his attempt to set the record straight about his financial problems. A printed circular of March 1834, signed by Miller and addressed to the 'select part of the trade', survives in Glasgow University Library.[41] It reveals that he has disposed of nearly 800 copies of *Latter Struggles* – an astonishing figure for such an unreadable work – and was now offering the booksellers who subscribed to it the opportunity to dispose of lots of the remainder of his stock of his own publications at a reduced price. Just over a year before his death on July 26 1835, he was still trying to sell off his stock.

In conclusion, one can clearly see that George Miller's latter struggles were his attempts to correct a disastrous business mistake, which was still dogging him twenty years later. His misguided optimism sometimes seems bewildering, particularly

---

[40] This was not a sudden decision. In MS. El.102/1 there is a letter of Miller's, from November 1830, in which he implies that he is giving up his business.

[41] Glasgow University Library Eph. N/70.

as it was almost inevitably followed by yet another setback which cast him into the depths of despair. On the other hand his persistence in the face of adversity and depression was admirable. It was in not in his nature to flee his troubles. Instead he faced them and tried to overcome them; that he failed in the end was not for lack of effort or will. He made his fair share of enemies, and comes across often as sanctimonious and irritating; but his motives in promoting literature amongst the working classes, however patronizing they may seem to twenty-first-century opinion, were genuine and heartfelt. Miller's surviving manuscripts and autobiography are, if somewhat difficult to penetrate, a valuable source of information for the provincial book trade in Scotland in the early nineteenth century and thus worthy of closer scrutiny.

Manchester Men and Manchester Magazines: Publishing Periodicals in the Provinces in the Nineteenth Century

MICHAEL POWELL & TERRY WYKE

'THE TIME WILL COME when the word London on the title page shall not be essential to successful publication – it has not yet arrived.' The words are not those of John Feather in 'Some Reflections on the Book Trade',[1] but are those of the proprietors of the *North of England Magazine* announcing the discontinuation of the Manchester-based publication in September 1843.[2] The periodical had lasted eighteen months, having been founded as a publication 'to represent the feelings and advocate the interests of the manufacturing and commercial classes' in February 1842.[3] It was politically a liberal, reforming journal, but not a political journal; on the contrary its coverage embraced music, the fine arts and drama. It was published every month as an octavo of sixty-four pages, with an annual cumulative volume.

Within a year of its initial publication, the *North of England Magazine* was in trouble and in May 1843 the proprietors informed the public that they had effected an arrangement with those of *Bradshaw's Journal* for carrying on the two periodicals in conjunction and the title became the *North of England Magazine*

---

[1] John Feather, 'Others: Some Reflections on the Book Trade', in *Book Trade Connections from the Seventeenth to the Twentieth Centuries*, ed. by John Hinks & Catherine Armstrong (London, 2008), pp. 1-19.

[2] *Waterloo Directory of English Newspapers and Periodicals: 1800-1900*: Series 2, http://www.victorianperiodicals.com/series2/

[3] '...nicely got up, printed with a clear type, on very nice paper, and tolerably well illustrated' was the view of the *Preston Chronicle*, 5 March 1842.

and Bradshaw's Journal, printed by George Bradshaw (of railway timetable fame) and Henry Blacklock of Manchester. But even this merger failed and four months later the proprietors announced its closure on the grounds that 'the simple fact is that the magazine does not pay its expenses, and that they are unwilling to incur further expenses on its account.'

The purpose of this essay is to ask how representative was the *North of England Magazine* of the Manchester periodical press? It will also explore whether the point made by the proprietors holds up: that the provinces simply could not sustain a viable periodical press. The periodical, after all, should be the genre that undermines the claim that publishing in Britain is essentially a metropolitan activity. It is a genre or series of genres intrinsically tied up with issues of regional identity. What is or what should be distinctive about a town's or a region's printed output is essentially determined by and reflected in the pages of its perio-dicals.

This essay seeks to put some flesh on the bones of the newspaper, magazine and journal output of Manchester in the nineteenth century. It does so by drawing on the work of historians of the book who have recognized that in the long nineteenth century the periodical was just as influential as the book. The figures on readers, collected so assiduously by the newly established rate-supported libraries, show that the newsroom was generally more popular than the bookroom by a ratio of two or even three to one.[4] Stephen Colclough's research has concluded that the business of the railway bookstall was primarily concerned with the sale of newspapers and periodicals.[5] No

---

[4] W. R. Credland, *The Manchester Public Free Libraries: A History and Description* (Manchester, 1899), p. 216.

[5] Stephen Colclough, 'Station to Station: the LNWR and the Emergence of the Railway Bookstall, 1840-1875', in *Printing Places: Locations of Book Production and Distribution since 1500*, ed. by John Hinks and Catherine Armstrong (London, 2005), pp. 169-184.

general discussion of the demographically and socially dynamic groups that comprise what for convenience we label the Victorian reading public can ignore their desire to read newspapers, magazines and journals. Since the 1960s the study of the Victorian periodical in particular has advanced, developing its own definite agenda and methodologies, focusing on issues such as production, content, contributors, distribution and readership. But in these researches surprisingly little attention has been given to periodicals published outside London. In the popular imagination, of course, Manchester's importance as a hub or even as a spoke for a print network derives from its place as a publishing and printing centre for the periodical. Just as historians of the book trade in Birmingham have to put up with the fact that the one thing everybody knows is that Baskerville printed in Birmingham, so the popular view of the self-proclaimed 'metropolis of manufactures'[6] is that it produced the *Manchester Guardian*. The most recent study of the newspaper industry in Manchester is entitled *The Other Fleet Street*, Manchester's position being so important as to emulate if not rival London and become Britain's second city for the trade of newspaper printing.[7]

This essay is dependent on a major unpublished resource, Frederick Leary's manuscript 'History of the Manchester Periodical Press', a work which sought to chart the output of the press from its origins in the eighteenth century to the 1890s.[8] There is clearly no possibility of either quantifying or characterizing the entire output of the Manchester trade in periodical

---

[6] *Manchester as it is, or, Notices of the institutions, manufactures, commerce, railways, etc. of the metropolis of manufactures : interspersed with much valuable information useful for the resident and stranger. With numerous steel engravings and a map* (Manchester: Printed and published by Love and Barton, 1839).

[7] R. Waterhouse, *The Other Fleet Street: How Manchester Made Newspapers National* (Altrincham, 2004).

[8] Frederick Leary, 'History of the Manchester Periodical Press', Manchester Central Library, MSf 052 L.161.

publications, but we seek instead to explore these issues by examining the output of the periodical press for three decades: the 1820s, the 1850s and 1880s. By sampling what was published in Manchester in these years we aim to clarify the nature and significance of the provincial press.

Frederick Leary was born in Manchester in 1841, and made a living as a mercantile clerk, a tailor and shopkeeper. He wrote a handful of books and pamphlets. The subjects include a biography of the Chartist Ernest Jones, the abolition of the House of Lords, and a book-length account of the history of the Chartist movement which was serialized in the *Sheffield Weekly Independent*. Leary also published pieces, many of which were concerned with Manchester periodicals in local newspapers and journals, which Leary researched for many years in peculiar isolation.[9] Leary appears to be another of those working-class autodidacts to be found in the pages of James Cash and Samuel Smiles,[10] though he preferred investigating and classifying local journals and newspapers in the warmth of the public library rather than searching for mosses and ferns on the cold shoulders of the Pennine hills. By the time Leary submitted his manuscript to Charles Sutton, Librarian of Manchester's Public Library, who seems to have offered to help get it published, Leary had produced a text of 160,000 words that provided a record of both current and extinct publications associated with Manchester.[11]

---

[9] For example articles in *Manchester Notes and Queries*, vol. 6 on Henry Whitworth (4435); The *Manchester Mercury* (3763), Old Manchester newspapers (pages 189-190), and The first Manchester daily paper (4004), vol. 7: Early Manchester printers (4984, 5000, 5007, 5014, 5018, 5038, 5044), and The editor of the *Gazette* [Mr Aston] (4766), vol. 8: Manchester Exchange (5295), James Perry (5482), Bradshaw's Guide (5691), St Ann's Square (5836), John Wesley (5852), and De Quincey's birthplace (5867).

[10] A. Secord, 'Thomas Edward and the making of a working-class scientific hero', *Science in Context*, 16 (2003), pp. 147-73.

[11] M. Powell and T. Wyke, 'Charting the Manchester Tributary of the Golden Stream: Leary's History of the Manchester Periodical Press',

Such a history, in Leary's words, 'their muse, their literary associations, their success and their failure, cannot fail then to form an interesting chapter in the annals of the city'.[12] Although he did not discuss explicitly his research methodology, he conceptualized the periodical in broad terms. For Leary it embraced newspapers in all their different forms: weekly, fortnightly and monthly magazines and journals, trade publications, commercial and trade directories, and almanacs. It was a generous boundary within which to research, one that was not far removed from that used by the Waterloo Periodicals project, in which John North's working definition was 'any publication which at its inception was intended to be published at regular intervals...'[13] Publications that for political or moral reasons would have been rejected by most public library committees were identified, examined and described. Leary was in pursuit of the bibliographer's nemesis – completeness. Defunct and long vanished titles outnumbered the surviving and thriving. Even so, Leary seemed conscious of the history's deficiencies, acknowledging the exclusion of publications such as the printed reports of local charities.

In a report of his work, published in 1889 in *Manchester Notes and Queries*, Leary summarized the output of the periodical press from 1720 until 1888.[14] Figure One identifies a total of 661 periodicals published during this period, made up of 101 newspapers (15.3%), 251 journals (38%), 123 magazines (18.6%), 52 literary, scientific and educational works including those published by societies (7.9%), 52 miscellaneous works (7.9%), and 82 other works such as annuals, calendars and directories (12.4%). Having

---

Manchester Region History Review, 17, No. 2 (2006), pp. 43-62.

[12] Leary, 'Periodical Press', p. 1.

[13] *Waterloo Directory of English Newspapers and Periodicals, 1800-1900*, series 2, ed. by J. S. North (Ontario, 2003) introduction.

[14] The table was published in an article by Leary on the Manchester periodical press *in Manchester Notes and Queries* (5415), 22 June 1889.

		Numbers published		In Progress
NEWSPAPERS		101		34
JOURNALS	94		27	
Art	10		2	
Athletic	8		2	
Commercial & Technical	33		25	
Satirical	20		0	
Sporting	27		8	
Temperance	20		7	
Theatrical	16		0	
Working Men / Co-operative	20		4	
Volunteer	3		2	
		251		77
MAGAZINES	50		6	
Anti- Religious	2		0	
Religious & Parish	58		23	
School	13		5	
		123		34
Literary & Scientific Societies	27		13	
Literary, Scientific and Educational	20		2	
Medical	5		1	
		52		16
MISCELLANEOUS	29		7	
Bazaars	9		0	
Gratuitous	7		2	
Societies	7		4	
		52		13
Annuals		13		6
Calendars and Almanacs		42		17
Directories		10		2
Railway Guides		17		7
TOTAL		661		206

Fig. 1 Manchester Periodical Press 1720-1888.

completed his investigations Leary was well aware of the fact that this summary did not represent the total number published in the city and neighbourhood and that the names of many were lost, often past all recovery. Leary's summary remains a useful document, however, not least for his attempt to break down newspapers and magazines into broad subject headings.

Leary's work was not published but if it had been, one could hazard a guess that it would have transformed our understanding of the importance of the periodical in relation to the book. His work suggested that Manchester was an important centre for the production of the periodical, an inference that is now supported by an analysis of the titles in the Waterloo periodicals database. It confirms that although Manchester's periodical trade was small in relation to London, it far exceeded the output of cities such as Birmingham, Liverpool and Leeds.[15] Such broad statistical comparisons are useful but they cannot tell us much about the significance of specific titles or types of periodicals. For Leary, the periodical was not of marginal importance; on the contrary his work argues for the centrality of the periodical to print culture in the provinces. Whatever the case, just as historians have long recognized the importance of regional newspapers to print culture, we now need to begin to study the local journal and magazine in more detail. What then can be said about the Manchester periodical?

---

[15] Figures from Waterloo would indicate that for the entire nineteenth century a total of 1,284 titles were published in Manchester. Other towns were as follows: Birmingham 857, Liverpool 952, Leeds 424. *Waterloo Directory of English Newspapers and Periodicals: 1800-1900: Series 2*, http://www.victorianperiodicals.com/series2/ It is significant that John Turner's research on the book trade confirms the clear supremacy of Manchester. 'Book Publishing from the English Provinces in the late Nineteenth Century: Report of Work in Progress', in *The Mighty Engine: the Printing Press and its Impact*, ed. By Peter Isaac and Barry McKay (London, 2000), pp. 185-196.

The 1820s

For Fred Leary the 1820s were dominated by the creation of the *Manchester Guardian* and its impact on newspaper publishing in the town. For that decade, he lists a number of new journals, of which three were devoted to art and three to commerce. Two of the new magazines were published: the *Catholic*, a weekly anti-Catholic magazine, which started in 1821 but which folded after only twenty issues in April 1822, and the *Catholic Phoenix and Papal Scourge*, another weekly that did exactly what it said on the title page, and which lasted all of a month. These two militant Protestant works were the only religious periodicals published in this decade. Two theatrical journals were started: the *Dramatic Censor* of 1822 and the *Manchester Theatrical Censor*, a four-page weekly which folded after a month. The latter was replaced by the *Phoenix, or Manchester Literary Journal*, a sixteen-page weekly that lasted only six months. The majority of magazines published in Manchester in the 1820s were, like the *Phoenix*, devoted to literature. These include *Jones's Literary Gazette* (1829), the *Manchester Iris* (1822-3), *Johnson's Selector* (1824) the *Scrap-Book* (1822) and the *Boeatian* (1824). The last of these was one of a number of periodicals started by the young Harrison Ainsworth that sought to impose an Oxbridge-style literary journal on a Manchester audience. It did not seek contributors – Ainsworth and his friend James Crossley provided all the content. To get the joke – that a Boeotian was a native of an ancient region of Greece and that it was a pejorative term meaning stupid, backwards, and dull – required a good classical education. Clearly the reader was being created in the image of the editor.[16] Each of these journals was short lived: *Jones's Literary Gazette,* and the *Boeatian* both lasted a mere six issues, whilst of the others, the *Manchester Iris* lasted longest, running from February 1822 until

---

[16] *The Boeatian* is one of the few periodicals published in Manchester to escape the attention of the Waterloo Directory.

December of the following year. In all, between 1820 and 1829 thirty-two periodical publications were launched, of which only nine appear to have survived into the following decade.

The weekly magazine or journal was a relatively expensive commodity – on average the Manchester examples were about half the price of a newspaper – and it seems fair to conclude that the actual market for their purchase was small. At the beginning of May 1821, six Manchester newspapers (four Conservative and two Liberal) were competing for public favour, when a prospectus printed by J. Pratt appeared for a new weekly paper to be entitled the *Manchester Guardian*. At the outset its politics were clearly identified: 'it will zealously enforce the principles of civil and religious liberty...it will warmly advocate the cause of Reform; it will endeavour to assist in the discussion of just principles of political economy and support without reference to the party from which they emanate whatever may...tend to promote the moral advantage or political welfare of the community'.[17]

The *Manchester Guardian* emerged into a competitive economic environment and a bitter political setting. Its impact is well documented and there is no need to repeat it here. In the Manchester newspaper war of the 1820s it is easy to overlook some important new initiatives and developments, but they did not escape Leary's attention. One was the publication in December 1821 of Manchester's first daily newspaper, the *Northern Express, and Lancashire Daily Post*. This was a four-page paper containing five columns, and was priced at 7d., of which 4d. was stamp duty. This was the second attempt to start a daily paper in Lancashire. Despite the fact that the latest news from London appeared less than twenty-four hours after it was first published, the *Northern Express* was dreadfully dull and folded

---

[17] *Manchester Guardian*, vol. 1 no. 1, 05 May 1821, cited in *Waterloo Directory of English Newspapers and Periodicals: 1800-1900:* Series 2, http://www.victorianperiodicals.com/series2/

after only three months. It would be some time before it mattered whether one's newspaper, complete with up-to-date news, was available at the daily breakfast table.

The second development was the publication in July 1825 of the *Manchester Advertiser*, the first free paper published in the town, which depended entirely on advertisements for its revenue. Like the *Northern Express*, this existed only for a few months and was killed off by the *Guardian* which countered the threat by bringing out a new Tuesday paper with the very same name of *Manchester Advertiser*.

By examining the 1820s newspaper war alongside the provision of failing literary magazines and short-lived religious journals, Leary helped to contextualize the publication of newspapers and provided a more realistic analysis of publishing success and failure. In particular his account showed how proprietors and publishers set about spoiling rival publications, how they competed for the all-important advertising revenue, and how their political views changed in order to defend and increase circulation. The *Manchester Guardian*, for example, saw its provision of commercial information as of equal importance to its politics.[18] It is significant that the proprietors of the *Guardian*'s competitors were all primarily printers or booksellers, whereas the *Guardian's* backers had experience in various branches of the textile trade.[19] In 1825 the *Manchester Guardian* and its Tuesday paper the *Advertiser* merged with Harrop's Tory papers the *Manchester Mercury* and the *British Volunteer*. Economic reality necessitated mergers. The new papers of the 1820s confirm that the way to success lay as much in providing

---

[18] The paper would report 'with accuracy and effect, the condition of trade and its prospects...they hope, thus, in some measure to supply that information on the subject, the deficiency of which is often so obviously apparent, both amongst public men and those connected with the press'.

[19] D. Ayerst, *Guardian: Biography of a newspaper* (London, 1971), p. 23.

accurate commercial information as in political persuasion. This applies to the *Manchester Advertiser* and the *Manchester Commercial Journal*, both of which were published on Tuesdays, the best day because the principal commercial market was held then, but also because this was the earliest day in the week that this commercial information could be published.

To conclude, the 1820s were clearly a difficult time to establish a periodical, magazine or newspaper in Manchester. Few survived the decade and few prospered. The middle years of this decade saw a sharp and severe economic depression. What impact did this have on the book trade? Needs had to be anticipated and then met and, as the attempts to set up literary magazines show, publishers could get things wrong and suffer the consequences. But if one got it right the rewards could be significant. The *Westminster Review* in 1830 analysed the profits that could be made from publishing a provincial weekly newspaper and estimated that those that sold steadily but which had a large number of advertisements, such as the *Leeds Mercury* and the *Birmingham Gazette*, the *Hampshire Telegraph* and the *Salisbury Journal*, could yield their owners between two and three thousand pounds a year each. In 1832 the *Manchester Guardian* paid £1,671 in advertising duties at a rate of 3s. 6d. per advertisement, over twice as much as its main competitor. The success of a paper could be judged as much by the number of advertisements as by the number of copies sold. The *Guardian's* proprietor, John Edward Taylor, set himself a target of 100 adverts an issue, a target he achieved after only three years in 1823. Sales of the *Manchester Guardian*, however, show an increase – it began with 1,000 and reached 3,000 by about 1825 – but, at 7d. per copy, sales of provincial stamped newspapers were always likely to be limited. Perhaps newspaper buying is as revealing an approximate indicator of the size of the middle class than better-known examples, such as the employment of a domestic servant. A good wage for a cotton spinner at this time was one pound per week and 7d. would be the equivalent of two nights' drinking. Seven pence was more than the cost of most of the books that James Weatherley, a Manchester bookseller, sold from his shops in the 1820s; and his autobiography shows how periodicals were a mainstay of the second-hand book trade.[20] We are conscious that the size of the reading public was increasing in the 1820s but for many potential purchasers living standards and real disposable income were only increasing slowly. What did the majority of working people have left of their wages after essential expenditure? It was seldom enough to purchase periodicals and newspapers. The *Manchester Guardian,* like every other stamped newspaper, was possibly read more in newsrooms and public houses than in the comfort of one's home.

The 1850s

Figures for the 1850s, the decade in which the stamp duty on newspapers was finally abolished, show a total of fifty-nine new periodical titles published in Manchester, approximately twice as many as in the 1820s.

Leary's data suggest some significant new developments both in the type of periodicals published and also their intended readership. For one thing, we see the emergence of more specialist journals. Of the fourteen new journals that were started, five came from moral pressure groups, in particular the temperance movement, five were devoted to commercial and technical issues, three to sport. Of the first group, four of the titles were short lived: the *Temperance Messenger, Teetotaler, Maine Law Almanac,* and *Temperance Advocate Circular,* all folded after a few issues. Only one survived – *Alliance: a Weekly*

---

[20] M. Powell and T. Wyke, 'Penny capitalism in the Manchester book trade' in *The Reach of Print. Making, Selling and Using Books,* ed. by P. Isaac and B. McKay (Winchester, 1998), pp. 135-56.

Journal of Moral and Social Reform, which was a penny folio started in July 1854. This journal, under the title of the *Alliance News*, continued to promote temperance in Manchester well into the twentieth century.[21] Manchester became the headquarters of the United Kingdom Alliance, no doubt in the expectation that it could do to brewing trades what the Anti-Corn Law League had done to the farming interests in the previous decade. The technical literature consisted primarily of trade journals: *Trades Advocate and Herald of Progress* established by the iron trades, the *Typographical Circular*, the penny monthly circular of the Provincial Typographical Association, and the *Cotton Supply Reporter*, an eight-page monthly that was free to members of the Cotton Supply Association but sold to non-members at 1*d*. This was an early and an important textile journal. Three sporting papers were also started – *Locket's Indicator and Sporting News*, which began life as a single sheet but which had become a one-shilling octavo by the 1890s, *Abbot's Sporting Chronicle*, a penny weekly handicap book, and *Paul Walmesley's Selections*, a weekly quarto. These represent a particularly interesting and under-researched group of periodicals, not the sort of publications that would find their way into the newsrooms of the newly created public libraries.

Magazines show a similar specialization, such as the *Teachers' Journal of Sunday School Education*, or *Endeavour: a Monthly Magazine for Pupils of Ashawe Hall Academy Flixton*. Manchester was the one of the centres of the homoeopathic movement from the 1840s, hence *Homoeopathic News*, brought out from 1859. We also see the emergence of new subjects – no fewer than three photographic magazines appeared in the 1850s. Both magazines and newspapers show that new markets and readers were being

---

[21] O. C. Niessen, 'Temperance' in *Victorian Periodicals and Victorian Society* ed. by J. Don Vann and R. T. VanArdsel (University of Toronto Press, 1994), pp. 263-4.

identified, such as the suburban reader, whose needs would be met by, for example, the *Droylsden Literary and Advertising Journal* (a half-penny monthly), or *Staveley's Hulme Advertiser* (a free weekly folio). This was an attempt to serve more specific constituencies of readers – Hulme for example had over 50,000 inhabitants at this time, a population that easily exceeded towns such as York or Chester. The *Droylsden Advertiser* was launched with the usual great hopes in May 1854. The area reached by the monthly half-penny folio contained a population of more than 25,000 and 'their daily augmenting business transactions rendered a vast amount of advertising and returns necessary'.[22] The editor also professed the obligatory high moral tone and aimed to infuse such trade among the thinking portion of the working classes as would lead them to abandon the pernicious publications which issued from the periodical press. Beside the local and general topics of the day, extracts would be given from new books and occasional biographical sketches of local celebrities would appear. A corner would also be devoted to local history, statistics and topography. 'We shall reserve to ourselves a discretionary power in rejecting certain kinds of advertise-ments, which one may consider pernicious to the minds and morals of the people and above all calculated to exercise a baneful influence upon our youth.'[23] But he soon fell off his high horse and after only issuing nine numbers the paper folded because it could not attract sufficient advertising. Circulation had steadily increased and 1,100 copies of the last number were printed. For a local newspaper advertising income remained essential and whatever one thought of the claims associated with products such as patent medicines, to exclude such advertise-ments had obvious consequences. The power of the advertiser was becoming more evident. Newspaper proprietors might be

---

[22] Leary, 'Periodical Press', p. 263. The editor was John Higson.
[23] Leary, 'Periodical Press', p. 264.

reluctant to criticise Manchester's main department stores, Kendal Milne or later Lewis's, given their advertising expenditure in the local press.

We know about the importance of advertisements to newspapers but less about their importance to the journal and magazine, especially to the small technical press. What proportion of total revenue was derived from advertisements? How much did one pay for adverts? This latter question is difficult to answer not least because so many libraries have bound these items in such a way that for some titles we have lost the wrappers, which contained the advertisements.

In the case of newspapers it is possible to trace the emergence of the daily newspaper in Manchester from its weekly and bi-weekly origins. Leary provided, for example, detailed information on the crucial year of 1854 when Manchester saw the publication of what is claimed to have been its first daily newspaper and the response it prompted from the existing bi-weekly titles. Indeed, the *Manchester Examiner and Times*'s decision to establish a daily news-sheet – the *Manchester Daily Times* – provided it with the experience of publishing a daily newspaper before the repeal of the stamp duty in 1855 signalled the conventional starting date of the daily morning newspaper in the region and country.[24] The abandonment of stamp duty had by no means an immediate impact on periodical publishing as a whole in the town.

If we turn from newspaper and periodical production to the evidence of readership we get a very different picture. Information on readership in Manchester for these years comes mainly from the Manchester wholesale and retail newspaper and periodical seller, Abel Heywood, to the 1851 Select Committee considering the abolition of newspaper stamp duty. Maintaining

---

[24] See A. E. Musson, 'The first daily newspapers in Lancashire', *Transactions of Lancashire and Cheshire Antiquarian Society*, 65 (1955) pp. 104-31.

that he handled ten per cent of the whole national issue of popular publications, he presented the committee with an account of his current sales.[25]

Family Papers	
Chambers's Journal	3,000
Chambers's Papers for the People	1,200
Eliza Cook's Journal	600
Cottage Gardener	1,800
Family Friend	1,800
Family Tutor	1,800
Home Circle	600
Household Words	600
Cassell's Working Man's Friend	1,800
News of the World	3,500
Weekly Times	4,000
Weekly Newspapers	
Family Herald	14,000
London Journal	14,000
Reynold's Miscellany	4,500
Religious Papers	
Catholic papers, total	22,000
Cassell's Pathway	700
Political and free-thinking papers	
Christian Socialist	70
Friend of the People	250
[Oastler's] Home	450
Robert Owen's Journal	250
[Holyoake's] Reasoner	400
TOTAL	77,320

[25] For a discussion of Heywood see Brian Maidment, 'The Manchester Common Reader – Abel Heywood's 'Evidence' and the early Victorian Reading Public', in *Printing and the book in Manchester 1700-1850*, ed. by Eddie Cass and Morris Garratt (Manchester, 2001), pp. 91-120.

It is interesting to note that in his evidence in 1851 Heywood underplayed the role and the sales of the radical press. The year before, when talking to Angus Bethune Reach, a journalist on the *Morning Chronicle*, Heywood gave sales of 3,000 per issue of the *Lancashire Beacon*, a free-thinking magazine that he published.[26] Conveniently he omitted to include this in his figures to Parliament. But even when one takes account of such omissions, Heywood's sales information demonstrated that the main titles distributed to newsagents and booksellers in the region were copies of London newspapers and magazines. A significant readership for London periodicals now existed in Manchester and the satellite cotton towns. At this time sales of the main Manchester newspapers were in the order of 5,000 copies each, a little more than a third of the sales of the *Family Herald* or the *London Journal*. Heywood's evidence confirmed Manchester's importance as a distribution centre for periodicals, magazines and newspapers. Manchester and Lancashire, in the words of Angus Bethune Reach, 'furnishes no unimportant part of the literary market of England'.[27] Many factors were at work here, including rising living standards, increasing literacy levels and a desire to own one's reading. The railway too contributed, relentlessly creating larger markets, by transporting ever-larger numbers of weekly and monthly magazines, which did not have the same delivery constraints as the daily newspaper. While Victorian Manchester was an important manufacturing centre, it was an economy in which trade and distribution predominated. In this case, it was one where books, periodicals and newspapers, like other goods, were simply moved on.

---

[26] First published in 1849, Charles Southwell being the 'responsible editor'.

[27] Reach's series of *Morning Chronicle* articles has been reprinted in *Manchester and the Textile Districts in 1849,* ed. by C. Aspin (Helmshore Local History Society, 1972).

The 1880s

The number of new serial publications brought out in the 1880s shows a dramatic if not altogether surprising increase over what had gone before, with a total of 228 new publications. This was made up of 28 newspapers, 69 journals, 93 magazines and 38 miscellaneous works – annuals, yearbooks, directories, calendars and guides. The reading public continued to increase, the result of a wide range of economic, technological and cultural factors, some of which – the provision of more reader-friendly gas lighting in the home and the manufacture of cheaper reading glasses – deserve more detailed study.[28] It was no longer necessary to read a newspaper in a newsroom – now it was read in the home or on the omnibus and train. Newspapers were no longer saved but used to light the fire in working-class homes. Possibly attitudes towards reading in Manchester were changing more quickly than in other regions simply because the district was at the forefront of new commercial realities and new consumer leisure opportunities. Of course, this apparent four-fold increase in publications compared with the 1850s may owe much to the survival of more recent periodicals, their preservation in Manchester Public Library and their acquisition by Leary himself, rather than a straightforward increase in the number published. But the change by the 1880s was on a fundamentally different scale from what had gone before and now we see in operation the fully-fledged cheap press, described so well by Jonathan Rose and others.[29] Forms of publication which were only just emerging in the 1850s were now commonplace and new ideas were coming through about how journals and magazines could be promoted and sold.

---

[28] T. Wyke, 'Publishing and reading books etc in nineteenth-century Manchester' in *Printing and the Book in Manchester*, pp. 29-49.

[29] Jonathan Rose, *The Intellectual Life of the British Working Class* (New Haven, 2001).

The most obvious change is that by the 1880s the specialist publication, aimed at a relatively small niche market, was commonplace. The titles include: *Manchester Accountants Students Society Transactions, Cohen's Journal of Phrenology, Two Worlds: a Journal Devoted to Spiritualism, Occult Science, Ethics, Religion and Reform*, and *Rainbow: a Juvenile Vegetarian Journal*. This latter was a testament to Manchester being home to the vegetarian movement, but sadly this particular title did not manage to make it as far as the second issue. Within this field of specialist publications there were a number of important categories. First, and perhaps surprisingly, was the parish magazine. Leary identified thirty-seven parish and religious magazines which started up in the 1880s, produced by both established and nonconformist churches in Manchester, although in this instance his figures may only touch the surface. The insertion of London-printed magazine supplements inside locally printed parish magazines is only one of the intriguing features of what was a widespread but almost completely under-researched genre. It was now possible for organizations and charities to produce small runs of magazines and keep them running. Second, and equally significant, was the growth in trade and technical journals. Almost forty were identified by Leary. Some, such as the *Cotton Factory Times*, were set up by the unions; others such as the *Textile Manufacturer*, were established by the employers.[30] Why did it take so long for specialist trade journals to develop in a major manufacturing town? Possibly the late development of a specialist business press, especially a press devoted to the cotton trade, was because the local daily and weekly newspapers provided very full commercial information.

In the 1880s the sporting press in Manchester was one of the largest and most successful features of the trade. Edward Hulton

---

[30] E. Cass, A. Fowler and T. Wyke, 'The remarkable rise and long decline of the *Cotton Factory Times*', *Media History*, 4, 2 (1998), pp. 141-59.

started a range of papers with a betting sheet printed in Ancoats, to be followed by the *Sporting Chronicle and Athletic News*.[31] This was the foundation of the Hulton publishing empire. Central to the sporting press, of course, was the betting newspaper or magazine and it is interesting to note that part of Leary's manuscript was written on the back of betting sheets. The provincial horse racing press is yet another area that needs a more detailed study.

Manchester's emergence as a place where periodicals for other areas could be printed and published was slow. By the 1880s there were certainly some works printed in Manchester for other regions: the *Manxman, Northern Advance, a Politico-religious Paper for the Northern and Midlands Counties*, and a supplement to *Life and Work*, and the *Caledonian Banquet and Fifeshire Chronicle*, though this last did not make it to a second issue. But such examples hardly support the idea that Manchester had become a centre for printing as well as distribution, especially outside the ring of cotton towns. In fact this raises more fundamental questions about the nature of the Manchester press as a whole. How far did Manchester-published periodicals travel? How large was the 'region' they served? Were the ones published in Manchester distributed in London and, if so, how and to what extent? In short, was it possible for a Manchester-based journal to become a market leader?

Evidence from a number of well-known cases such as *Tit-Bits* would suggest that to be successful one had to move to London. Started by George Newnes in Manchester in October 1881, *Tit-Bits* was an immediate success. Six weeks after its first appearance Newnes was offered £16,000 for outright purchase of the publi-

---

[31] T. Mason, 'Sporting news', in *The Press in English Society from the seventeenth to the nineteenth centuries*, ed. by M. Harris and A. Lee (London, 1986).

cation by a Manchester publishing firm.[32] Six months later a London firm offered him £30,000. Within a year sales had reached over 400,000. But after only three years Newnes moved the whole operation to London. *Tit-Bits* shows that it was possible to produce a successful magazine in the provinces but that a London base was needed in order to move on and become a mass-market title.

There are further examples of publishers whose careers testify to the economic importance of London. To Newnes could be added another purveyor of cheap literature, Manchester-born John Cassell, and, in a different field and several decades earlier, William Dugdale, one of the leading publishers of pornography in Victorian England. As for the press, the Chartist paper, the *Northern Star*, moved from Leeds to London while journals associated with pressure groups ranging from the Anti-Corn Law League to the Women's Social and Political Union, both of which had strong Manchester connections, ended up being published in the metropolis. Even some trade journals moved to London: the *Meat Traders' Journal & Cattle Salesman's Gazette* was founded in 1888 and moved in 1892, as did *Journeyman Bakers Magazine* (Organ of the Amalgamated Union of Operative Bakers and Confectioners), *Ironmongery and the Machinery and Hardware Trades Advertiser* and *Sale and Exchange*. People of talent, drive and initiative in the book trade and in other fields were irresistibly drawn to London. A southward drift of talent – of artists, academics, musicians and sculptors, as well as of publishers and writers – is evident, even if there were those who were content to work amidst the sooty streets of Manchester.

Periodicals were a risky businesses and there was no guarantee of success. A host of others followed Newnes's initiatives, only to fail. Trade journals also flopped. *The Outfitter: a Journal for Cloth-*

---

[32] Kate Jackson, *George Newnes and the New Journalism in Britain, 1880-1910: Culture and Profit* (Aldershot, 2001), p. 68.

iers, Hosiers and Assistants folded after a year, leaving the publisher with high stocks of unsold copies. In some cases the relatively low entry costs to establish and publish the specialist periodical meant that losses were small. Perhaps more cautionary is the tale of the *North Times and Latest News,* a victim of a local newspaper war in 1882, which ceased trading with debts of £16,000. Why one magazine or paper succeeded and another failed is a difficult question to answer. In Manchester in the 1880s there were many that sought to imitate *Tit-Bits,* running the same insurance scheme, depending largely on readers for their content, and coming up with novel ways of marketing and promoting sales. Though imitation may be a form of flattery, it is no guarantee of success and few of these magazines survived the decade. What we see in the 1880s is the way that publishers and proprietors spent time, energy and money trying to keep their publications alive. The penny humorous magazine, *Manchester Figaro,* demonstrates this. It changed its day of publication, produced special numbers to coincide with the local races and pantomime calendar, altered its title and cover price, and introduced coloured illustrations. All of these changes occurred within an eighteen-month period before it finally ceased publication.

What then were the principal features of the Manchester periodical press? Can we now return to the question posed at the outset and say which of the *North of England Magazine* or the *Manchester Guardian* is more representative of the Manchester periodical press? Clearly on one hand, the answer is that the *North of England Magazine* is more typical. As the *Waterloo Directory* project has made clear, we need to look at the entire body of nineteenth-century newspapers and periodicals, including the short-lived failures, rather than focus on the small number of publications that survive and prosper. 'We would be imprudent to assume that the periodicals already known to us were the most important at the time'.[33] With the statistical and biblio-graphical evidence of *Waterloo* and of Leary, we are better placed to answer the questions 'important to whom?' and 'important by what criteria?' But, on the other hand, the most characteristic publication of the Manchester periodical press is not a political and literary magazine, such as *North of England Magazine*. Rather the archetypal Manchester periodical is a commercial or trade journal or even a sporting paper. The argument that Manchester and the provinces could not sustain a viable periodical press is simply not true. The industrial towns of the North and Midlands might not have been able to produce general literary magazines to rival *Chambers's Edinburgh Journal* or the *Penny Magazine*, but they could produce specialist journals and magazines that were by no means insignificant in terms of sales. We should not un-derestimate, for example, the importance of either the racing press or the temperance press. Leary estimated that the magazine *Every Band of Hope Reader*, which had commenced in 1883, sold over a million copies in the next twelve years or so. Betting sheets sold in huge numbers in newsagents throughout the work-ing-class districts of Manchester. The idea of a Manchester which produced an autonomous periodical literature may need to be de-fined differently but its existence cannot be doubted. There is something splendidly symmetrical about the Manchester man working in the Exchange and gambling on the price of various commodities and the Manchester working man in his home, bet-ting his wages on the horses. Both could do this because in front of them was up-to-date, accurate information in the form of regularly produced periodicals that would shape their choices.

---

[33] *Waterloo Directory of English Newspapers and Periodicals: 1800-1900:* Series 2, http://www.victorianperiodicals.com/series2/

National Enterprise and Domestic Periodicals in Nineteenth-Century Ireland

ELIZABETH TILLEY

T HE MARKET FOR domestic periodicals in Ireland for the period 1830 to 1870 has not been studied in any great detail. This is largely due to a widely held belief that the publishing industry in Ireland virtually collapsed after the Act of Union in 1802. While the number of firms certainly decreased dramatically, with bankruptcy reports and emigration records supporting production figures, the years following 1829 are relatively rich in titles published. This is the post-Catholic Emancipation period, of course, so one finds a significant increase in the number of periodicals and books sponsored by or produced by the Church. The period is also thirty years after the Act of Union, and one would expect that publishing would have recovered somewhat from the devastation of the reprint industry at the beginning of the century. These years are also distinguished by a discernible rise in Irish nationalist politics, with the Repeal Movement and Young Ireland sponsoring great amounts of reading material. Finally, census statistics indicate a considerable rise in literacy rates during this time. All of these conditions are calculated to increase titles and circulation. But in fact the usual starting place for talking about nineteenth-century periodical literature is the series of comments made by John Power in his *List of Irish Periodical Productions*: 'Never was there a more tragical history than that of Irish periodical literature: like that of our ancient monarchs, it comprises little more than a narrative of untimely deaths.' In case more fuel is needed, Power adds a note from the *Irish Quarterly Review* of October, 1858: 'It is melancholy to look back on the mass of brilliant but unsuccessful periodicals which rose and fell in Ireland like meteor lights.' [1]

If Power is right, and periodical literature was unsustainable in Ireland, one has to wonder why publishers or proprietors bothered. And yet the *Waterloo Index of Irish Periodical Literature* lists almost four thousand newspapers and periodicals published in the country between 1800 and 1900. The argument that follows forms notes towards a case study of the experience during this period of one publisher: James Duffy (1809-1871). It asks how he handled the business, how long his titles lasted, and it concludes with some speculations regarding how he contrived to survive in the face of apparently inevitable failure.

If one looks closely it appears that at least eight of the domestic titles in the *Waterloo Index* were directly controlled for the period in question by Duffy, the publisher best known for his association with Young Ireland. Periodicals were not his only interest and diversification was certainly one of the reasons why he could afford to keep bringing out new titles, but this does not explain why he bothered to do so in the first place. Personal information about Duffy is scarce but we know that he was a nationalist and he seems to have had a genuine desire to see a national literature grow. The easiest place for that to happen was in the periodical press. Secondly, he was a businessman and he recognized the potential in the part-issue for branding, as well as the constant appeal of the new.

Duffy was born in 1809 in Monaghan and came to Dublin around 1830. From there the story of his beginnings as a bookseller and publisher reflects, in peculiar ways, the cultural context of Ireland at the time. There are at least three versions of

---

[1]   John Power, *A List of Irish Periodical Publications (chiefly literary) from 1729 to the present time; reprinted from "Notes and Queries", March and April, 1866, and "The Irish Literary Enquirer", No. IV, with additions and corrections* (London, 1866).

these beginnings, none of which is wholly satisfactory. The first simply mentions that Duffy set up shop in a small way in Dublin, and that his initial success came in 1830 with a reprint of Napoleon's *Book of Fate*, subtitled *Boney's Oraculum*. This he sold for two pence per copy, trading on the revolutionary memories of the populace and the timeless appeal of the mystically bogus.[2] The second version of Duffy's origins declares that he bought up Protestant Bibles, which the Bible Society gave free to Catholics and which the Catholics would then pawn. Duffy's practice was to take the Bibles to Liverpool and trade them there for, as the source calls it, 'more saleable volumes.'[3] The discarding of Protestant Bibles to feed the national taste for less serious fare would have seemed appropriate at the time. The third version declares that Duffy was in fact a pedlar, trading around the counties of Cavan and Meath. The source notes that 'During his wanderings [Duffy] picked up sundry old Irish manuscripts which he took to Bryan Geraghty, of Anglesea Street, Dublin, an old bookseller of antiquarian proclivities, getting from him in exchange Catholic prayerbooks.'[4] The idea of Duffy trading valuable antiquarian material for cheap devotional works is entirely in keeping with his later reputation as a bookseller-publisher of quantity but not necessarily quality. In this third version of Duffy's origins, his first publication is listed as *The Key of Heaven*, a popular old prayerbook, whose stereotyped plates Duffy had purchased from Geraghty. The source article goes on to say that Duffy could not have succeeded had it not been for

---

[2] Anon. 'How James Duffy Rose to Fame', *Irish Book Lover*, vol. 18, no. 6 (Nov, Dec 1930), p. 168. The British Library Catalogue lists the *Catechism of the Council of Trent* (trans. By J. Donovan) as issuing from James Duffy and Co. Ltd., in 1829.

[3] 'James Duffy' in *Dictionary of Irish Literature*, ed. by Robert Hogan (London, 1996), p. 386.

[4] Anon., 'Contributions to Irish Biography. No 29 – James Duffy the Publisher,' in *The Irish Monthly*, 23 (November 1895), p. 596.

the invention of stereotyping, a process which meant that print runs and prices could be kept low, as copies of books could be reprinted, without the costly resetting of type, whenever demand required. The twentieth-century journal *The Irish Book Lover* gives similar attention to commerce in its account of Duffy's origins as it notes that:

until this time the price of books had been very high, prohibitive indeed as far as the majority of the Irish people were concerned; and except for weekly papers and cheap monthly journals, popular reading, in the sense that we understand it to-day, did not exist. Duffy set himself to cater for the masses and his enterprise quickly justified itself.[5]

All of this information, if it is true – and there is probably a good deal of invention here – makes it clear that Duffy was a fairly shrewd businessman, not overly concerned with the intellectual content of his wares, and clever enough to take advantage of new technology as it presented itself. Most importantly he was catering to a domestic Catholic market, producing great volume at low prices for a relatively impoverished population.

These small amounts of information about Duffy always emphasize the two aspects of his career noted above: firstly, he is lauded as a nationalist, and secondly, it is acknowledged that his list was extensive and keenly priced, if not always intellectually uplifting. Nationalism is one thing, and business is another, and it seems clear that in Duffy there existed an individual who could, unusually, combine both. He seems to have done this largely through choosing the right allies. By 1843, when demand for copies of *The Spirit of the Nation* became more than Gavan Duffy and Thomas Davis could handle from the *Nation* offices, they turned to James Duffy as a sympathizer in the nationalist cause, and as a publisher already known for producing cheap editions of books. They had emphasized the importance of education to the country

---

[5] 'How James Duffy Rose to Fame', p. 168.

from the outset, and saw Duffy's existing machinery as suitable for their purposes. Gavan Duffy recalls the association of the Young Irelanders with James Duffy as follows:

The *Spirit of the Nation* was issued in the first instance from the *Nation* office, but as the demand for it became embarrassing, I looked out for a publisher and fixed upon Mr. James Duffy. This was the beginning of his connection with the Young Ireland party. He was a man of shrewd sense and sly humour, but without cultivation or judgment in literature; and it was a subject of constant vexation to the men who were making his name familiar to the world, that side by side with books of eminent merit, he would issue some dreadful abortion of an Irish story or an Irish pamphlet which was certain to be treated at a distance as the latest production of Young Ireland.[6]

Individual authors could also find Duffy's choices and methods of publication rather puzzling. Charles Gavan Duffy remembers an incident witnessed:

Mr James Duffy whose liberality contributed largely to create a national literature in Ireland, sometimes held his hand when it was too late to save judiciously. When he issued an illustrated edition of 'Valentine M'Clutchy,' [William] Carleton was of the opinion that it was not duly advertised or distributed for review, and remonstrated without result. I walked into Duffy's back shop one day about the time the second number appeared, and found the publisher and the author in high controversy on the subject. Carleton on seeing me took up a copy, and looking at me with a face mantling with suppressed fun, muttered, in a slow stage whisper: 'This, my friend, is an illustrated edition of *Valentine M'Clutchy* that's coming out just now; but don't mention it to any one, James Duffy does not wish it to be known.'[7]

Gavan Duffy's increasing embarrassment at the public association of Young Ireland – that serious political movement – with Duffy's

---

[6]   Charles Gavan Duffy, quoted in *The Irish Monthly*, 23 (November 1895), pp. 597-598.
[7]   *Ibid.* p. 598.

brand of domestic Catholicism and his dubious taste in novels, comes about largely as the result of Duffy's insistence on branding publications from his firm. Consequently titles by the Young Irelanders are usually found under series prominently described as from Duffy, and are often part of groups that include Catholic devotional and historical works, such as: *Duffy's Weekly Volume of Catholic Divinity, Duffy's Historical Works, Duffy's National Library of Ireland,* and the very successful *Duffy's Library of Ireland,* which comprised twenty-three volumes by 1850 (see Fig. 1).

Duffy acknowledged the church as partner in a letter he wrote to the *Nation* in response to the favourable report of his activities printed by that paper: 'I have to thank you for connecting my humble name with our national literature; but the praise is due to the kind patronage and extensive support which I have received from the Catholic hierarchy, clergy, and the laity of Ireland.'[8] Indeed, Duffy's catalogue for 1851 reflects this bias, as it is entitled: *A Catalogue of Standard Catholic Works, and Books Relating to Ireland.* Duffy's cultivation of allies also enabled him to fend off competition from other Irish publishers; at least one challenge to Duffy's monopoly on piety and nationalism has come to light. In 1846 James McCormick, a bookseller with a shop in Christ-Church Place, is recorded as publishing, concurrently with *Duffy's Library of Ireland* series, a series entitled the *National Library of Ireland.* McCormick's volumes should have outsold those of Duffy, as they were of good quality, though priced at four pence a volume, whereas Duffy's were one shilling a volume; however as the *Irish Builder* notes, 'they were looked upon by a large number of the Young Ireland school, represented by the *Nation,* as an ungenerous opposition' and soon disappeared.[9]

---

[8]   *Nation,* 29 April 1843, pp. 456.

[9]   CHC [Christopher Clinton Hoey], 'The Rise and Progress of Printing and Publishing in Ireland', *Irish Builder,* 1 March 1878, pp. 67-8. I am grateful to Dr Anthony McNicholas of the University of Westminster for identifying Hoey.

CONTENTS.

BOOKS FOR THE MILLION!!

JOHNSON'S DICTIONARY of the English Language, a new and beautiful edition, with 2000 additional words by Townsend Young, LL.D., 18mo. large type, fancy roan, 1s.

Just Published, in One Volume, 18mo., fancy cloth, 2s.

BALLADS and Romances of Ireland, by James Clarence Mangan, &c. Edited by Hercules Ellis, Esq.

IRVING'S (Washington) Sketch Book, 1s.

IRVING'S (Washington) Bracebridge Hall, 1s.

IRVING'S (Washington) Tales of a Traveller, 1s.

THE NUN OF MONZA, a Tale of the 17th century, translated from the Italian of Rosini, by M. C., 2 vols. post 8vo. 7s. 6d.

STARK'S Tour in the South of Ireland in 1850, beautifully printed in one volume post 8vo. with numerous illustrations by M. Angelo Hayes, Esq. fancy cloth, 5s.

CARLETON'S Valentine M'Clutchy, the Irish Agent; or, Chronicles of Castlecumber: together with the pious aspirations, permissions, vouchsafements, and other sanctified privileges of Solomon M'Slime, a religious Attorney. With 20 illustrations by "Phiz," 8vo. cloth gilt, *reduced to 6s.*

CARLETON'S Tales and Stories, illustrating the Traditions, Sports, and Pastimes of the Irish Peasantry, with numerous illustrations by "Phiz," 8vo. fancy cloth, 6s.

Duffy's Library of Ireland,

23 Volumes, 18mo. fancy cloth,

PRICE ONLY ONE SHILLING EACH!!

TO BE HAD OF ALL BOOKSELLERS, AND AT THE PRINCIPAL RAILWAY STATIONS.

BARRY'S Songs of Ireland.

CARLETON'S Art Maguire, or the Broken Pledge.

CARLETON'S History of Paddy-Go-Easy.

CARLETON'S Rody the Rover, the Irish Detective.

DAVIS'S Literary and Historical Essays.

DAVIS'S Poems and Ballads.

DOHENY'S History of the American Revolution.

DUFFY'S Ballad Poetry of Ireland, sixth edition.

ELLIS'S Songs of Ireland.

FRENCH'S (Rt. Rev. Dr.) Bleeding Iphigenia.

FRENCH'S (Rt. Rev. Dr.) Unkind Deserter.

HAY'S History of the Irish Rebellion of 1798.

MADDEN and DAVIS'S Lives of Grattan and Curran.

M'CARTHY'S Book of Irish Ballads.

M'CARTHY'S Poets and Dramatists of Ireland.

MACMAHON'S Casket of Irish Pearls.

MACNEVIN'S History of the Confiscation of Ulster.

MACNEVIN'S History of the Volunteers of 1782.

M'GEE'S Irish Writers of the 17th century.

M'GEE'S Life of Art MacMurragh, King of Leinster.

MEEHAN'S (Rev. C. P.) Confederation of Kilkenny.

MEEHAN'S (Rev. C. P.) Geraldines, Earls of Desmond.

MITCHEL'S Life and Times of Hugh O'Neil.

☞ DUFFY'S LIBRARY OF IRELAND may be had, bound in 11 vols. *fancy cloth, richly gilt, price 21s.*

☞ From the immense circulation of the "FIRESIDE MAGAZINE," at home and abroad, it will be found a desirable medium for advertising. A limited number will be inserted in each Publication, at the following rate, viz.:—

For Ten Lines, or under, . . . 5s.
Each additional Line, ... 3d.

It will be necessary, in all cases, to send Advertisements to the Office on or before the 15th, as the Magazine must be delivered in London on the 26th of the month.

DUBLIN: JAMES DUFFY, 7, WELLINGTON-QUAY.

Fig. 1 Advertisement from *Duffy's Fireside Magazine* (November, 1850) (Reproduced courtesy of the James Hardiman Library, National University of Ireland, Galway.)

Again, with such a solid foundation in books, it seems puzzling that Duffy should have turned his hand to periodicals (see Appendix). In fact, Duffy had been involved in the business of publishing periodicals, with varying amounts of success, since the 1840s. He tried his hand at all sorts of formats, from penny magazines to monthlies, and at all sorts of prices. His distribution network was also fairly extensive. The title page of the first volume of one of Duffy's longest running periodicals, *Duffy's Fireside Magazine* (1850-54), lists agents in London, Birmingham, Liverpool, Edinburgh, Glasgow, and four agents in Manchester. All of these cities are traditional resting places for Irish emigrants. Clearly, Duffy chose his markets wisely. Further, Duffy's dependence on the Catholic hierarchy for support made his publication of titles aimed specifically at Catholic audiences frequent. The most famous is probably the *Catholic University Gazette*, the journal published by Duffy but set up by the hierarchy expressly to publicize the foundation of the Catholic University, and containing Newman's serially published *The Idea of a University*. Once that goal was complete, the *Gazette* ceased publication. *Duffy's Irish Catholic Magazine* (February 1847 to December 1848), by contrast, reflected an ambitious alliance of culture and religion that was intended to serve a wider audience. The full title of the journal was: *A Monthly Review, Devoted to National Literature, Arts, Antiquities, Ecclesiastical History, Biography of Illustrious Irishmen, and Military Memoirs*. At one shilling per issue, the journal was expensive, though it offered high quality woodcuts and an encyclopaedic format as part of its appeal. It appeared at a difficult time, though, both in the fortunes of the country, and apparently in Duffy's own financial affairs, and the December 1848 issue concludes with the following notice from Duffy:

The PUBLISHER begs to announce, that the present number concludes the SECOND VOLUME of the IRISH CATHOLIC MAGAZINE;

and from the present depressed state of the trade in Ireland, he does not deem it prudent to continue the publication any longer.[10]

The date Duffy chose to discontinue the publication is important. The *Irish Catholic Magazine* fits neatly into a two-volume format, and just as smoothly presented itself anew as a book, rather than a periodical. Stereotyped issues were thus recycled in a new form that cost Duffy very little. Obviously, other publishers did the same, and the date of conclusion of *Duffy's Irish Catholic Magazine* could easily have been coincidence, except that it happened fairly frequently with Duffy's titles. *The Catholic Guardian; or, The Christian Family Library*, for example, ran for approximately one year, from the first of February to the end of November 1852, and advertised itself prominently as 'Complete in One Volume'. Again, what could be called transference of form took place and the periodical became a book, with, presumably, a new set of buyers; moreover, the original publication costs were spread over a considerable period and the result was something that looked more like a volume sold by subscription than a periodical. As volumes were then offered bound in Duffy's distinctive green cloth, with a gold harp prominent on the cover, they looked uniform on the shelf: periodicals were indistinguishable from nationalist essays or ecclesiastical histories. Occasionally Duffy offered half-yearly volumes for sale, as he did with the *Irish Penny Magazine*, and one has to wonder whether he was slightly worried about the viability of the periodical. Duffy's dealings elsewhere show him as an astute, if not overly intellectual, businessman, and it is hard to imagine a businessman letting one aspect of his portfolio slide without having a recovery plan in place.

The 1850 launch of *Duffy's Fireside Magazine*, which ran until 1854 and marked Duffy's return to the penny journal format of the early 1840s has already been mentioned. The *Fireside Maga-*

---

[10] 'Conclusion,' *Irish Catholic Magazine* (December, 1848)

zine typifies the sort of material Duffy offered the public, material that Barbara Hayley declares comprised 'a new kind of cosy family Catholicism.'[11] Certainly there is great emphasis on the domestic. The scene chosen for the title page of *Duffy's Fireside Magazine* is an astonishingly crude depiction of three generations of an Irish family, surrounded by dancing couples and serenaded by pipers and fiddle-players. Three rather sinister figures, bearing more than a passing resemblance to the caricatures of the Irish in *Punch*, support banners declaring the issue number, price, and subtitle of the journal.

Fig. 2 Title-page, *Duffy's Fireside Magazine* (November, 1850). (Reproduced courtesy of the James Hardiman Library, National University of Ireland, Galway.)

---

[11] Barbara Hayley, 'A Reading and Thinking Nation: Periodicals as the Voice of Nineteenth-Century Ireland' in *Three Hundred Years of Irish Periodicals*, ed. by Barbara Hayley and Enda McKay (Mullingar, 1987), p. 42.

Inside, there are the usual tales and stories of the Irish peasantry, didactic articles on temperance, and, always, excerpts from
volumes, or long reviews of volumes, published by Duffy himself. The *Fireside Magazine* ceased publication almost exactly four
years after it had begun, neatly filling four volumes. Its final address to readers was self-congratulatory, proclaiming the magazine the first of its kind to make a profit, or, as the editor said,
the first to survive 'without entailing positive loss on those connected with it.'[12] In other words, it appears that Duffy planned
the obsolescence of the *Fireside Magazine* as deliberately as he set
up his audience to expect a successor to it.

Fig. 3 Title-page, *Illustrated Dublin Journal* (7 September 1861). (Reproduced courtesy of the British Library.)

---

[12] 'A Few Last Words to our Readers', *Duffy's Fireside Magazine* (October,
1854), p. 380.

In 1861 Duffy again produced a penny magazine, this time called *The Illustrated Dublin Journal*, a weekly paper intended to be a 'Miscellany of Amusement and Popular Information' (see Fig. 3). Each issue began with serial fiction, often by William Carleton, with illustrations and capital letter vignettes making the whole quite distinctive. Circulation rose to 100,000 by the second month of production, aided perhaps by the promise of a free first part of *Webster's Critical Pronouncing Dictionary* to be included with the 19 October issue. In fact it proved impossible to prepare the 100,000 copies needed in the time allotted, and the editor announced that a delay of two weeks would be required to print the first part of the *Dictionary*. By November the publisher announced that additional machinery had been brought in to deal with the increase in circulation and to keep delivery times consistent. Running concurrently with the *Illustrated Dublin Journal* was Duffy's attempt at a more serious monthly: *Duffy's Hibernian Magazine*. Priced at nine pence with no illustrations it presented a much more sober face to the reader. Gone were the extravagant initial letter vignettes, the generous format and engravings. Also gone, for the most part, were the caricatures, though the determinedly Irish character of the whole remains. Its title-page similarly suggested higher things and its list of contributors, prominently displayed, includes Lady Wilde, Carleton, John O'Donovan, Wakeman, Griffin, and others (see Fig. 4).

In the 7 December 1861 issue of *The Illustrated Dublin Journal* a new publication was announced: *Duffy's Hibernian Sixpenny Magazine: A Monthly Journal of Literature, Science, and Art*. Its great boast was that it was "THE CHEAPEST MAGAZINE OF THE DAY" at three pence cheaper than the *Hibernian Magazine*. There was no indication that its inauguration would mean the demise of the *Illustrated Dublin Journal*, though around the same time the latter seemed to experience difficulty in obtaining sufficient copy from its contributors. In one case, for example, the editor complained directly to his readers about Blanchard Jerrold, whose serial, *Faversham on his Way to Fame*, had begun in November of 1861.

By March of 1862 the following notice appeared. Mr Jerrold, the editor said, 'by his agreement with the Publisher of this Journal, undertook to furnish the necessary amount of copy, but has not adhered to his stipulation.'[13] The lack of material meant that readers were disappointed and continuity, something vital in sales, was compromised. The public rebuke seems to have had an effect on the author, who protested that he was very sorry, but was out of town and was not aware that copy had been exhausted.

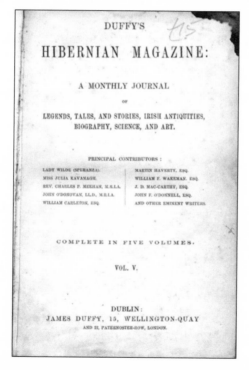

Fig. 4 Title-page, *Duffy's Hibernian Magazine: A Monthly Journal of Legends, Tales, and Stories, Irish Antiquities, Biography, Science, and Art* (Vol. 5, 1864).

---

[13] *Illustrated Dublin Journal*, 29 March 1862, p. 480.

Again, this problem arose during the first months of 1862, and by May of that year the magazine itself had ceased publication. So we have, rather confusingly, *Duffy's Hibernian Magazine* running at the same time as *The Illustrated Dublin Journal*, followed closely by the arrival of *Duffy's Hibernian Sixpenny Magazine* and the disappearance or absorption of the other two. The branding is there: these journals are all neatly identified as Duffy publications; the contents of at least two of the three are roughly the same, and many of the same authors appear. The ethos is the same: Catholic, nationalist, offering home-grown material. In other words, what Duffy offered was the appearance of newness with none of the difficulties surrounding the launch of the genuinely new. The audience already existed, the good will was there, and the desire for novelty and reduction in price guaranteed steady sales, at least for a time. If these speculations are correct and Duffy practised planned obsolescence, or at least took advantage of difficulties once they presented themselves, these are the measures calculated to be the most effective ones in terms of survival.

Finally, we return to stereotyping and the use of technology as a crude sort of sales technique. In the *Waterloo Index of Irish Periodicals*, the *Irish Penny Magazine* is listed as one of Duffy's publications. In fact the *Irish Penny Magazine* was first stereotyped in 1833 by T. & J. Coldwell. It ran from January of 1833 to December of the same year. Eight years later, in January of 1842, the first volume of the *Irish Penny Magazine* was republished, with no mention made of the long hiatus, and with an addition of three more issues back dated to 1834. The name of the publisher had also changed, first to Tegg and then apparently to Duffy. In other words, the stereotyped plates of the *Irish Penny Magazine* were bought by at least two firms after the original publication in the 1830s. The fact that the reissue makes no mention of the lapse in time between Coldwell's guardianship and that of the later publishers adds to the illusion that the title is a new one, and including it under the Duffy umbrella necessarily transfers to it all of the associations the public had with Duffy's name.

Again, the business strategy was transference. Firstly, transference of form, from periodical to book; Duffy's numerous part-issue offerings sold 'complete in one volume' should perhaps be seen as volumes sold by subscription rather than periodicals in perpetual decline. Secondly, transference of title: journals offering essentially similar material were repackaged under a new title and therefore took advantage of the appeal of the new. And thirdly, the transference of publisher, as with Duffy's adoption of the *Irish Penny Magazine*, allowed for a cheap re-packaging of existing material. All of these strategies were possible because of the extreme fluidity and adaptability of the periodical form, capable of withstanding market depressions, audience decrease or increase, and change in personnel. If these factors are taken into account, the periodical industry in Ireland needs to be viewed in a new light.

There is no evidence that Duffy ever edited or wrote for any of his own publications. The author of the biographical notice of Duffy in the *Irish Monthly* says that he was shown a copy of the first number of *Duffy's Hibernian Magazine*, endorsed, he says, 'in the publisher's handwriting "My own copy with the names of contributors and the amounts paid to each. James Duffy, July 2nd, 1860." It was uncut; to print and pay for it was enough – he could not be expected to read it.'[14] In 1871 the *Bookseller* ran an article on what it called the 'decay of the book trade in Ireland; a lament for the past' and noted that what was required was the awakening of the attention 'of the rising James Duffys – and there must be many of these in the country...[to] induce them to

---

[14] *Irish Monthly*, 23 (Nov 1895), p. 600.

cultivate a branch of native industry that cannot fail to pay those who embark in it.'[15] The notice neatly encapsulates Duffy's dual enterprise, nationalism and business, and states baldly that they are not incompatible aims. As Duffy considered his main competitors to be English magazines rather than other Irish ones, his nationalism came in handy as an advertising strategy. Duffy's enterprises reflect a particular audience and political and economic situation that tells us much about the changed climate of Ireland as a publishing centre after the Act of Union. Every contemporary commentary I have examined on nineteenth-century Irish publishing emphasizes the cultural duty of the industry to the larger Irish community. *Duffy's Hibernian Sixpenny Magazine*, in a self-reflexive article actually copied from *The Freeman's Journal* in February of 1864, uses the example of Duffy's own rapidly expanding premises as the basis for an argument about the natural profits that will accrue when businesses take cognizance of the needs of their customers – and the identity of their customers: Irish, Catholic, nationalist, if geographically scattered. The nineteenth century was certainly a difficult time for publishers of periodicals in Ireland, but the case of Duffy illustrates the ways in which the particular circumstances of the Irish market could be used to advantage and it invites the book historian to shift the critical focus from Power's narrative of failure to other ways in which the concept of longevity might be construed.

---

[15] 'The *Bookseller* on Irish Literature' in *The Irish Builder*, 15 September 1871, p. 242.

APPENDIX

James Duffy: List of Periodical Publications

from *The Waterloo Directory of Irish Newspapers and Periodicals, 1800-1900*, ed. by John North (Waterloo, Ontario, 1986)

The Catholic Guardian; or, The Christian Family Library
Weekly
February 1852-November 1852

Catholic University Gazette
Weekly, then monthly from April 1855
June 1854-August 1856

Duffy's Fireside Magazine
Monthly
November 1850-October 1854

Duffy's Hibernian Magazine
Monthly
July 1860-December 1861
Then becomes: *Duffy's Hibernian Sixpenny Magazine*
Monthly
January 1862-June 1864

Duffy's Irish Catholic Magazine
Monthly
January 1847-December 1848

Illustrated Dublin Journal
Weekly
September 1861-May 1862
In May 1862 incorporated with *Duffy's Hibernian Sixpenny Magazine*

Irish Penny Magazine
Weekly
January-December 1833
Resumed January 1842-March 1842

Irish Penny Journal
Weekly
July 1840-June 1841

Selling the News: Distributing Wrexham's Newspapers, 1850-1900

LISA PETERS & KATH SKINNER

PROVINCIAL PRESS HISTORIANS have stated that the success of a provincial newspaper depended to a significant extent upon its reliable delivery service to customers.[1] If a newspaper was unable to establish a strong distribution network this would severely restrict circulation and profits. The second half of the nineteenth century saw four weekly newspapers established in the north Wales town of Wrexham: the *Wrexham Advertiser* (1850-1936), the *Wrexham Telegraph* (1855-63), the *Wrexham Guardian* (1869-1954), and the *Wrexham Free Press* (1870-3). The methods used to distribute these newspapers across north Wales and the border area will be examined, as will the way a newspaper's area of circulation can be ascertained from the location of its agents. The variety of professions not naturally associated with the book trade yet were involved in distributing Wrexham's newspapers will also be discussed.

Newspaper distribution is intrinsically linked with geographical circulation, and newspapers used several methods to ensure that their issues reached a wide audience. Hannah Barker maintained that provincial newspapers were heavily reliant upon sales outside their town of publication[2] and consequently newspapers were always seeking to expand their area of circulation; but the

---

[1] Most notably, G. A. Cranfield, *The Development of the Provincial Newspaper 1700-1760* (Oxford, 1964), p. 190 and C. Y. Ferdinand, 'Local Distribution Networks in Eighteenth-century England', in *Spreading the Word: the Distribution Networks of 1550-1850*, ed. by Robin Myers and Michael Harris (Winchester, 1990), p. 134.

[2] Hannah Barker, *Newspapers, Politics and English Society* (Harlow, 2000), p. 41.

larger and more rural the area, the greater the distribution difficulties. Wrexham's newspapers used five main methods of distridistribution:

1. Collection. Many copies, possibly the majority, were distributed within the town of publication. Consequently one of the most common methods of obtaining a newspaper would have been to purchase a copy at the newspaper office or from newsagents within the town itself. Most newspapers were published on market day when the town would be busier than usual with more potential customers in the locality. David Ayerst estimated that between 1830 and 1845 the number of copies of the *Manchester Guardian* sold 'over the counter' at the newspaper's office declined, probably as a result of expanded geographical circulation, and this phenomenon could have been repeated with Wrexham newspapers.[3] Rural subscribers could either collect their copies from a local Post Office or, if they subscribed to either the *Advertiser* or the *Telegraph*, their copies would be sent to the nearest railway station for collection. Both the *Advertiser* and the *Telegraph* offered this service in conjunction with the Great Western Railway Company who issued half-penny labels to allow single copies to travel between two of their stations, with delivery by first train on Saturday.[4]

2. Post. Before the abolition of stamp duty in 1855, newspapers could be sent through the post to subscribers for no extra charge. This practice continued after 1855 in Wrexham though newspapers charged subscribers extra for postal delivery. As late as 1875, Wrexham newspapers were still posting out copies to subscribers in Liverpool and Manchester. Unsurprisingly, there were prob-

---

[3] David Ayerst, *Guardian, Biography of a Newspaper* (London, 1971), p. 83.

[4] 'Notice', *Wrexham Advertiser*, 13 January 1866, p. 2 and *Wrexham Telegraph*, 3 January 1866, p. 2.

lems with late deliveries, in 1872 to Mold[5], and again in 1875[6] and 1876.[7] The newspapers made clear that they accepted no responsibility for late or absent deliveries: they blamed the postal service.

3. Messengers. They were similar to the paperboys and girls of today or to the eighteenth-century newsmen who travelled to neighbouring towns and villages to deliver copies to subscribers and to sell the newspaper in the streets. Some newsmen covered extremely large routes: for example, one delivered the *Manchester Mercury* to Bolton, Wigan, Preston and Kendal.[8] In contrast, Wrexham's messengers covered only nearby villages. Messengers were especially used by the *Telegraph*, possibly to deliver copies in areas where they had few subscribers and therefore where it was not worth having an agent.

4. Hawkers. They were used to sell copies in the street and were usually young boys. Sir John Gibson, proprietor and editor of the Aberystwyth-based *Cambrian News* sold newspapers on the streets of his hometown of Lancaster in this way in the 1850s[9] and Jones commented that hawking allowed young boys to combine employment and education.[10] In 1896, the *Advertiser* sought boys to sell it on Saturday mornings, probably on the streets of Wrexham.[11]

---

[5] 'Post Office Delays', *Wrexham Advertiser*, 6 July 1872, p. 4.

[6] *Wrexham Advertiser*, 23 January 1875, p. 4.

[7] *Wrexham Advertiser*, 18 March 1876, p. 4.

[8] Cranfield, *Provincial Newspaper*, p. 193.

[9] Aled G. Jones, 'Sir John Gibson and the *Cambrian News*', *Ceredigion*, 12:2 (1994), p. 59.

[10] Aled G. Jones, *Powers of the Press: Newspapers and the Public in Nineteenth-Century England* (Aldershot, 1996), p. 139.

[11] *Wrexham Advertiser*, 19 September 1896, p. 8.

5. Agents. The most popular method of distribution was establishing a network of agents in Wrexham and throughout the locality to sell the newspaper in their own shops and/or organize distribution to subscribers. Ferdinand described agents as other business people who gained an income from discounts on the newspapers and a commission on advertising or other goods they sold on behalf of the newspaper.[12] Agents allowed newspapers to establish a readership outside the local area without charging for delivery. As well as selling the newspaper in their place of business or home, agents might also have organized deliveries to nearby villages without an agent to local subscribers. As two leading newspaper historians have noted, the existence of an agent in a particular location did not necessarily mean that the newspaper sold many copies in that area.[13] Wiles argued that lists of towns and counties with agents did not constitute convincing evidence of large circulation in the area as many newspapers indulged in bluffing and window-dressing.[14] In addition, if a newspaper attempted to circulate over a wide area and acquire a large number of geographically dispersed agents this could have placed a heavy strain on its resources. As with postal delivery, distribution problems could arise, leading to disgruntled customers switching to another newspaper. However, as a consequence of the growth of the urban and industrial society in Wales, commercial distribution through agents became the dominant newspaper distribution method in the late nineteenth and early twentieth centuries.[15]

---

[12] Ferdinand, 'Local Distribution Networks', p. 135.

[13] Cranfield, *Provincial Newspaper*, p. 203 and R. M. Wiles, *Freshest Advices: Early Provincial Newspapers in England* (Columbus, 1965), p. 113.

[14] Wiles, *Freshest Advices*, p. 113.

[15] Aled G. Jones, *Press, Politics and Society: a History of Journalism in Wales* (Cardiff, 1993), p. 105.

The impetus behind the establishment of agents in areas some distance from the newspaper's publishing office was almost certainly the development of the railway network in north Wales from the late 1840s, an occurrence described by Jones as 'the single most important contribution to the growth of a mass newspaper market'.[16] Preston pointed out that railways allowed a quicker and more efficient distribution network to be created, especially in rural areas, as newspapers could quickly be sent in bulk to agents in towns and villages with a railway station, including those some distance from the town of publication, and then be sent, probably by road, to agents in nearby settlements.[17] Wrexham newspapers were especially fortunate in that Wrexham was an important nodal point on the north Wales railway network and the growth of railways gave Wrexham's newspapers the opportunity to expand outside the immediate locality and aspire to be regional, as opposed to local, newspapers.

However, it does appear that trains were as unreliable in the late nineteenth century as they can be in the early twenty-first century. In March 1876, the *Advertiser* devoted an editorial to bewailing the impact that late trains were having on its sales. Its Mold agent reported that his delivery of *Advertisers* was over two hours late one week and consequently he did not sell as many as usual, a complaint shared by the newspaper's Ruthin agent whose delivery was nearly three hours late. The *Advertiser* appealed to its agents to provide them with evidence of late deliveries so it could complain to the railway company.[18] Another disadvantage of the railway system was that it allowed

---

[16] Jones, *Press, Politics and Society*, p. 106.

[17] Michael Preston, 'The Newcastle journal 1832-1950' in *Newspapers in the Northeast: the 'Fourth Estate' at work in Northumberland and Durham*, ed. by Peter Isaac (Wylam, 1999), pp. 112-39 (p. 120).

[18] *Wrexham Advertiser*, 18 March 1876, p. 4.

newspapers from other areas, both local and national, to seek new readers in Wrexham and its locality.

Agents and the Circulation Area

The existence of an agent in a certain location does not necessarily mean that the newspaper sold many copies in that area but it must have been selling some copies there. From 1850 until 1900, Wrexham's newspapers regularly published lists of their agents, their addresses and professions. This information can be used to plot each newspaper's area of circulation and show how this area altered over time.[19]

Wrexham's first two newspapers, the *Wrexham Registrar* and the *Wrexham Recorder* (both established in 1848) did not list any agents which suggests that their circulation was limited to Wrexham. The first agent listing appeared in the *Wrexham Advertiser* in December 1850.

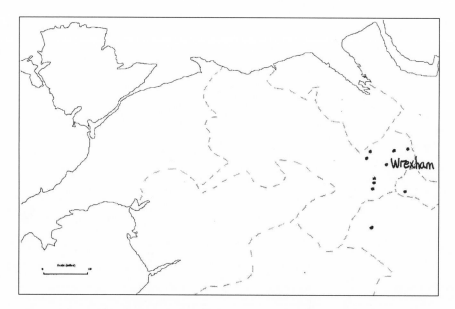

Fig. 1 Geographical Distribution of *Advertiser* Agents in December 1850.

---

[19] Ferdinand, 'Local Distribution Networks', p. 136.

Most of the agents were located close to Wrexham, so clearly the infant newspaper was focussing on developing its circulation in the Wrexham area. By 1854 the *Advertiser* had started to expand into the towns of north Wales and beyond: Ruthin, Holywell, Chester. By 1870 the *Advertiser* had four and a half times more agents than 1854 and had established a strong distribution network in north-east Wales.

The main impetus behind this was the development of railways. Railways allowed a quicker, more efficient and large distribution network to be established. Wrexham was an important nodal point on the north Wales railway system: the Wrexham, Mold & Connah's Quay line to the north, the coastal line to Holyhead from Chester, and lines south to Llangollen and down to Dolgellau. This railway system was built to support the north Wales coalfield, a densely populated area of north Wales, and it meant that in 1870 the *Advertiser* had its widest geographical area of circulation, with agents located up to fifty miles away. By 1900 the vast majority of *Advertiser* agents were

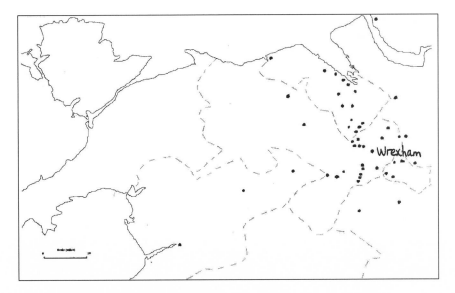

Fig. 2 Geographical Distribution of *Advertiser* Agents in 1870.

located within twenty miles of Wrexham and it appears that the newspaper's area of circulation had been reduced to focusing upon its town of publication.

It is possible that the geographical circulation of the newspaper could have been limited by its politics and its rivals. The *Advertiser*, like most of Wales, supported the Liberal party. To the west, the *Carnarvon & Denbigh Herald*, established in 1831 and with publishing offices in Caernarfon in the west and Denbigh in the east, had a wide circulation and also supported the Liberal party, as did the *Oswestry Advertiser* to the south. Over the border, Chester also had a number of long-established newspapers. Why should an English-speaking Liberal-supporting inhabitant of Caernarfon buy a Wrexham newspaper when he had a local newspaper that supported his political affiliation? It was its rivals, rather than its distribution network, that restricted the *Advertiser*'s circulation to the Wrexham area. It is possible that the *Advertiser* may not have wanted to spread into northwest Wales – to do so would have placed pressure on its distribution network as it would have needed to recruit extra agents in a

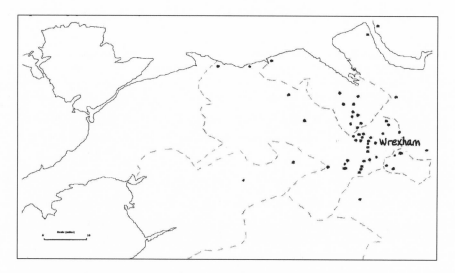

Fig. 3 Geographical Distribution of *Advertiser* Agents in 1900.

predominantly Welsh-speaking area. If the *Advertiser* had suffi-cient subscribers in the fast growing towns and villages of north-east Wales to turn a sufficient profit its owner may not have wished to expand its circulation area further.

Despite existing from 1855 to 1867, the *Wrexham Telegraph* (originally published as *The Wrexhamite*) only published agent listings between 1857 and 1863. In 1857, the *Telegraph* had a wide geographical distribution of agents for a newspaper that had only existed for two years and it appears that it was focusing on de-veloping its readership in the larger settlements of north-east Wales: the towns of Denbigh, Ruthin, Holywell, and over the border in Chester. By 1863, the *Telegraph*'s number of agents had fallen to fourteen (compared to fifty-five for the *Advertiser* in 1866) and focused again on towns. The *Telegraph* did not have agents in the mining villages near Wrexham; this could be be-cause the *Telegraph* was a Conservative newspaper and therefore unlikely to be purchased by working class miners, or just an ac-ceptance that it was not likely to be successful in those areas so no effort was made to gain agents there. Instead it focused on gaining agents in the towns of north-east Wales and, as its edito-rial said, 'through agents and correspondents identifying our-selves as much with Mold, or Denbigh, or Ruthin and the other considerable places as with Wrexham'.[20]

This identification was formally acknowledged in October 1863 when the newspaper changed its title from the *Wrexham Telegraph* to the *Denbighshire and Flintshire Telegraph*. Its geo-graphical circulation may have been due largely to its Conserva-tive politics – an issue further explored with the geographical circulation of the *Telegraph*'s Conservative successor, the *Wrex-ham Guardian*.

---

[20] 'To Our Readers and the Public', *Wrexham Telegraph*, 2 January 1864, p. 4.

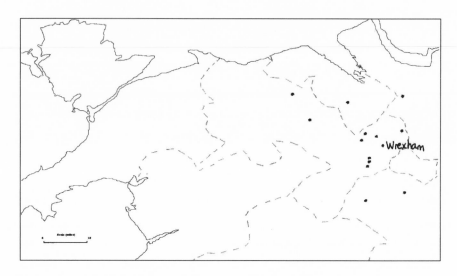

Fig. 4 Geographical Distribution of *Telegraph* Agents in 1857.

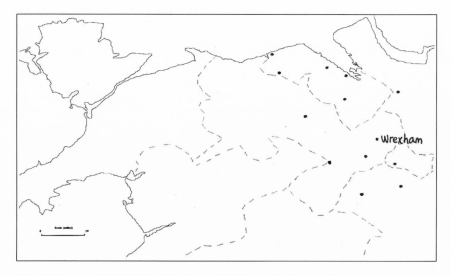

Fig. 5 Geographical Distribution of *Telegraph* Agents in 1863.

From its creation in 1869 as a Conservative response to the Liberal successes in Wales in the 1868 general election, the *Guardian* established a wide distribution network including the main towns of north Wales, and gained agents as far away as Abergele, Llanrwst, Bangor and Dolgellau. The *Guardian*, it seems, was trying to establish a regional network across all of north Wales and the border area, from Holyhead to Chester and Shrewsbury. It also followed the *Advertiser* practice of establishing agents in the north Wales coalfield, along the railway lines. By 1875, the *Guardian*'s network of agents had continued to expand westwards into west Flintshire, and along the north Wales coast as far as Holyhead. However, by 1890 the agents in Holyhead, Caernarfon, Bangor, and Llandudno had disappeared and the *Guardian* had a distribution pattern similar to that of the *Advertiser*, focusing in on towns and villages near to Wrexham and the larger towns of north-east Wales. The only area where it had agents that the *Advertiser* did not was along the north-east Wales coast, in Flint, Holywell, and Connah's Quay.

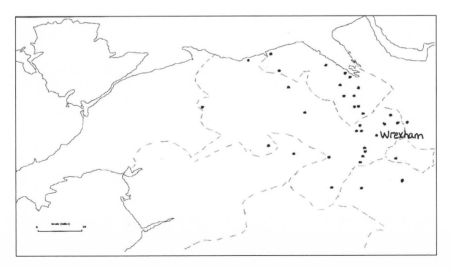

Fig. 6 Geographical Distribution of *Guardian* Agents in 1869.

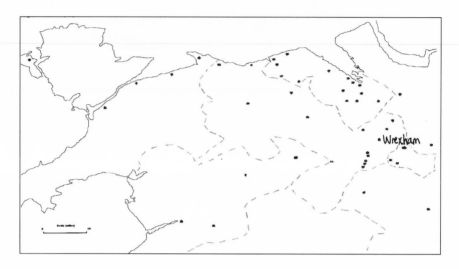

Fig. 7 Geographical Distribution of *Guardian* Agents in 1875.

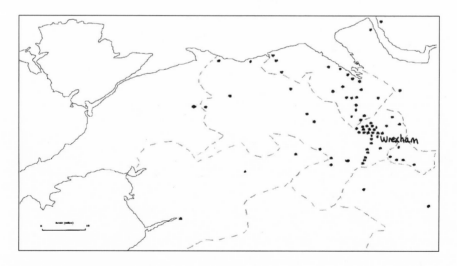

Fig. 8 Geographical Distribution of *Guardian* Agents in August 1890.

There are two possible explanations for this expansion and then contraction in circulation areas: firstly that the *Guardian* may have sought to be a regional north Wales newspaper establishing agents throughout north Wales before realising that it had over extended itself and scaled back. The second reason is politics. As a Conservative newspaper, the *Guardian* had fewer rivals than the Liberal *Advertiser* with the same political beliefs (only the *North Wales Chronicle* in Bangor). Consequently its circulation was less hemmed in by competition than the *Advertiser*. With fewer Conservatives in north Wales to purchase the newspaper it needed to circulate over a wider area in order to gain sufficient buyers. Between 1869 and 1878, the *Guardian* was financially supported by some of north Wales's leading Conservatives, such as the Hon. George Kenyon and Sir Watkin Williams Wynn, as a political mouthpiece for their party and to spread the message of Toryism. In 1878, heavily in debt, the *Guardian* was sold and had to survive without a subsidy from its political masters. The realization that it now had to survive on its own merits as a commercial enterprise could have forced the new owners to reorganize the distribution network. In addition, by 1887, the *Guardian*'s owner was probably Sir Evan Morris, Wrexham's mayor, who is likely to have been more concerned with promoting Conservatism in Wrexham itself rather than the whole of north Wales.

Wrexham had a fourth newspaper which used agents: the *Wrexham Free Press*. In 1870, *Free Press* agents were predominantly located near to Wrexham in eastern Denbighshire. Maybe the *Free Press* deliberately limited its circulation to Wrexham; unlike all the other Wrexham newspapers it did not have a long regional subtitle that tried to include every other north Wales county. Unfortunately, the newspaper only published agent listings for 1870 so it is unknown whether its agent network expanded or contracted in later years.

Both the *Advertiser* and the *Guardian* could be bought in London, the *Advertiser* from 1885 and the *Guardian* from 1890. While only a small number of copies would have been sold in London, it does show that the Welsh community in London maintained an interest in the homeland.

Agents' Professions

Was selling newspapers the agents' main profession or was selling newspapers merely a method of raising extra money for their main business? Cranfield commented that those involved in the book or communication trades such as booksellers, stationers, postmasters, and innkeepers were a popular choice to be newspaper agents, but also that newspapers did employ agents who had no obvious link either to the book, printing, or communication trades. He listed as examples of agents: writing masters, a livery lace weaver, a snuff-maker, a tobacconist, a peruke-maker (wig-maker), a salter, an engraver, a bell-founder, an attorney, a surgeon, and a governor of a workhouse.[21] Wiles found a clockmaker and a barber amongst *Leeds Mercury* agents in 1725[22] and Ferdinand discovered that a baker, a tallow chandler, and a dealer in rum sold the *Hampshire Chronicle* in the 1770s.[23] Could Wrexham's newspaper agent listings possibly contain any more unusual occupations than these?

In the following statistics, the book trade is defined as including newsagents, booksellers, printers, reporters, stamp offices, and stationers, while shopkeepers are defined as including grocers. In cases where agents were listed as having more than one profession, the first one has been used. The occupations of some agents were not listed so trade directories and the census were used to attempt to discover them. Unfortunately, only a small

---

[21] Cranfield, *Provincial Newspapers*, p. 198.
[22] Wiles, *Freshest Advices*, p. 117.
[23] Ferdinand, 'Local Distribution Networks', p. 142.

number of agents' professions were discovered this way and consequently a category of 'unknown' has been used.

Surprisingly, the dominant occupation in the agent listing in the early years of the Wrexham press was not the book trade. Of the ten *Advertiser* agents in 1850, only two were involved in the book trade and five of them were shopkeepers. Four years later, thirty-one per cent of *Advertiser* agents were involved in the book trade, fewer than the thirty-eight per cent of shopkeepers, and therefore it was shopkeepers not booksellers, printers, stationers, or newsagents who were primarily responsible for distributing Wrexham's newspapers in their early years. Upon closer analysis, this is to be expected. Villages would have usually had a shopkeeper but not necessarily a bookseller or newsagent so shopkeepers were best placed to distribute and sell newspapers, particularly in smaller settlements. The number of shopkeepers engaged as agents fell as the newspapers became established and increasingly turned to book-trade professions as distributors.

By 1866 the book-trade professions made up over half of the *Advertiser*'s agents, but from then on, this percentage fell, reaching thirty per cent by 1900. This is a pattern repeated with other newspapers. The *Telegraph* and the *Guardian* did not have the *Advertiser*'s initial reliance on shopkeepers, with book-trade professions initially making up half of *Telegraph* agents and over two-thirds of *Guardian* agents. After such a heavy reliance on book-trade professions, there was a decline to less than half as the *Guardian* began to use W. H. Smith railway bookstalls as agents. First and second class rail travel opened up a new market for reading material. Although the first railway bookstall was opened in 1841 in Fenchurch Street station and operated by Horace Marshall & Son, it was the name W. H. Smith & Son that became synonymous with railway bookstalls. W. H. Smith gained its first tender to operate a railway bookstall in 1861[24] and rapid expansion in the 1870s meant that 'as travellers passed through city stations and country transfer points, they never failed to see the familiar W. H. Smith stalls'.[25] The bookstall business expanded nationally from 35 bookstalls in 1851 to 290 in 1870, 540 in 1880, and 615 in 1894.[26] As railway companies increased their rental charges for bookstalls, W. H. Smith began to move into towns and cities, marking the start of a presence on the high street. Their operation in Wales began in December 1861 when it opened a bookstall at Neath railway station. Two years later W. H. Smith acquired the contract to sell newspapers and books at GWR stations.[27] GWR lines in north Wales included the Ruabon-Llangollen, Corwen-Llangollen, Bala-Dolgellau, and the Chester-Shrewsbury lines. By 1890 W. H. Smith had railway bookstalls in Corwen, Denbigh, Dolgellau, Ruabon, Rhosllanerchrugog, and Rhyl. Both the *Advertiser* and the *Guardian* used W. H. Smith railway bookstalls as agents. The *Guardian* did so to reach towns far from Wrexham – Bangor, Caernarfon, Llandudno, and Holyhead. By 1890 W. H. Smith made up thirteen percent of *Guardian* agents and by 1900 they made up fourteen per cent of *Advertiser* agents. The *Free Press* used mainly the book trade and an unusually high percentage of shopkeepers to distribute issues, possibly because it was established by Wrexham tradesmen to promote their goods.

Amongst other occupations, the *Telegraph* was particularly reliant on messengers to distribute copies to the villages surrounding Wrexham between 1857 and 1861 and, although the

---

[24] Charles Wilson, *First with the News: a History of W.H. Smith 1792-1972* (London, 1985), p. 112.

[25] Richard Altick, *The English Common Reader: a Social History of the Mass Reading Public, 1800-1900*, 2nd ed. (Columbus, 1998), p. 301.

[26] Wilson, *First with the News*, p. 182.

[27] Wilson, *First with the News*, p. 120.

Guardian's agent listings never included any messengers, in 1891 the newspaper stated that it was distributed by 'numerous boys'.[28] As mentioned earlier, Wrexham newspapers used the Royal Mail to send copies to distant subscribers so it is not surprising to see Post Masters and Mistresses acting as agents, making up an average of ten per cent. The *Advertiser* was especially reliant on these postal agents and they made up thirteen per cent of agents in 1870. Cranfield argues that Post Offices were unsuitable for newspaper distribution[29] but this appears not to have been true for Wrexham newspapers. Wrexham's newspapers used publicans as agents, but only in small numbers. The advertising agents, first appearing in 1866, were all located in Liverpool and London and their main involvement with Wrexham newspapers was probably the collection of advertising and they sold only a small number of copies.

Wrexham's newspapers were also sold by a clerk, a coachman, a waggoner, a painter and paperhanger, a Baptist Minister, a mortgage broker, an insurance agent, a tobacconist, a saddler, a basket-maker, a toy dealer, a retailer of beer, a miller, an ink-maker, a chemist, a draper, a brick manufacturer, a ship chandler and broker, a nail maker, a cheese factor, a joiner and carpenter, a retired farmer, an eleven year old boy, a fitter, and a coroner. While a number of these descriptions seem unusual for a newspaper agent, perhaps it is Mr Edwards, the Coroner of Holt who would be considered the least likely person to be a seller of newspapers. Often these other categories of profession made up a significant percentage of agents, nearly a quarter of *Advertiser* agents in 1854. Most of them were located in villages without a book-trade professional, such as James Williams the basket-maker in Cefn Mawr and Mr Scott the ink maker in Queensferry. These agents may only have been recruited because the

---

[28] *Wrexham Guardian*, 18 July 1891, p. 1.
[29] Cranfield, *Provincial Newspaper*, p. 201.

village lacked a book-trade professional and therefore the most obvious candidate to sell newspapers was not available. The newspaper proprietors may have been forced to settle for whoever was willing to sell the newspaper and collect advertising to be their local agent. Some were located in the larger towns and villages that already had one or more book-trade agents, like Mr Davies, the Wrexham hairdresser, and Mr Lloyd, the Ruthin chemist. Apart from being able to boast of an increasing number of agents, it is unclear why newspapers would have recruited agents from other professions when they already had a book-trade agent in town.

In addition, despite trawling through censuses and trade directories, it has not been possible to identify the occupations of some agents. It is unlikely that these agents were involved in the book or shopkeeping trades as they would have been listed as such. Instead, were they engaged in these unusual professions? If so, these other professions played a more significant role in newspaper distribution than originally suspected: for example, in 1890 the unknown and other professions made up sixteen per cent of *Guardian* agents and twenty per cent of *Advertiser* agents in 1900.

Although the vast majority of these agents were men, Wrexham's newspapers had a total of forty-one female agents, two of whom acted for more than one newspaper. Only a quarter of these had their profession noted in the agents listings and the professions of a further quarter can be deduced from trade directories. Therefore over half of these female agents were in trade. Of the other half, it is difficult to discover their profession. However, the census does tell us that some of them were wives, for example Mrs Jackson, *Advertiser* agent, in Gwersyllt, was the wife of a rail labourer, and was replaced as agent by Mrs Simpson, wife of a coalman; Mrs Evans, *Guardian* agent, was the wife of a carter. These wives probably sold odd copies and accepted advertisements as a way of bringing in small sums of money for their family. They were not professional agents and therefore it is not surprising that the tenure of these wives as agents was usually short.

Little is known about the relationship between Wrexham newspapers and their agents. We do know that in 1890 the *Guardian* stated that it had received reports about its agents delivering rival newspapers instead of the *Guardian* when the *Guardian* was what had been ordered, and appealed to readers for further information. Some newspapers actually acted as agents for their rivals. This was not unusual: Cranfield comments 'one can only assume that their willingness to act in this capacity stemmed less from a disinterested generosity than a desire to keep an eye upon one another's activities'. [30] Charles Bayley, part-owner of the *Advertiser*, sold the *Guardian* in his Oswestry bookshop from 1875, and in Wrexham the *Advertiser* was sold by Railton Potter, owner of the *Telegraph* and by Hughes & Son, whose earlier newspaper had been effectively put out of business by the *Advertiser*'s owners' earlier newspaper; the *Guardian* was sold at the offices of the *Flintshire Observer* and the *Llangollen Advertiser*. Several booksellers acted as agents for more than one Wrexham newspaper. In fact, Mold booksellers Pring & Price acted as agents for all four – the *Advertiser*, *Telegraph*, *Guardian*, and *Free Press* – and were also a publishing office for both the *Advertiser* and the *Guardian*. It is unfortunate that the surviving small collection of Wrexham newspaper company records makes no reference to their relationship with their agents.

Between 1850 and 1900 the railway significantly altered the distribution system of Wrexham's newspapers. In 1850, the method of delivering each issue was relatively haphazard, but by

---

[30] Cranfield, *Provincial Newspaper*, p. 198.

the end of the century it had become far more co-ordinated and cohesive. The railway system was still in its infancy when the first Wrexham newspapers were produced but as the network expanded, so newspapers could be delivered to agents in towns far away from Wrexham. This was a great advance for the newspapers themselves especially as they could receive advertising and even local news from agents beyond the Wrexham area. Added to this expansion of the railway, the introduction of bookstalls on railway stations was significant.

Of all the methods of distribution, it was the use of agents which vouchsafed the widest coverage and was almost certainly the most cost effective. Messengers and hawkers could only provide a local service and subscription collection was purely on an individual basis. Posting single copies was expensive and unreliable. By using agents, newspapers were able to reach readers far away from their publication centres.

Expansion and contraction of the network was caused by different factors, such as the political bias of each newspaper. The Tory supporting *Guardian* was able to spread into towns far away from Wrexham, whilst its Liberal rival concentrated its agents on the industrial heartlands of Wrexham and north-east Wales. This paper has also demonstrated the eclectic mix of agents used by newspapers, particularly in the later years, to distribute each issue. Important and as seemingly obvious as the book trade was in the dissemination of news, it was never the sole, and often not even the main, outlet. In towns, the book trade was an obvious agency for selling newspapers, but in the rural areas where there were no such outlets, the newspapers turned to shopkeepers and others whose jobs brought them into daily contact with villagers to provide the service – the miller and the tobacconist would certainly have come into this category – but possibly not the nail maker and the coroner! Their participation in newspaper distribution has yet to be explained.

'The retail newsagents of Lancashire ARE ON STRIKE': The Dispute between the Lancashire Retail Newsagents and the 'Northern Wholesalers', February-September 1914

STEPHEN COLCLOUGH

Newsagents, arise, for drudgery is over...
Arise, newsagents and be slaves no more
Long, long have been the hours that you have laboured,
Small, small have been the wages you received;
Wholesalers the cream, you with the skim are favoured,
Now for the cream strike out, don't be deceived.
Strike the fatal blow,
Let your fetters go.
Arise newsagents! for your day has come.

THOMAS SHEPLEY'S 'ARISE, NEWSAGENTS!' appeared in *The National Newsagent* on 11 April 1914 as part of a article on 'The Great Fight Against Injustice' that detailed the latest events in the dispute between the retail newsagents of Lancashire and the wholesalers that supplied them, which many newspapers reported as 'the Newsagents' carriage fight in the North'.[1] This essay outlines the major events of this dispute and places them in the context of the distribution of newspapers on the eve of the First World War.

From the moment that W. H. Smith (1792-1865) and the Manchester wholesaler Abel Heywood gave evidence to the Newspaper Stamp Committee in 1851, the transport of daily and weekly newspapers by train from London to Manchester began to fas-

---

[1] *The National Newsagent*, 11 April 1914, p. 8.

cinate Victorian commentators.[2] Both of these companies remained particularly important to the distribution of texts in and around Manchester in 1914. From the late 1840s onwards, the railway bookstalls of W. H. Smith & Son played an important role in distributing texts throughout England and Wales, but because Manchester was such a significant market the firm set up a separate wholesale warehouse in the city in 1859. By the end of the nineteenth century, as the number of halfpenny papers and other cheap periodicals increased, Smith & Son found it increasingly difficult to deal with both retail and wholesale at their stalls and the firm increased the number of provincial wholesale houses that it owned. By March 1914 there were seventeen, all largely independent of head office. The development of the provincial wholesale house system signals that by the early twentieth century the railway bookstall was no longer the most important site for the retailing of newspapers and other cheap texts. These were now also sold by back-street newsagents, who combined the sale of halfpenny and penny papers (such as the *Daily Mail* and the *Daily Herald*) with other goods, and in Smith's own high street shops.[3] Most of these texts were still printed in London. Some were delivered direct from the publisher to the newsagent via 'syndicate trains' that left the capital in the early hours. However, despite this direct supply, which was handled by special depots such as the *Daily Herald* depot in London Road, Manchester, the majority of texts sold by the Lancashire newsagents still passed through the hands of a major wholesaler such as Heywood or Smith. As J. D. Symon noted in *The Press and Its Story* (1914), many of the bundles of newspapers and magazines constructed at Smith's wholesale house on the Strand, and in the packing vans attached to trains

---

[2] *Report From the Select Committee on Newspaper Stamps* (London, 1851), pp. 371-89, pp. 420-37.

[3] Charles Wilson, *First with the News: the History of W. H. Smith, 1792-1972* (London, 1985), pp. 208-18.

leaving London in the early hours of the morning, were destined for retailers in the north of England in much the same way as forty years earlier.[4]

In 1914 *Newspaper World* argued that the wholesalers were powerful enough to dictate prices to both publisher and retailer, but one sign of the increased power and importance of the small retailer at this time was the growth of retail newsagents' associations, such as the United Kingdom Federation of Newsagents (UKF) that became involved in the 1914 dispute.[5] Although it was too small to represent the whole of the British Isles at this time, the UKF was expanding, and it had the use of a powerful propaganda tool, the weekly *National Newsagent, Bookseller, Stationer & Fancy Trades Journal*, which provides the best account of the UKF's activities during this period. The issue for 4 January 1913 claimed that during the past year it had been particularly influential in obtaining good rates from the publishers, such as 8*d* for twelve copies of some of the penny papers, and in establishing a national timetable of publication so that newsagents received periodicals on the day before they were due for sale.[6] At the beginning of the following year the *National Newsagent* was celebrating new terms with Harmsworth's Amalgamated Press. It claimed that every agent within a fifty-mile radius of Manchester was now receiving Amalgamated Press publications at three farthings per copy for the penny papers and 'all the halfpenny pubs at 13 for 4½*d*'. Another article, on the possibility of charging for delivery noted an increasing dissatisfaction with the terms offered by the wholesale trade, who it was claimed 'take their 15 per cent, rob us

---

[4] J. D. Symon, *The Press and Its Story* (London, 1914), pp. 43-5. For an earlier description of this process, see 'How we get our Newspapers', *All the Year Round*, 25 December 1875, pp. 305-09.

[5] *Newspaper World*, 2 May 1914, p. 15.

[6] *National Newsagent* (hereafter *NN*), 4 January 1913, p. 2

of the 13th copy, [and] wrong us on the returns'.[7] Throughout 1914 there were many similar articles that suggest a deep mistrust of both wholesalers and street vendors (such as newsboys) who were thought to have often combined to rob the back-street trader of sales. The *NN*, as the *National Newsagent* tended to refer to itself, is the best source of information about the 1914 'carriage fight in the north', and this essay is particular concerned with the way it was reported in its pages, but it also draws upon a number of other trade papers and national dailies in order to map out and explore the events of February to September 1914.[8]

In February 1914 there were about 4,000 newsagents in the Manchester area who were being supplied by five main wholesalers: Abel Heywood & Son, John Heywood Ltd, W. H. Smith & Son (who still owned a major warehouse in Manchester), F. & G. Pollard and Edwards & Bryning (the last two based in Oldham and Rochdale respectively). The dispute referred to in the poem 'Arise Newsagents!' had begun on 14 February 1914 when John Heywood Ltd 'in conjunction with the other Northern Wholesalers' sent out a circular to the trade that detailed a new set of carriage charges that were to come into operation on 23 February (See Fig. 1). It explained that within four miles of Manchester Town Hall the charge for delivery was to be 1s. per week, whereas those newsagents working outside that radius 'and within 50 miles of the Manchester Town Hall' were to be charged on a scale running from 1s. per week, on a weekly order of less than 20s., through to 2s. 6d. on orders of 81s. and above. On top of this a 'collecting fee of 6d. per week' and a 'Collecting Charge of 2½%' was to be made 'in addition to the Carriage (minimum charge 6d.), on all split or incomplete orders for weekly periodicals'. It also noted that these charges were deemed necessary because of 'in-

---

[7]   *NN*, 21 February 1914, p.12; *NN*, 31 Jan 1914, p. 4.

[8]   Both *The Daily Herald* and *Newspaper World* covered the dispute in some detail.

creased Railway Charges, Working Expenses, &c'.[9] Because this circular was issued in 'conjunction with the other Northern Wholesalers', those who supported the dispute often referred to this group as 'the Manchester ring of wholesalers'.[10]

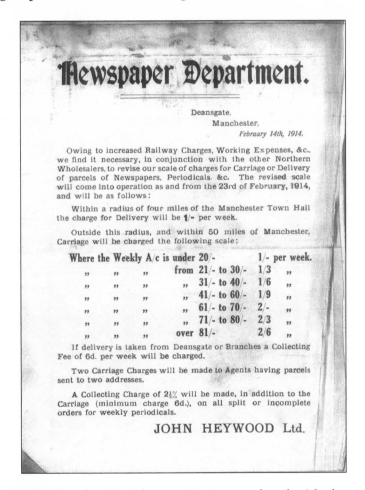

Fig. 1 Trade Circular, 24 February 1914, reproduced with the permission of the W. H. Smith Archives.

---

[9] 'Circular from Newspaper Department, John Heywood Ltd, 14 Feb 1914', W. H. Smith Archive, Swindon (hereafter WHSA), A298. I am particularly grateful to Gail Collingburn of the WHS archive for her kind assistance in locating documents on the dispute.

[10] *Newspaper World*, 2 May 1914, p. 15.

As a result of this notice, the Manchester branch of the UKF, which was still celebrating the new terms negotiated with the Amalgamated Press, went on the offensive. The *National News-agent* for 21 February reproduced the 'notice sent out by the Manchester wholesalers' as part of an article explaining that the Lancashire agents were 'in Revolt'. It argued that the current maximum charge for delivery was 1s. per week and that the 'extra 2½%' on 'split or incomplete periodical sheets' was an attempt to stop the newsagents' dealing directly with the publishers through 'special agents'. Groups such as the Manchester and District Newsagents' Protection Society organized meetings urging those affected to organize deliveries to their shops from the 'Special Depots', using the additional 1s. 6d., which they would otherwise have to pay to the wholesalers, to hire lads to 'get the papers home'. The *NN* itself urged the agents to 'receive papers under protest' deducting the extra carriage from their bills. Before the new charges had even come into operation, however, it was clear that the newsagents would not be able to maintain their current supplies by the 'Special Depots' alone, and the *National Newsagent* was already hoping that another London wholesaler would enter the picture in an attempt to poach business from the existing wholesale houses.[11] How the supply of newspapers was going to be maintained during a dispute, or the current set of wholesalers replaced in order to free retailers from 'the ring', dominated debate over the next few months.

During the following days and weeks the public meetings came thick and fast. On 17 February, 100 out of the 115 members of the South East Lancashire County Federation of Newsagents met. Two days later it was the turn of the Cheshire Newsagents' Federation to discuss the 'carriage protest'. Most significant, however, was the 'mass meeting' that took place at the Crosby Hotel in

---

[11] *NN*, 21 February 1914, pp. 4-5.

Manchester on 18 February. This meeting, which included members of the Sale, Droylsden, Ashton-under-Lyne, Stalybridge, Openshaw, Clayton, Denton, Heywood, Hyde and Middleton branches, pledged 'not to pay any carriage whatsoever' after 23 February as a protest against the 'unreasonable and exorbitant' new charges. By 25 February, 400 newsagents had signed up to this proposal. The same meeting also adopted a resolution that this was 'an opportune time for the formation of a co-operative supply'. On the following day a deputation of four newsagents, the head of the National Carter's Union and representatives of the wholesalers met at the Queen's Hotel, where it was announced that the imposition of the new charges had been suspended until 16 March, thus giving time for the various newsagents' federations to decide on the mood of their members.[12]

The pages of the *National Newsagent* reveal something of the debate that was going on at a national level during this time. One correspondent wrote in suggesting that the Lancashire Agents should become their own wholesalers; another that the real issue was charging the public for delivery. The latter complained that the smaller shops lost a great deal of business to street newsvendors who were supplied direct from the publishers and provided an important argument in favour of using a wholesaler rather than getting texts via the 'direct supply' method, which forced the newsagent to deal with 'a dozen different deliveries' per day.[13] The author was optimistic about the wholesalers' ability to stop the trade to street vendors in order that carriage costs could be recouped via the newsagents' instigation of a delivery charge. However, the *NN*'s own editorials tended to argue that the wholesalers were profiting unfairly from better terms with the publishers which were never passed on: 'we know papers to be put on the market which could have been priced at 6d. per dozen to the re-

---

[12] *NN*, 28 February 1914, p. 3.
[13] *NN*, 28 February 1914, p. 16.

tailer and then allowed the wholesaler a fair profit, and yet these papers were given no advantage on the wholesalers' sheets'.[14]

During the first week of March the *National Newsagent* carried a number of reports from the various newsagents' federations in Lancashire, noting that they were determined not to make 'any compromise with the wholesalers on the increase'.[15] The 'Manchester Notes' section of the paper encouraged the newsagents to buy their supply of *The Daily Herald* (which was supporting the dispute) from Sam Brierley at 24a London Road, Manchester. The *Daily Herald* and Brierley, who was responsible for the Manchester column, were to play an increasingly important role in the dispute over the coming months. Indeed, in the next issue this column drew attention to the fact that Brierley had joined together with George Brady, a former employee of Heywood's, to become a joint wholesale and retail newsagent.[16] By mid-March 1914, the *National Newsagent* was able to boast that the dispute had the support of more than 1,000 Lancashire newsagents and that the wholesalers had found it impossible to charge both the new percentage on incomplete sheets and the 6d. collecting charge.[17]

The rhetorical strategies used by the *National Newsagent* to persuade more newsagents to join the strike during this period are particularly interesting. In its editorial of 21 March it argued that the wholesalers were making the demands of 'a twentieth-century pharaoh' while the retailers were said to be 'fighting the fight of the little Mafekings'.[18] The idea of the wholesaler as 'tyrant' and the newsagent as 'slave' was also being used in Shepley's poetry which became more and more a feature of the *NN*'s

[14] *NN*, 7 March, p. 3.
[15] See also *NN*, 7 March 1914, pp. 12, 15, 21.
[16] *NN*, 14 March 1914, p. 4.
[17] *NN*, 21 March 1914, p. 4; 14 March 1914, p. 4.
[18] *NN*, 21 March 1914, p. 4.

coverage as the dispute progressed.[19] At other times Manchester's long history of political radicalism was invoked. One of the earliest accounts of the dispute encouraged those involved to 'Remember Peterloo! Remember your fathers who faced fire and prison for justice and fair play'.[20]

Signs of modern day radicalism, such as placards and posters, were also mobilised to publicise and encourage the dispute. On 21 March 1914 the *National Newsagent* encouraged retailers to cut out and display the full-page 'appeal to the public' included in its pages (see Fig. 2).[21]

This and many of the posters issued by the *Daily Herald* encouraged support from those involved in trade union activity and labour politics. Indeed, such was the importance of the *Herald's* posters that it was claimed that those newsagents supplied with copies of the paper from the major wholesalers often found that they had been removed.[22] A number of these posters, with slogans such as 'Northern Carters Support the Newsagents' and 'Rebel Newsagents Great March Past', can be seen in a photograph that appeared in the *National Newsagent* in April 1914.[23] Some local branches of the UKF also produced their own posters and circulars. For example, the South-East Lancashire County Federation produced a poster addressed 'to the public and trade unionists' asking them 'NOT to support any shop not showing this poster'.[24] A similar poster issued by the Stockport Newsagents' Defence Committee in March 1914 refers to the new carriage charges and to the opening of 'Blackleg

---

[19] See for example Shepley's 'How Th' Wholesalers Were Beaten', *NN*, 30 May 1914, p. 3.

[20] *NN*, 21 February, p. 4.

[21] *NN*, 21 March 1914, p. 21.

[22] 'The Ring Will Be Smashed: "Herald" Posters Lost, Stolen, or Strayed', *Daily Herald*, 14 April 1914, p. 4.

[23] *NN*, 4 April 1914, p. 5.

[24] *NN*, 28 March 1914, p. 4.

shops' as part of the wholesalers' 'attempt to crush the local news-agents'.[25] Both an article in the *Daily Herald* and an open letter to the UKF from the Stockport and District Newsagents' Society confirm that 'Messrs Abel Heywood' had tried to end the dispute 'before anything had really happened' by opening several shops in Stockport in March 1914.[26] As the use of the *NN* to disseminate information about the dispute and the display of *Daily Herald* posters suggests, the newsagents involved in this dispute knew how to manipulate and use the various media forms that they distributed to publicize their cause.

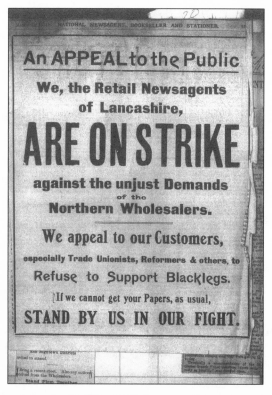

Fig. 2 An Appeal to the Public 21 February 1914, reproduced with the permission of the W. H. Smith Archives.

[25] WHSA, A298.

[26] *NN*, 18 April 1914, p. 12; 'The Newsagents' Fight', *Daily Herald*, 23 March 1914, p. 2.

The next series of big meetings in support of the strike took place in Manchester on 24-26 March 1914. The first, a 'mass meeting' at Milton Hall, was followed by a smaller one at the Mecca Café in Pall Mall where 200 newsagents who had decided not to pay their bills gathered to hear the editor of the *NN*, Fred Easton, explain his plans for them to be supplied by a new London wholesaler (the 'Federation supply' plan). The following day, these same newsagents, now carrying *Daily Herald* posters, gathered in Stevenson Square to form a procession that sent out 'a great shout of defiance' as it passed the much-lampooned 'White House' of Abel Heywood and Sons on its way to the Crosby Hotel. Once there, they publicly declared that instead of paying their accounts to the wholesalers they would use the money to help establish the Federation supply.[27] That evening there were meetings in Oldham and Manchester at which Sam Brierley, who was now leader of the strike committee, spoke and Federation order sheets were distributed. The *NN* declared 24 March 'Federation Day', but it is important to note that the supply of newspapers that was put in place at this time was always described as a temporary measure via an 'Emergency Depot'.[28]

The meeting at Milton Hall also took some important decisions. Those in attendance agreed to adopt a proposal by which all the newsagents 'covering a radius of fifty miles round Manchester' would 'refuse to purchase any stationery or fancy goods whatever from any wholesale newsagents'.[29] They also hoped that other members of the UK Federation would make this a national campaign.[30] This was a well thought out strategy. As

[27] 'Newsagents and Heywood's', *Daily Herald*, 26 March 1914, p. 3; *NN*, 28 March 1914, p. 4.

[28] *NN*, 21 March 1914, p. 17.

[29] *NN*, 28 March 1914, p. 3.

[30] 'Is it to be "Down Placards"? Hint of a National Newsagents Strike', *Daily Herald*, 1 April 1914, p. 5.

Charles Wilson has shown, sales of stationery were particularly important to the financial well-being of Smith's provincial wholesale houses during this period.[31] One effect of this strategy was that alternative suppliers of stationery, such as William Ritchie, began to advertise their wares in the *National Newsagent*. By late April 1914 there were reports of new wholesale stationers opening accounts in Cheshire.[32] This meeting also resolved 'to give a week's notice' to the wholesalers if the new carriage rates persisted and to switch their trade to the Federation supply.[33]

For the next few months the establishment of this supply was at the heart of the campaign to defeat the 'ring'. The *NN* for 28 March included a 'final appeal to Lancashire' by Easton, which informed the retailers that 'the Federation agreement' was ready and waiting to be signed at the Mecca Café. He promised that once a new Federation depot was established in Manchester 'all the difficulties of local supply would disappear'. However, in order for this supply to become a reality, the Federation firm, Willing & Co., whose identity had still not been made public at this stage, were demanding a guarantee that they would get at least £1,000 worth of orders per week (known as the £1,000 'deposit'). Easton urged even those who had not yet broken with the ring to contribute to this sum. Some shops were now without their supplies and those still receiving deliveries were asked to give local papers in order to keep them in business.[34]

On April 4 the *National Newsagent* published several accounts by newsagents in the Manchester area declaring that they were satisfied with the Federation supply at the 'Emergency Depot', alongside a request that all those involved in the dispute meet at Brierley's *Daily Herald* Depot on London Road, which was now

---

[31] Wilson, *First With the News*, pp. 222-5.

[32] *NN*, 18 April 1914, p.5; 25 April 1914, p. 10.

[33] *NN*, 28 March 1914, p. 7.

[34] *NN*, 28 March 1914, pp. 7-8

the Strike Committee HQ. From there they were to proceed to the railway station in order to meet the 9.35pm 'federation train' which was carrying the Sunday papers for those newsagents (such as Brierley) whose supply had been stopped, or who had switched to the Federation.[35] The next issue covered these events in some detail under the headline 'the Federation Depot a Reality', giving a whole page over to a 'flash-photograph' of the Manchester agents meeting the train.[36] However, despite Brierley's optimistic account of that night, which included much cigar smoking after the newspapers had been delivered to each shop using a hired furniture van, the dispute had clearly entered a difficult phase. Heywood's, and possibly some of the other wholesalers, were refusing to deal with those customers who had transferred part of their order to the Federation depot. Both the *Daily Herald* and the *NN* reproduced letters in which the wholesalers declared that 'we must have the whole of your order or none at all'.[37] Not surprisingly, this led the *NN* to accuse the wholesalers of operating as a 'ring', because 'if any agent was dissatisfied with the service of "A" he would be prevented from transferring his business to "B", "C" or "D"'. It argued that the only way to break this combination of the wholesalers was to open up a new 'source of supply'.[38] However, there was clearly some nervousness amongst those in charge of the Federation supply about whether it could handle large numbers of new orders, and the newsagents were asked not to 'overload the new depot'.[39]

---

[35] *NN*, 4 April 1914, pp. 5-6.

[36] *NN*, 11 April 1914, pp. 8, 10.

[37] *NN*, 4 April 1914, p. 6; 'Newsagents and Heywood's: How the Fight Goes on in the North', *Daily Herald*, 2 April 1914, p. 3; 'The Fight Against the Newspaper Ring', *Daily Herald*, 11 April 1914, p. 2.

[38] *NN*, 4 April 1914, p. 16.

[39] *NN*, 11 April 1914, p. 4.

These letters from the northern wholesalers, which also included a suggestion that the newsagents would have to pay in full for any order that had already been dispatched, were clearly intended to intimidate anyone participating, or thinking of participating, in the dispute. That the wholesalers really meant business is also suggested by the fact that they had successfully persuaded one of the largest publishers, D. C. Thomson & Co. Ltd, not to supply both the Emergency Depot and Willing & Co.'s distribution centre at King's Cross.[40] Again this was clearly an attempt to undermine the new service, as Thomson was a very important supplier of many of the best-selling weekly papers aimed at women and boys, as well as other cheap periodicals.[41] The *NN* urged retailers throughout the UK to counteract this strategy by dropping any title supplied by a publisher who refused to deal with Willing & Co. They gave particular praise to the Amalgamated Press and reported that a proposal 'to push' Harmsworth's publications as reward for their role in the fight had been applauded by a mass meeting at Manchester on 8 April.[42]

The wholesalers were also attempting to intimidate the *National Newsagent* by suing the newspaper for libel over remarks made in the 7 March issue, although this seems to have little affected the way in which the dispute was written about in its pages.[43] Of course, as a trade magazine, the *NN* did not have a large circulation and was largely dependent upon advertising for most of its income. This meant that throughout the dispute it

---

[40] *NN*, 11 April 1914, p. 8.

[41] On the importance of Thomson, see Joseph McAleer, *Popular Reading and Publishing in Britain 1914-1950* (Oxford, 1992), pp. 162-204.

[42] *NN*, 11 April, p. 12.

[43] *NN*, 4 April 1914, p. 5. In this article Fred Easton reiterated the potentially libellous statement that the wholesalers had cut off some newsagents' 'means of living in a cruel manner'.

continued to place full and half-page adverts for W. H. Smith & Son as wholesalers. On 18 April 1914, for example, an advert appeared on the *NN*'s front page with the tag line 'A live newsagent knows that he must have a live wholesaler and therefore places his order with W. H. Smith & Son'. Its message was, however, somewhat undermined by the note, 'You must help the Federation Guarantee Fund', which the *NN* chose to run directly below it.[44]

Another way in which the wholesalers attempted to defeat the strike involved asking some newsagents to enter into new deals. One local agent claimed to have been offered thirteen for 8d. with free carriage on deliveries and returns. The Federation terms were thirteen for 9d. plus additional transport costs.[45] A more widespread strategy to stop the dispute was the 'Pay Under Protest' ('PUP') deal that some of the wholesalers offered in order to try and stop newsagents moving their orders to the Federation supply. The 'PUP' scheme encouraged the agents to pay the new carriage charges with the promise that they would get their money back if the new rates were rescinded. Although rejected at the Manchester meeting of 8 April, the recurrence of stories about 'PUP' suggests that some newsagents continued nominally to support the strike, whilst protecting their own supplies.[46]

It is difficult to tell how many newsagents the Federation actually supplied during the spring of 1914. According to the open letter from the Stockport and District Society, before the strike began Heywood's supplied fifty newsagents, but only fifteen of these appear to have transferred their supply to the Federation 'Emergency Depot' by the middle of April 1914. We are told

---

[44] *NN*, 18 April 1914, p. 1.

[45] *NN*, 2 May 1914, p. 8, p. 4.

[46] *NN*, 18 April 1914, pp. 10-11. The *NN* had, of course, supported a 'pay under protest scheme' during the first few days of the dispute.

that at least one female newsagent had begun to pay the new charges, but it is very difficult to tell how many of the other thirty-four newsagents were directly involved in strike action.[47] Even the local secretary, Herbert Lees, seems to have been continuing to get at least part of his supply from Heywood's until they refused to supply him any more.[48] Given that in Stockport there were some shops that had not joined the strike, and that ten new ones had been established by Heywood's in opposition to the strike, it is not surprising that those retailers involved in the dispute decided to display a new 'Newsagents' Class certificate' in their shop windows to show that they were not being supplied (or run) by the major wholesalers.[49]

April was clearly a difficult month for the strikers. Although they now had an alternative supply of newspapers from London, they were still operating out of the 'temporary Depot' on London Road and the various strategies used by the wholesalers appear to have been quite successful in preventing the spread of the strike. Indeed, in order to counteract the activities of the wholesalers, the *NN* was forced onto the offensive once more. For example, on 18 April it was warning against new attempts to get the retailers to enter into PUP agreements in an article that encouraged them to reply to any such offer with a series of bad puns that played on the names of some of the participants: "All right, Mr Smith, if you are Abel, go and Bray under protest". This issue also makes the first mention of an earlier carriage dispute that had taken place in 1908. The retailers were told that they should not listen to the suggestion that they establish a 'co-operative supply' because a similar distribution system set up by John Morris at the end of the earlier dispute had been smashed

---

[47] *NN*, 18 April 1914, p. 12.

[48] 'Agents' Dispute Develops: The Ring Opens Rival Shops in Stockport', *Daily Herald*, 28 April 1914, p. 2.

[49] *NN*, 25 April 1914, p. 4.

by the ring.[50] On 25 April the *NN* was forced to revise an earlier statement suggesting that the Federation Depot could not cope with the demand in an article that argued that 'even with carriage rate on separate parcels there is a distinct five per cent saving to the retailer', 'no vexatious charges such as 1d. per sheet' and 'full allowance for returns'.[51] This same issue also confirmed that Willing & Co. would handle the supply and that they had already obtained 500 accounts worth £900 in total, but that guaranteed orders of at least £1,000 a week were needed before a new depot could become a reality.

During this period the strike leaders were also busy trying to extend support for the dispute by attending the executive meeting of the UK Federation of Retail Newsagents in Leeds, where it was agreed that a UKF 'fighting fund' should be created, and by travelling to London to encourage the publishers to supply the Federation Depot.[52] During this trip to the south they also met with Fred Easton of the *NN*, who published a photograph of 'Sam [Brierley] and some of the victims' in front of the 'the Federation Supply Company's Temporary Premises' on London Road.[53] Puns being very much in fashion in the spring of 1914, the same issue carried an advert headed 'Willing Service' in which Willing & Co. guaranteed that their prices were 'based on a fair trading profit'.[54]

Given that the *NN* noted that only an additional £25 had been added to Willing's orders during the first week in May, and that in some areas (such as St Helens) only a single newsagent had transferred to the Federation supply, the celebratory

[50] *NN*, 18 April 1914, pp. 10-11, 13.

[51] *NN*, 25 April 1914, p. 4.

[52] *NN*, 2 May 1914, p. 6.

[53] *NN*, 2 May 1914, p. 9.

[54] *NN*, 2 May 1914, p. 1.

tone of the 9 May issue is surprising.[55] It opens with a poem by
Easton called 'A Win for the Rank and File' that declares that
the fight against 'the tyrants' greed' was won the moment that
'the Flag of Federation' was flying 'oer the new supply'.[56] The
NN often refers to its stories as having a 'propaganda' purpose –
a word that had not yet taken on its negative, post-war associations – and this piece was clearly intended to persuade retailers
to continue transferring their orders to Willing. In fact, in
terms of establishing the new Depot things were little different
than they had been a few weeks before, as the £1,000 guarantee
had still not been achieved, although a new address in Ducie
Street was now being given for the Depot. The real reason that
the *NN* was keen to stress the role of the Depot was that a major aim of the strike had actually been achieved: the wholesalers
had cancelled the 'new carriage rates'.[57]

Why was this particular piece of news not the main headline?
Those running the strike (such as Brierley) had already acknowledged in print that they were worried that if the wholesalers
restored carriage charges to their pre-14 February 1914 levels, the
majority of newsagents would be content to continue business
with the 'ring'. Easton's triumphant article on the victory of the
'rank and file' was followed by 'a warning' that told the retailers
to think again of 1908 and its aftermath, this time quoting a statement from John Morris which declared that as soon as that
dispute ended the wholesalers 'smashed my depot then raised their
prices.'[58] This and the next few issues of the *NN* were used as
'propaganda' against the wholesalers. A London branch report
claimed that the better terms given to the wholesalers for distribution of *The Times* had not been passed on to the retailers, and

---

[55] *NN*, 2 May 1914, p. 8, p. 4.

[56] *NN*, 9 May 1914, p. 3.

[57] *NN*, 9 May, 1914, p. 15.

[58] *NN*, 9 May 1914, p. 14.

another suggested that some wholesale houses were refusing to supply the *NN*.[59] It was also reported that a newsagent in Oldham Street, Manchester was displaying a poster distributed by the wholesalers which warned that history was repeating itself and that Willing's Depot would disappear as quickly as that established by John Morris.[60] Brierley even went as far as to republish an earlier libellous statement which accused 'a certain wholesaler' of having a 'schedule list', that is a list of newsagents who were given better rates than their neighbours.[61] The only 'real victory' according to the strike's most vocal supporters was 'to smash the ring' using the 'trump card' of an alternative wholesaler.[62]

In order to make this work a number of strategies were suggested, including wider collective action. Branches in London and the south declared that they were willing to penalize any firm 'stopping the depot'. The *Daily Herald* had already encouraged the newsagents to stop ordering books published by Abel Heywood and the Weavers' Union was now demanding that its members refuse to enter 'scab shops' such as those established in Stockport.[63] On 23 May 1914, the *NN* reported that the new Depot was being built even though Willing's had not yet received their guarantee. Readers were requested to:

Come unto the Depot
Don't fall in the trap O!
Come on and save many a shilling
Remember the fable
That you may be Abel
But you need more than that to be Willing.[64]

---

[59] *NN*, 9 May 1914, p. 14.

[60] *NN*, 23 May 1914, p. 16.

[61] *NN*, 16 May 1914, pp. 6-7.

[62] *NN*, 16 May 1914, p. 6.

[63] *NN*, 23 May 1914, p. 20.

[64] *NN*, 23 May, p. 20.

Also called the 'Red House' in mockery of Heywood's 'White House', the *NN*'s readers were informed that 'the Depot' would sell 'fancy goods' as well as newspapers.[65]

When the 'Red House' became a reality on 17 June 1914 it was said to be big enough to supply 3,000 agents whose orders would be delivered by the 'Federation red motors'.[66] Its staff included several men who had defected from firms who were part of the 'ring'. Barker, who had previously worked for Pollard's, was running the news department, whilst Stationery was controlled by Lawson, 'late of Edwards and Bryning'. Lawson was said to be pleased with the way in which the 'wholesale manufacturing firms' had come forward to supply the Red House, but there were clearly problems with the supply of papers.[67] Indeed, the 13 June issue of the *NN* had noted that 'the ring' was threatening to refuse to take publications from anyone who supplied the new Depot.[68] This was a serious threat. As Charles Wilson has argued, Smith's provincial wholesale houses were powerful enough to break a new publication if they refused to supply it.[69] Earlier notes about Willing's referred to the fact that they supplied books, but there is no reference to there being a 'book department' at the Red House. Local retailers had already expressed worries about not being able to obtain the same range of texts as they were usually able to acquire from Smith's and Heywood's and it is significant that even after all this campaigning, the £1,000 guarantee had still not been reached.[70]

Smith & Son were quick to exploit this weakness in a series of adverts that appeared in the *NN*:

---

[65] *NN*, 23 May, p. 22.

[66] *NN*, 13 June 1914, p. 6.

[67] *NN*, 20 June 1914, p. 4.

[68] *NN*, 13 June, p. 13.

[69] Wilson, *First With the News*, p. 233.

[70] *NN*, 2 May 1914, p. 8; *NN*, 20 June 1914, p. 4.

W. H. Smith & Son, Manchester. Have been, are, and will be MORE THAN WILLING to supply you with ALL your orders, or with SINGLE COPIES of any publication whether you be FEDERATED, CONFEDERARTED, OR NON-FEDERATED.[71]

By early August 1914, the optimistic tone of the Federation had begun to disappear. Although some newsagents were 'still transferring to Willings' the fact that some publishers were refusing to supply the 'Red House' meant that one of the main aims of the strike – to allow the newsagent to choose the source of his or her supply – had not been achieved.[72] Some shops in Manchester were no longer *advertising* those newspapers and magazines whose publishers refused to supply the Depot, but they do not appear to have stopped *selling* these texts. Presumably many of the smaller retailers could not afford to do so.[73] There is a note of desperation in the article on 'Messrs Willing & Co.'s Depot' that appeared in the *NN* for 15 August. It informed the newsagents that they should 'come over' to the Federation supply because they 'would be paying the extra carriage but for Willing's', whilst at the same time noting that the number of orders being processed by the Depot had dropped to £550 per week rather than the promised £1,000.[74]

It is difficult to follow the dispute after the outbreak of the war, when other concerns tended to dominate the trade press. The cost of carriage became less of an issue as paper shortages led to smaller and lighter newspapers. However, at a meeting of the Midland Newsagents at Birmingham in November 1914, which announced that a Midland federation was to be formed, the president of the UK Federation was able to celebrate a victory over 'increased freightage' in Manchester. The 'ring' had been hit

---

[71] *NN*, 27 June 1914, p. 11.

[72] *NN*, 1 August 1914, p. 5.

[73] *NN*, 1 August 1914, p. 8.

[74] *NN*, 15 August 1914, p. 6.

particularly hard, he claimed, by Federation members transferring their stationery orders to other businesses, but it had been broken by a 'National Federation' of the UKF, the *National Newsagent*, Willing & Co and the Amalgamated Press.[75] This is clearly something of a rhetorical flourish, and more research will be necessary to establish whether the 'Red House' was a success in the post-war period, but the Lancashire carriage strike of 1914 clearly had a major impact on the trade. Even if the 'ring' was not so easily broken as the Birmingham report suggests, the Federation of northern newsagents had proved effective in stopping the new carriage charges and in introducing a new wholesaler to the North. It was this level of success that encouraged several of these regional unions to join together to become the National Federation of Retail Newsagents, Booksellers and Stationers in 1919.[76]

---

[75] *NN*, 21 November, 1914, p. 6.

[76] On the importance of the National Federation in the period up to the Second World War, see McAleer, *Popular Reading*, p. 51.

Index